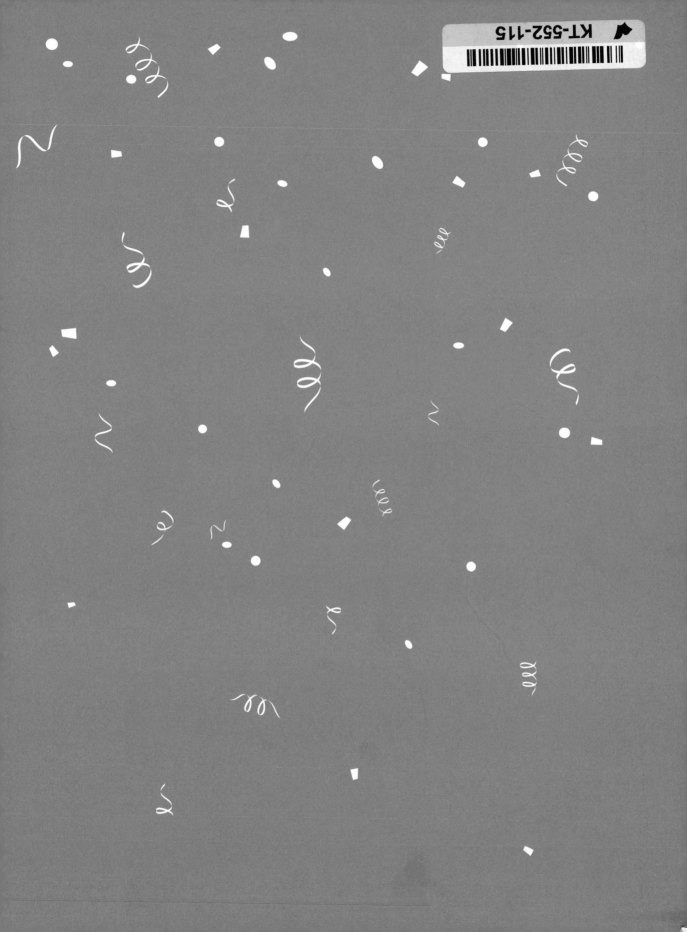

THE GREAT BRITISH
BAKE OFF
CELEBRATIONS

THE GREAT BRITISH BAKE OFF CELEBRATIONS

LINDA COLLISTER

INCLUDES RECIPES BY

MARY BERRY & PAUL HOLLYWOOD

HODDER &
STOUGHTON

This book is published to accompany the television series entitled The Great British Bake Off, first broadcast on BBC ONE in 2015

Executive Producer: Anna Beattie
Series Producer: Paolo Proto
Series Director: Andy Devonshire
Food Producer: Chloe Avery
Home Economists: Faenia Moore & Becca Watson
Unit Manager: Deborah St John Gray
Commercial Director: Rupert Frisby
Commissioning Editor: Claire Patterson

First published in Great Britain in 2015 by Hodder & Stoughton
An Hachette UK company

2

A CIP catalogue record for this title is available from the British Library

Hardback ISBN 978 1 473 61533 5
Ebook ISBN 978 1 473 61534 2

Editorial Director: Nicky Ross
Editor: Sarah Hammond
Copy Editor: Norma MacMillan
Art Director & Designer: Alice Laurent
Photographer: Rita Platts
Food Stylist: Emma Marsden
Props Stylist: Louie Waller
Production Manager: Claudette Morris
Art Editor: Kate Brunt
Art Director: Alasdair Oliver

Typeset in Gill Sans, Kushtie and Mostra Nuova

Printed and bound in Germany by Mohn Media GmbH, Gütersloh

Hodder & Stoughton policy is to use papers that are natural, renewable and recyclable products and made from wood grown in sustainable forests. The logging and manufacturing processes are expected to conform to the environmental regulations of the country of origin.

Hodder & Stoughton Ltd
Carmelite House
50 Victoria Embankment
London EC4Y 0DZ

www.hodder.co.uk

CONTENTS

WELCOME

Don't just celebrate – bake!

Every year The Great British Bake Off celebrates anew the special place baking holds in our national identity.

From family meals to birthday parties and home-cooked teas to the big dates in the community calendar, nothing says celebration like a home-made bake. So this year, we have devoted our book to recipes that will help you make the most out of every occasion, no matter how large or small.

There are fantastic centrepieces for the times when you need a real showstopper – a Tiered

Raspberry & White Chocolate Cheesecake (see page 179) or a 16-layer Mocha Torte (see page 193) – as well as simpler recipes like a citrus Madeira cake or White Chocolate Butterscotch Blondies for when all you want is a failsafe yet delicious bake to welcome unexpected visitors.

The Judges' recipes provide the perfect excuse to impress, whether it's serving your own freshly made bread or whipping up a batch of handmade biscuits, whilst the Bakers' recipes will inspire you with their creativity and ingenuity. Introducing new flavours and techniques, the recipes are a showcase for how

the Bakers embrace different ideas and ingredients from around the world.

So many of our Bakers started out because they had something significant to celebrate – making a sister's wedding cake, for example, or baking for a big family gathering, but you don't have to restrict your baking to the big events. Whatever the occasion, we hope this book will encourage and inspire you to celebrate for yourselves everything that we love about baking.

MEET THE BAKERS

'There are so many avenues to go down to express yourself. I wish I had started baking much earlier. When I go back to the Philippines I love to flip through my mum's old recipe books.'

v ALVIN

'I am always looking for ideas for new flavour and texture sensations, all the clever little surprises that can add finesse to baking.'

DORRET >

< IAN

'Baking breads and brioche is what I really love. Luckily my son doesn't have a sweet tooth, so for his birthday he was very happy with an artistic pile of scones!'

FLORA ∧

'Birthdays, Christmas, Easter, Bonfire Night, Burns' Night . . . our family jump at any excuse for big get-togethers. My mum and I like nothing better than to get our pinnies on and spend a whole day cooking and baking.'

'When my wife and I were getting married, we wanted a macaroon tower instead of a conventional wedding cake . . . I'd never baked anything before, but I decided to do the macaroons myself and my first batch were perfect! That is how I started baking.'

MAT >

'Decorating cakes for my grandchildren's birthdays gives me the chance to experiment. I've done daleks, zombies and even Cinderella running down the stairs. That took some doing!'

v   MARIE

< PAUL

NADIYA ∧

'My father is an amazing cook, but he doesn't believe in rules. He is always curious, and I'm the same. I like to take a recipe and then put my own twist on it.'

'Ever since a friend asked me to make a wedding cake decorated with sugar orchids, I've been hooked on the creation of sugar flowers. I'm obsessed with getting them as botanically correct as possible, down to every tiny vein and detail.'

'It is such a feelgood thing, total escapism. You leave the world outside behind and get lost in what you are doing, and then at the end of it you have all these treats to share with everyone you love.'

STUART >

'I like a sense of adventure. I read baking books as if they were novels and I'm forever trying new things. If they don't go according to plan, we have a saying in our family that pretty much anything will be okay if you have it with custard!'

∨ SANDY

< UGNE

TAMAL ∧

"We are quite an anglicised family, but I use the spicing and flavours of Indian cooking in my baking. I love experimenting and making something new and surprising."

'I love to bake with the children — everyone getting their hands in the mixing bowl. I want my children to grow up thinking that mummy's baking is better than shop-bought.'

BAKER'S GUIDE

Note

In the recipes, an asterisk is used to refer you back to the instructions and information in this section.

What Does It Mean?

• fold This is a way to delicately combine 2 (or more) ingredients so you don't knock out all the air you've carefully beaten or whisked into a mixture — for example, adding sifted flour to a creamed mixture of butter, eggs and sugar for a cake, or adding sugar or other ingredients to whisked egg whites for meringue. A large metal spoon or plastic spatula is best for folding. Turn the spoon so one side cuts down through the mixture. When you touch the bottom of the bowl, turn the spoon upwards and draw it up through the mixture to the top, then flip the spoon over so the mixture flops on to the surface. Give the bowl a quarter turn (so you start folding from a different place) and repeat. Using a light touch and as few movements as possible, keep lightly cutting down, lifting and flopping over until you can no longer see any streaks of unmixed ingredients.

• rub in This is how you combine butter and flour when making pastry and simple cake mixtures

(like that for plain fruit cakes). Use the fingertips and thumbs of both hands — try to keep your palms clean (your fingertips are cooler than your palms). Pick up a little of the butter and flour mixture, lift your hands up to the top of the bowl and gently rub your fingers and thumbs together so the mixture is combined as it falls back down into the bowl. Continue doing this until the mixture has a crumb-like consistency. The rubbing-in will add air, which will make the pastry or cake mixture lighter.

• sift This means shaking flour, a raising agent, cocoa powder, icing sugar, ground spices or other dry ingredients through a sieve into a bowl. Sifting will remove any lumps, as well as adding air, and it helps to combine ingredients — important for raising agents added to flour to be sure they

are evenly dispersed (you can also do this in a food processor by 'pulsing' the flour with the raising agents a few times).

• work This is a way of saying to mix, stir, blend or combine ingredients using a spoon, plastic spatula or your hands until they have come together (or look smooth, or soft, or thickened, depending on the recipe instructions).

How Do I Do This?

PREPARING TINS

• grease and base-line a springclip tin, a deep round or square tin, a sandwich tin or a traybake/ brownie/rectangular cake tin Lightly and thoroughly brush the base and sides of the tin (including the rim) with melted butter. Set

the tin on a sheet of baking paper and draw around it, then cut out the disc (or square or rectangle). Turn the baking paper over, to be sure any pencil or pen marks are underneath, and press it on to the base of the tin.

• grease and line a springclip tin or a round, deep cake tin Brush the base and sides with melted butter, then cut out 2 discs of baking paper very slightly smaller than the base of the tin (measure as for base-lining, left, then cut inside the drawn line). Also cut out a double-thickness strip of baking paper long enough to go around the tin and stand about 5cm above its rim. Make a 2.5cm fold along one edge of this strip, then snip diagonally up to the fold at 1cm intervals (it will look like a thick fringe). Press one paper disc on to the base of the tin, then place the strip around the inside of the tin so the snipped edge lies flat on the base and the paper is pressed smoothly to the sides of the tin (no creases). Brush the paper on the base and the snipped edge of the side strip with a little more melted butter, then press the second paper disc on top. Lightly brush the paper on the base and sides with melted butter to hold it all in place.

• grease and line a loaf tin with a long strip of baking paper Lightly brush the base, sides and rim of the tin with melted butter. Cut a strip of baking paper the width of the tin and long enough to cover the base and 2 short sides. Press the paper into the greased tin to line it. The paper will help you lift out the loaf after baking.

• grease and line the base and sides of a loaf tin Lightly brush the base and sides with melted butter. Cut a rectangle of baking paper as long as the length of the tin plus twice its depth plus an extra 2cm, and as wide as the tin plus twice its depth plus an extra 2cm. Set the tin in the centre of the rectangle and draw around its base. With scissors, cut in from each corner of the paper rectangle to the corner of the drawn tin base. Fold the paper along the lines of the drawn tin base to make a case, folding around the overlapping snipped corners neatly. Slip the case into the tin and press against the sides.

CHOCOLATE

• melt chocolate Chop or break up the chocolate into even pieces so it will melt at the same rate. Put it into a heatproof bowl and set this over a pan of steaming hot but not boiling water – the base of the bowl shouldn't touch the water. As the chocolate starts to soften, stir gently so it melts evenly. It is ready as soon as it is liquid and smooth. Take care not to leave it over the heat any longer because if the chocolate overheats it will 'seize up' – turn grainy and hard – and be unusable. White chocolate melts at a lower temperature and seizes more readily than dark chocolate.

EGGS

• whisk egg whites Separate your eggs carefully – any trace of yolk (or speck of grease in the bowl) will stop the whites

from being whisked to their full volume – and use the whites at room temperature. Put them into a large, spotlessly clean and grease-free bowl. Whisk, on low speed if using a hand-held electric whisk or mixer, for about 30 seconds until frothy. If you add a pinch of cream of tartar, or dash of vinegar or lemon juice, at this point, the slight acidity will help the structure of the whites to stiffen. Then increase the speed and continue whisking – the whites will become a mass of tiny bubbles, with a very smooth and fine texture. *Soft peak* is when you lift the whisk and the peak of whites on it slightly droops down. The next stage, after more whisking, is *stiff peak* when the peak stands upright. You should also be able to turn the bowl upside down without the whites falling out.

• whisk to the 'ribbon stage' For whisked sponges, eggs and sugar must be whisked thoroughly to build up a thick mass of tiny air bubbles that forms the structure of the cake. Use a large bowl – after 4 or 5 minutes of whisking on high speed, the initial volume of eggs and sugar will increase five-fold. Using a large free-standing electric mixer is the easiest and quickest way to whisk eggs and sugar to the ribbon, but you can also use a hand-held electric whisk or, if you're not making a large quantity, a rotary whisk. The ribbon stage is reached when the whisked mixture becomes very thick: if you lift the whisk out of the bowl, the mixture on it will fall back on to the surface of the mixture in the bowl to make a distinct thick, ribbon-like trail.

CREAM

• whip cream Make sure the cream is well chilled before you start (in warm weather, pop the bowl and whisk into the fridge to chill too). This will prevent the butterfat from separating and the mixture from curdling as you whip. You can use a hand-held electric whisk, a rotary whisk or a wire whisk. If you are going to fold the cream into another mixture, whip the cream to soft peak stage (see Whisk egg whites, page xi). For piping, whip the cream to a slightly firmer peak.

PIPING

• fill a piping bag Put the piping bag in a large glass or tall mug and fold the top of the bag over the rim (the glass/mug will support the piping bag, making it easier to fill). Spoon the icing/cream/meringue into the bag, filling it about two-thirds full. Unfold the bag from the glass/mug, then twist the top of the bag to push the icing down to the tip or nozzle end, getting rid of any air pockets. Twist the top again to compact the icing.

MAKING A PASTRY CASE

• line a flan tin or pie plate Roll out the pastry dough on a lightly floured worktop to a disc about 8cm larger than your tin. Roll up the pastry around the rolling pin and lift it over the flan tin, then unroll the pastry gently so it drapes over the tin. Flour your fingers and gently press the pastry on to the base and up the side of the tin, smoothing out any pockets of air. Leave the excess pastry hanging over the rim of the tin, or roll the pin over the top of the tin to cut off the excess (if there are any holes in the pastry case, use these dough trimmings to patch them). With your thumbs, ease the pastry up the side of the tin, just slightly higher than the rim, to allow for shrinkage during baking. Curve your forefinger inside this new rim and gently press the pastry over your finger so it curves slightly inwards – this will make it easier to unmould after baking. Prick the base of the pastry case well with a fork, then chill for 20 minutes. If you need to keep the pastry case in the fridge for any longer, loosely cover with clingfilm to prevent the pastry from drying out.

• bake a pastry case 'blind' Crumple up a sheet of baking or greaseproof paper, then flatten it out (this makes the paper easier to fit). Line the pastry case with the paper and fill with ceramic baking beans or dried beans. Place in the heated oven and bake for 12–15 minutes (or as the recipe directs) until the pastry is firm. Carefully remove the paper and beans, then return the tin to the oven and bake for a further 5–7 minutes (or as the recipe directs) until the pastry is thoroughly cooked and starting to colour (this is vital to avoid the dreaded 'soggy bottom'). Pastry containing sugar

needs to be watched carefully as it can burn on the edges before the base is cooked through. If this happens, reduce the oven temperature slightly, or cover the rim with a long strip of foil.

• 'knock up' a pastry edge Use the back of a small knife to make small horizontal cuts all around.

• flute or scallop a pastry edge Place 2 fingers on the pastry edge to press it down and draw a small knife between them. Continue all around the edge.

BAKING CAKES

• skewer test For richer, heavier cakes, fruit cakes and dense chocolate cakes, the way to test if the cake is done is to stick a wooden cocktail stick or fine skewer into the centre of the cake. If the stick or skewer comes out clean rather than damp with cake mixture adhering, the cake has finished baking. Note though that for some recipes, such as Brownies, the cocktail stick should come out slightly sticky; this is to avoid over-cooking a cake that is supposed to be moist and fudgy.

• fingertip test For delicate sponge cakes the most reliable test to check if the cake is done is to gently press the top, in the centre, with your finger – the cake is ready if the sponge springs back into place. If a slight dent is left, the mixture is still soft, so bake for a couple of minutes more and test again. When done, a sponge will also have started to shrink from the side of the tin.

• cool a sponge on a wire rack To avoid a wire rack leaving marks on the top of a sponge, cover a clean board (or a second wire rack) with a clean, dry tea towel. Hold the upturned towel-covered board over the sponge (in its tin) and turn the whole thing over so the sponge falls out on to the tea towel. Lift off the tin and remove the lining paper. Set the upturned wire rack on the sponge and turn the whole thing over again. Carefully remove the board and tea towel and leave the sponge to cool, now the right way up, on the wire rack.

• cut a sponge into 2 layers First, make a small vertical nick or cut in the side of the sponge with the tip of a small sharp knife (this will help you align the layers when sandwiching). Gently but firmly press down on the top of the sponge with the flat of your hand and, using a long serrated knife (such as a bread knife), carefully saw the sponge horizontally in half to make 2 equal layers.

MAKING BREAD

• mix a quick bread dough Doughs raised with a mixture of bicarbonate of soda and buttermilk need to be mixed, shaped and baked without delay. It's important to work quickly because once the acidic buttermilk starts to react with the alkaline bicarbonate of soda,

bubbles of carbon dioxide gas are produced and it is these that will raise the dough as it bakes.

• mix a yeasted dough Many doughs raised with yeast specify lukewarm liquid (milk, water, etc). It's important that the liquid not be too hot or it could kill the yeast. After warming the liquid, check the temperature by dipping your little finger into it: it should feel comfy. For lukewarm water, you can mix half boiling water with half cold water from the tap.

• hydrate the flour If you leave the mixed yeasted dough in its bowl for 5 minutes (uncovered) before you start to knead, you'll find it an easier process because the flour will have had time to absorb the liquid properly – a particularly important step for wholemeal and rye flours, which are slow to hydrate. You can judge whether or not the dough needs a touch more flour or water at this point.

• knead dough Working a dough develops the gluten (in the flour's protein) and turns it from a messy ball into neat bundles of strands that are capable of stretching around the bubbles of carbon dioxide gas (produced by the growing yeast). The dough will then rise slowly, thanks to the yeast and gluten, and set in the oven. You can knead by hand or in a free-standing electric mixer fitted with the dough hook attachment. Note that some unyeasted quick doughs are also kneaded, just to mix them but not to develop the flour's gluten.

• knead yeasted dough by hand First lightly dust the worktop with flour to prevent the dough from sticking. Turn the dough out on to the worktop. Stretch the ball of dough away from you by holding down one end with your hand and using the other hand to pull and stretch out the dough as if it were an elastic band. Gather the dough back into a ball again and give it a quarter turn (so you start from a different section of the dough), then repeat the stretching and gathering-back movements. As you knead you'll notice the dough gradually changes in the way it looks and feels – it will start to feel pliable and then stretchy and very elastic, and silky smooth. Most doughs need about 10 minutes of thorough kneading by hand.

• knead yeasted dough in a mixer Set the mixer on the lowest possible speed and knead with the dough hook for about 5 minutes. While it's almost impossible to over-knead by hand (your arms will give out first), take care when using a mixer because

you can stretch the gluten beyond repair, which means the dough won't rise well at all.

• test if yeasted dough has been kneaded enough Take a small piece and stretch it between your fingers to make a thin, translucent sheet. If it won't stretch out or it tears easily, continue to knead a while longer.

• bake a loaf with a good crust Make sure the oven is thoroughly heated so the dough quickly puffs (called 'oven-spring') and then sets, bakes evenly and forms a good crust. If you are worried about the oven temperature dramatically dropping as you load the bread in the oven, heat it slightly higher than the recipe says, then turn it down to the specified temperature once the oven door is closed again.

• bake a loaf with a crisp crust Creating a burst of steam in the oven at the start of baking will help give your loaf a crisp crust – the steam keeps the surface moist, helping the bread to rise easily; once the surface has set the moisture evaporates, leaving a crisp finish. To do this, put an empty roasting tin on the floor of the oven when you turn it on to heat it. Then, when you're putting the loaf in to bake, pour cold water – or throw a handful of ice cubes – into the hot tin. Quickly close the oven door to trap the resulting steam inside.

• **bake a loaf with a crisp bottom crust** When you turn on the oven, put a baking sheet or baking stone in to heat up. Then carefully transfer your loaf (in a tin or on a sheet of baking paper) on to the hot baking sheet or stone for baking.

• **test bread to see if it is done** Carefully remove the bread from the oven and turn it over or out of its tin, upside down, on to one hand (thick oven gloves needed here). Tap the underside of the loaf with your knuckles. If the bread sounds hollow, like a drum, then it is cooked through. If you just get a dull 'thud', put the bread back into the oven – straight on to the oven shelf. Bake for a few

more minutes, then test again. A rule of thumb: a slightly over-baked loaf will taste far better than an undercooked one. Cool on a wire rack, not in the tin or on a baking sheet, so the steam from the loaf cannot condense during cooling and turn the crust soggy.

Cook's Notes

SPOON MEASURES

All teaspoons and tablespoons are level unless otherwise stated.

EGGS

Some recipes contain raw or partially cooked eggs. Pregnant women, the elderly, babies and toddlers, and people who are unwell should avoid these recipes.

SALT

If a recipe calls for a small or hard to weigh amount of salt, remember that ½ teaspoon fine salt weighs 2.5g, and ¼ teaspoon weighs 1.25g. If you are using

sea salt it is best to crush the flakes into a fine powder before measuring and adding to your recipe (unless otherwise specified).

OVEN TEMPERATURES

Recipes give temperatures for a conventional oven. If you have a fan-assisted oven, set the temperature 20°C lower than specified in the recipe. Don't forget that ovens vary – from the front to the back of the oven, as well as between top and bottom shelves – so an oven thermometer is very useful. Get to know your oven, and where the 'hot spots' are. Always preheat the oven, and be sure your oven gloves are dry.

CAKES

Nothing says celebration like a cake, and in this chapter you will find a wealth of simple, fun and flavourful ideas to inspire you, from a rich fruit cake for Christmas or Hogmanay (pages 50 and 52) to a Midsummer Celebration Cake (page 20) to round off a sunshine barbecue or picnic, or a Malted Milk Chocolate Cake (page 14) for a children's birthday party.

The texture and flavour of a good cake is all about chemistry, which means careful weighing of ingredients and watchful timing. But once your cake is on the cooling rack, it is time to unleash your inner artist. Even a classic sponge like a Madeira cake can be given a simple touch of elegance with some gorgeous candied orange peel (page 16). And while most of the recipes give ideas for decoration, you don't have to

follow them to the letter – you can let your imagination run riot with icing, chocolate and cream, gold and glitz.

You could follow Flora's example and build an individual creation for a special person or occasion: 'For my mum's 50th birthday cake, I made three tiers of iced blackcurrant sponge, one of which was sprayed with gold. The others were white, and the whole thing was covered in blackcurrants and gold and deep-purple coloured macaroons, with flowers wired all around,' she says. 'Mum is a florist and she has taught me how to work with fresh flowers.'

Today's baking shops are treasure troves of tools, cutters and moulds, pastes, sprinkles, sparkles and stencils – everything you could wish for to create the most intricate and adventurous creations, like the Gingerbread Cake Haunted Houses (page 46). They are also meccas for a whole community of cake-makers keen

to swap tips and share ideas, as Tamal discovered when he made his first celebration cake for his sister's wedding: 'I had never done anything as ambitious before', he says, 'but I talked to the lovely ladies in my local cake-decoration shop, who gave me great advice.'

As well as a labour of love and artistry to share with the people around us, the making of a cake can be an emotional link to the past or to family and friends far away. For Alvin and his wife, who moved to the UK from the Philippines, ironically it's the French Dacquoise (layers of meringue, buttercream and nuts) that connects them to home. 'During the 1930s many wealthy Filipinos went to France to study and they brought back the recipe', he explains, 'but whereas in France they use hazelnuts or almonds, we substitute cashew nuts and add some rum and chopped-up jackfruit, which makes the whole cake so fragrant. I make it once or twice a year for a birthday or other celebration.'

Thanks to the long, rich, cross-cultural history of cake-making, whether you follow a recipe from this chapter, or one that has been handed down through the generations of your family, you will be tapping into centuries of just such sharing of influences and traditions – so every cake, in a way, is a celebration of who we are today.

EASTER LEMON & COCONUT CAKE

As a change from the traditional Easter Simnel cake, why not make this rich centrepiece lemon sponge, filled with sharp lemon curd and iced with a thick, glossy marshmallow/meringue that is swirled all over the cake and finished with a flurry of coconut flakes? The quantities of butter, sugar and flour for the sponge are all based on the weight of the eggs.

Serves about 12

Kit you'll need: 2 x 20.5cm round, deep sandwich tins, greased with butter and base-lined*

FOR THE SPONGE
4 medium eggs,
    at room temperature
about 240g unsalted butter,
    softened
about 240g caster sugar
about 240g self-raising flour

finely grated zest of 2 medium
    unwaxed lemons
2 tablespoons milk,
    at room temperature

FOR THE LEMON CURD
FILLING
70g unsalted butter, diced
125g caster sugar
finely grated zest of 3 medium
    unwaxed lemons
100ml lemon juice
2 medium eggs, plus 2 yolks,
    at room temperature

FOR THE ICING
3 medium egg whites,
    at room temperature
200g white caster sugar
1 tablespoon golden syrup
¼ vanilla pod, split open
¼ teaspoon cream of tartar
4 tablespoons water

TO FINISH
150g desiccated coconut flakes
    (unsweetened) OR long-shred
    desiccated coconut

1. Heat your oven to 180°C/350°F/gas 4. Put the 4 eggs (in shell) on your kitchen scales and use their total weight – about 240g – to calculate the weight of the butter, sugar and flour you need.

2. Put the softened butter and lemon zest in a mixing bowl, or the bowl of a large free-standing electric mixer, and beat with a hand-held electric whisk, or the whisk attachment of the mixer, until creamy and mayonnaise-like. Gradually beat in the caster sugar, scraping down the side of the bowl from time to time, then continue beating until the mixture is very light and fluffy.

3. Break the eggs into a small bowl and beat with a fork just to mix. Gradually add the eggs to the butter mixture, beating well after each addition and scraping down the side of the bowl as before. To prevent the mixture from curdling, add a tablespoon of the weighed flour with each of the last 2 additions of egg. Sift the rest of the flour into the bowl and add the milk. Carefully fold* everything together with a large metal spoon until well combined, without any streaks of flour.

4. Divide the mixture equally between the 2 prepared tins and spread evenly. Bake the sponges in the heated oven for 25–28 minutes until well risen and golden brown and they feel springy when gently pressed in the centre with your fingertip.

>>>

5. Remove from the oven and leave to cool for a few minutes – the edges of the sponges will contract and start to firm up. Run a round-bladed knife around the inside of each tin to loosen the sponge, then turn it out on to a wire rack and leave to cool completely.

6. Meanwhile, make the lemon curd for the filling (this makes more than you need for this cake, but the rest can be kept in a covered container in the fridge for a week). Put the butter, sugar, and lemon zest and juice into a heatproof bowl. Set the bowl over a pan of simmering water (the base of the bowl shouldn't touch the water) and stir with a wooden spoon until the sugar has completely dissolved. Remove the bowl from the pan and set it on a heatproof surface.

7. Beat the whole eggs with the yolks in a small bowl until well mixed, then strain into the lemon mixture and combine thoroughly. Set the bowl over the pan of simmering water again and stir the lemon mixture until it becomes very thick and opaque. Don't be tempted to turn the heat up because the eggs will scramble if the mixture gets anywhere near boiling. The lemon curd is ready when you can draw a finger through the curd on the wooden spoon and make a clear path. Immediately lift the bowl from the pan and leave the curd to cool completely.

8. When you are ready to assemble and finish the cake, set one sponge upside down on a cake turntable, if you have one, or on the wire rack. Spread over 200g of the lemon curd, then place the second sponge on top, crust-side up.

9. To make the marshmallow icing, put the egg whites in a large heatproof bowl and whisk them, using a hand-held electric whisk, for just a few seconds until slightly frothy. Add the sugar, golden syrup, seeds scraped from the vanilla pod, cream of tartar and water to the bowl and whisk for 10 seconds just to combine.

10. Set the bowl over a pan of simmering water – the base of the bowl should not touch the water – and whisk on full speed for exactly 7 minutes to make a very thick and glossy meringue-like mixture. Remove the bowl from the pan and whisk for another 7 minutes. As the mixture cools it will become even thicker and more shiny.

11. Working quickly, before the icing firms up, spread and swirl it very thickly over the top and side of the cake to cover completely – use an offset palette knife if you have one or a regular palette knife or round-bladed knife. Scatter some of the coconut evenly over the top of the cake and gently press the remainder on to the icing around the side.

12. Leave uncovered to firm up for a couple of hours before serving, or carefully putting into an airtight container and keeping in a cool spot (not the fridge). Eat within 3 days.

Note

You can use 200g ready-made lemon curd instead of making your own.

DAIRY-FREE CITRUS & SPELT CAKE

For lemon drizzle fans, a moist loaf cake packed with flavour is perfect for any celebration. This one is made with white spelt flour and a light olive oil instead of butter – the oil should be mild enough to add to the lovely fruity taste of the sponge without overpowering it. As usual the drizzle comes from quickly made lemon water-icing, spread over the cake while still hot.

1. Heat the oven to 180°C/350°F/gas 4. Break the eggs into a large mixing bowl, or the bowl of a large free-standing electric mixer. Add the sugar and orange and lemon zests. Whisk, using a hand-held electric whisk or the whisk attachment of the mixer, on full speed for about 8 minutes to the ribbon stage*.

2. Gradually whisk in the orange and lemon juices, then slowly add the oil in a thin, steady stream, still whisking on full speed – the mixture will become thinner and much less foamy. Sift the flour, baking powder and bicarbonate of soda into the bowl and gently but thoroughly fold in* using a large metal spoon or plastic spatula until you can no longer see any specks of flour.

3. Pour the mixture into the tin and ease it into the corners so it is evenly filled. Bake in the heated oven for 50–55 minutes until

the cake is golden brown and a skewer inserted into the centre comes out clean.

4. While the cake is baking make the lemon water icing. Sift the icing sugar into a bowl, add the lemon juice and stir to make a smooth, runny icing.

5. When the cake is ready, take the tin out of the oven and set it on a wire rack. Spoon the lemon icing over the top of the hot cake and gently spread out evenly with an offset palette knife or a round-bladed knife. Leave to cool completely.

6. Run a round-bladed knife around the inside of the tin to loosen the cake, then carefully lift it out using the ends of the lining paper to help. Keep in an airtight container and eat within 4 days.

Serves 10

Kit you'll need: 1 x 900g loaf tin, about 26 x 12.5 x 7.5cm, greased with butter and lined with a long strip of baking paper*

4 medium eggs,
    at room temperature
225g caster sugar
finely grated zest of 1 large
    orange, plus 2 tablespoons juice
finely grated zest of 1 large
    unwaxed lemon,
    plus 1 tablespoon juice
225ml mild, fruity extra virgin
    olive oil
250g white spelt flour
½ teaspoon baking powder
½ teaspoon bicarbonate of soda

FOR THE ICING
100g icing sugar
2–3 tablespoons lemon juice

JAM-FILLED CINNAMON MUFFINS

Fruity muffins are great for a children's party or half term sleepover, when the kids can get involved with making them. They're hard to resist - the smell as they bake is so tantalising. You can use shop-bought jam, but you don't need anything special to make your own – a good-size pan is enough for the small, 3-jar batch in the recipe opposite.

Makes 12

Kit you'll need: 1 x 12-hole muffin/cupcake tray, lined with 'tulip' muffin cases

FOR THE APPLE MIXTURE
1 large tart eating apple, such as Braeburn
½ teaspoon ground cinnamon

FOR THE MUFFIN MIXTURE
100g unsalted butter, softened
125g light brown muscovado sugar
2 medium eggs, at room temperature, beaten to mix
150ml natural yoghurt (not Greek-style), at room temperature
300g self-raising flour
1 teaspoon ground cinnamon
¼ teaspoon bicarbonate of soda
4 tablespoons Blackberry and Apple Jam (see opposite) OR ready-made jam or conserve

FOR THE TOPPING
40g unsalted butter, melted
40g demerara, granulated or caster sugar
1 teaspoon ground cinnamon

1. Heat the oven to 200°C/400°F/gas 6. Peel, quarter and core the apples, then cut into dice about the size of your small fingernail. Put into a small bowl, sprinkle over the cinnamon and toss until thoroughly combined. Set aside.

2. Put the soft butter into a mixing bowl, add the sugar and beat well with a wooden spoon or a hand-held electric whisk, scraping down the side of the bowl once or twice. Gradually add the eggs, beating well after each addition. Stir in about a third of the yoghurt using a plastic spatula. Sift the flour, cinnamon and bicarbonate of soda into the bowl and gently stir in. Add the rest of the yoghurt and mix in followed by the cinnamon apples.

3. Spoon 2 tablespoons of the muffin mixture into each muffin case. Bang the tray on the worktop to settle the mixture in the cases, then put a teaspoonful of jam into each. Spoon the rest of the muffin mixture on top of the jam so the muffin cases are equally filled.

4. Bake in the heated oven for about 25 minutes until the muffins are a good golden brown and well risen, and they feel firm when gently pressed in the centre.

5. Remove from the oven and set the tray on a wire rack. Quickly brush the top of each muffin with melted butter. Combine the sugar and cinnamon and sprinkle over the muffins. Carefully lift them out of the tray, still in their paper cases, and set on the wire rack to cool. Best eaten the same day.

BLACKBERRY & APPLE JAM

The best time to make this jam is in late summer/early autumn when the fruit is free – the hedgerows are full of blackberries and you can collect windfall cooking apples.

1. Rinse and pick over the berries, removing any remaining centre 'cores'. Put into a large pan. Peel, quarter and core the apples, then slice thinly into the pan. Add the lemon zest and juice with the water. Set the pan over medium heat and cook gently, stirring from time to time, for 15–20 minutes until the fruit is tender.

2. Turn down the heat to low, add the sugar and stir gently until it has completely dissolved. Turn the heat back up to medium to bring the mixture to the boil. Adjust the heat so the mixture boils rapidly (without spluttering or boiling over) and boil for about 10 minutes.

3. While the jam is boiling, put 2 or 3 saucers into the freezer to chill (unless you are going to test for a set with a thermometer).

4. When the jam is bubbling with large, noisy bubbles, and it will fall from the wooden spoon in flakes rather than drips, it's time to test for setting point. Remove the pan from the heat and carefully put a small spoonful of the jam (use the wooden spoon, not a metal spoon) on to a chilled saucer.

Leave to cool for 30 seconds, then drag your finger through the middle of the blob of jam. If this leaves a clear path with wrinkles either side, then the jam is ready; if it just leaves a clear path, return the pan to the heat and boil for another couple of minutes before testing again. (On a thermometer, setting point is about 105°C.)

5. Once the jam has reached setting point, remove from the heat and leave to cool and settle for 30 minutes, then ladle into warm, sterilised jars. Leave until cold before covering. Store in a cool place; once opened, keep in the fridge for up to a week.

Makes about 1.25kg

Kit you'll need: a large pan; about 3 sterilised jars

500g blackberries
300g cooking apples
   (about 1 large Bramley)
finely grated zest and juice
   of 1 large unwaxed lemon
100ml water
800g granulated sugar

MALTED MILK CHOCOLATE CAKE

Not too rich, not too sweet, but really chocolatey, this is easy to make and portion for handing around – the perfect birthday cake. Ice it simply with melted chocolate and decorate with malted milk chocolate balls, then add candles or, once the icing has set, greetings and names, using tubes of writing-icing. The cake can be made in advance, then finished on the day.

Serves 16

Kit you'll need: I traybake tin or cake tin, 20.5 x 25.5 x 5cm, OR a roasting tin, greased with butter and base-lined*

FOR THE SPONGE

60g malted milk drink powder
(use 'original', not diet or flavoured versions)
50g cocoa powder
225ml milk
(whole or semi-skimmed)
175g unsalted butter, softened
125g caster sugar
125g light brown
muscovado sugar
3 medium eggs, at room
temperature, beaten to mix
185g self-raising flour

FOR THE TOPPING

100g good-quality milk chocolate
(at least 40% cocoa solids) OR
dark chocolate (about 70%
cocoa solids) OR 50g of each
20g unsalted butter, softened
80–90g malted chocolate-
covered honeycomb balls –
milk or white chocolate
or a mix of the two

1. Weigh the malted milk drink powder and cocoa in a small pan (preferably non-stick) and stir in the milk with a wooden spoon. When thoroughly combined, set the pan over very low heat and stir until the mixture comes to the boil and thickens slightly. Remove from the heat and leave to cool until barely warm.

2. Heat the oven to 180°C/ 350°F/gas 4.

3. Put the softened butter and both sugars into a mixing bowl, or the bowl of a free-standing electric mixer, and beat with a hand-held electric whisk, or the whisk attachment, until light and fluffy. Scrape down the side of the bowl, then gradually add the eggs, about a tablespoon at a time, beating well after each addition. Scrape down the side of the bowl from time to time.

4. Sift half the flour into the bowl and mix in, using the whisk on medium/low speed. Add half of the milk mixture and whisk in, followed by the remaining flour and then the rest of the milk.

5. When everything is thoroughly combined, scrape the mixture into the prepared tin and spread it out evenly. Bake in the heated oven for 25 minutes, then turn down the oven temperature to 170°C/325°F/gas 3. Bake for a further 15 minutes until a skewer inserted into the centre of the sponge comes out clean.

6. Set the tin on a wire rack. Run a round-bladed knife around the inside of the tin to loosen the sponge, then leave until cold before turning out. (The cake can be stored in an airtight container for up to 48 hours before decorating.)

7. When you are ready to finish the cake, set it on a serving plate or board. To make the topping, melt* the chocolate gently, then stir in the butter until smooth. Spread over the sponge. Scatter the malted chocolate balls (cut in half, if you like) over the cake. Leave until set before cutting. The malted chocolate balls quickly soften when exposed to the air so the cake is at its best as soon as it has been decorated.

LEMON MADEIRA CAKE WITH CANDIED PEEL

In Victorian times, when the ritual of taking tea became fashionable amongst the gentry, this cake was devised to accompany a glass of Madeira wine. Here the rich sponge is made quickly using the all-in-one method, and elegantly finished with strips of home-made candied peel. The remaining peel can be dipped in melted dark chocolate, set and served with coffee after dinner, or used to decorate other confections.

1. Start by making the candied peel for the decoration. Cut the lemon into 8 wedges, then cut out (and discard) the flesh, leaving just 5mm thickness of white pith and the yellow peel. Cut each wedge into 4 strips.

2. Pour 300ml water into a small pan, add the granulated sugar and set over low heat. Stir with a wooden spoon until the sugar has dissolved. Add the strips of lemon peel and simmer for 30–45 minutes until the peel is soft and translucent. Drain in a wire sieve and leave to cool while you heat the oven to its lowest setting.

3. Spread out the peel on the lined baking sheet and sprinkle evenly with the caster sugar. Dry out in the warm oven for about 1 hour. Remove and leave to cool. Turn up the oven to 180°C/350°F/gas 4.

4. To make the cake mixture, put all the ingredients into a large bowl, or a free-standing electric mixer. Beat with a hand-held electric whisk, or the mixer whisk attachment, for about 1 minute until smooth and thoroughly combined. Transfer the mixture to the prepared tin and spread evenly.

5. Bake the cake in the heated oven for 35 minutes. Remove from the oven and decorate the top of the cake with 3 pieces of candied peel. Bake for a further 20–25 minutes until a skewer inserted into the centre of the cake comes out clean.

6. Leave to cool in the tin for 15 minutes before turning out on to a wire rack to finish cooling. Store in an airtight container.

Serves 8–10

Kit you'll need: 1 baking sheet, lined with baking paper; an 18cm round, deep cake tin, greased and lined*

FOR THE CANDIED PEEL
1 large unwaxed lemon
200g granulated sugar
100g caster sugar

FOR THE CAKE MIXTURE
175g unsalted butter, softened
175g caster sugar
225g self-raising flour
50g ground almonds
4 large eggs, at room
    temperature
finely grated zest
    of 1 large unwaxed lemon

Tip

The remaining pieces of candied peel can be stored in an airtight container for up to a week. Dip them in melted dark chocolate and allow to set, then pack in small jars to give as gifts.

SUGAR-FREE CARROT CAKE

For this gorgeous spicy, nutty carrot cake, the sponge is sweetened with agave syrup rather than sugar, and the cream cheese frosting is made with maple syrup. Both these syrups add wonderful flavour as well as sweetness. Take care to check the sponges as they bake to avoid the tops catching and becoming too dark.

Serves 8–10

Kit you'll need: 2 x 20cm round, deep sandwich tins, greased with sunflower oil and base-lined*; a piping bag fitted with a 1cm plain nozzle

FOR THE SPONGE
200ml sunflower oil
3 medium eggs,
   at room temperature
150g agave syrup
400g carrots, peeled and grated
275g self-raising flour
2 teaspoons baking powder
1 teaspoon ground cinnamon
1 teaspoon ground mixed spice
150g sultanas
150g walnut pieces
finely grated zest
   of 1 medium orange

FOR THE FILLING AND FROSTING
400g full-fat cream cheese
50g unsalted butter, softened
50ml maple syrup

FOR THE DECORATION
25g walnut pieces, chopped fine
ground cinnamon, for dusting

1. Heat the oven to 180°C/350°F/gas 4. To make the sponge mixture, pour the oil into a large mixing bowl, add the eggs and agave syrup, and beat with a wire whisk until thoroughly blended. Add the grated carrots and mix well.

2. Sift the flour, baking powder, cinnamon and mixed spice into another bowl. Add the sultanas, walnuts and orange zest and stir to coat the sultanas and nuts with flour. Tip into the carrot mixture and gently stir everything together until thoroughly combined.

3. Divide the mixture equally between the 2 prepared tins and spread evenly. Bake in the heated oven for about 40 minutes until the sponges are well risen – cover the tins lightly with foil after 20–30 minutes to prevent the tops from becoming too dark or burning. Remove the tins from the oven and leave to cool for 5 minutes before turning out on to a wire rack to finish cooling.

4. To make the filling and frosting, spoon the cream cheese into a large piece of muslin or a new J-cloth and gather up the ends to make a bag. Press gently to squeeze out excess moisture – this is a good trick to prevent the cheese frosting from being damp. Tip the cheese into a mixing bowl and beat with a hand-held electric whisk until smooth. Add the softened butter and maple syrup and beat well until smooth and creamy. Cover the bowl and keep in the fridge until needed.

5. When ready to assemble the cake, set one sponge crust-side down on a cake plate or board. Spoon a quarter of the chilled cream cheese mixture into the piping bag fitted with the plain nozzle and set aside. Spread about two-thirds of the remaining cream cheese mixture over the surface of the sponge layer, then pipe a ring of 'kisses' around the edge. Top with the second sponge, crust-side up. Spread the remaining cream cheese mixture over the surface to make a very thin layer and cover it neatly.

6. Sprinkle the finely chopped walnuts over the top of the cake. With the last of the cream cheese mixture, pipe a ring of small 'kisses' around the edge. Finish with a light dusting of cinnamon.

MIDSUMMER CELEBRATION CAKE

A gloriously frivolous midsummer night's dream of a cake for a summer party, this looks impressive but doesn't require hours in the kitchen. The three layers of genoise sponge, flavoured with honey and ground toasted hazelnuts, are sandwiched with raspberry jam and cream whipped with fresh raspberries.

1. Heat the oven to 190°C/375°F/ gas 5. Put the eggs into a large mixing bowl, or a free-standing electric mixer, and whisk with a hand-held electric whisk, or the mixer whisk attachment, just until frothy. Add the honey and sugar and whisk on full speed for 7–8 minutes to the ribbon stage*.

2. Sift the flour into the bowl and gently fold in* with a large metal spoon or plastic spatula. When you can no longer see any specks of flour, fold in the ground nuts until thoroughly combined.

3. Transfer a spoonful of the mixture to a smaller bowl, add the butter and mix well. Return to the whisked mixture and carefully fold in – the mixture will lose a lot of its volume.

4. Divide the mixture equally among the tins and spread evenly. Bake in the heated oven for 12–15 minutes until golden and just firm when lightly pressed in the centre. Transfer to a heatproof surface. Run a round-bladed knife around the inside of each tin to loosen the sponge, then turn out on to a wire rack and leave to cool.

5. Place one sponge crust-side down on a serving plate. Spread over half of the jam. Spread the rest of the jam over the crust side of a second layer – don't sandwich them yet.

6. Pour the cream into a large mixing bowl and whip until soft peaks* form. Add the raspberries, honey and icing sugar to taste, and whisk on medium/low speed just for a few seconds to slightly crush the berries and thicken the cream to stiff peak stage.

7. Spread a third of the raspberry cream over the sponge on the cake plate, then top with the second sponge layer (jam side up). Spread half the remaining cream over this, then place the third sponge layer, crust-side up, on top. Spread the last of the cream over the surface and heap the raspberries for finishing on the top. Halve the toasted hazelnuts and scatter over. Finish with a dusting of icing sugar. If not serving immediately, store in an airtight container in the fridge or a cool spot. Best eaten the same day, but any leftover cake can be kept overnight in the fridge.

Serves 12

Kit you'll need: 3 x 20.5cm round, deep sandwich tins, greased with butter, base-lined* and dusted with flour

FOR THE SPONGE
6 medium eggs,
    at room temperature
60g clear honey
50g caster sugar
90g plain flour
175g ground toasted hazelnuts
40g unsalted butter, melted
    and cooled

FOR THE FILLING
5 tablespoons good-quality
    raspberry jam or conserve
300ml double cream, well chilled
250g fresh raspberries
1 tablespoon clear honey
1–2 tablespoons icing sugar,
    to taste

TO FINISH
100g fresh raspberries
30g toasted whole hazelnuts
icing sugar, for dusting

BLACK FOREST GATEAU

This iconic gateau has flung off its Seventies' image. After all, what is not to like about a rich confection of chocolate, cream and cherries that lends itself to all manner of decorative extravagance? The showstopper here is made with four light-as-air chocolate whisked sponges and decorated with chocolate piped trees and chocolate-dipped cherries.

Serves 12

Kit you'll need: 2 x 23cm round, deep sandwich tins, greased with butter and base-lined*; 2 small disposable piping bags; a disposable piping bag fitted with a star nozzle

FOR THE SPONGE
6 large eggs, at room temperature
150g caster sugar
100g self-raising flour, sifted
50g cocoa powder, sifted

FOR THE FILLING AND TOPPING
2 x 390g jars black cherries in Kirsch
2 heaped tablespoons cornflour
750ml double cream (pourable not extra-thick or spooning cream), chilled

FOR THE DECORATION
150g white chocolate
250g dark chocolate (about 46% cocoa solids)
24 fresh cherries with stalks

1. Heat the oven to 180°C/350°F/gas 4. Break the eggs into a large mixing bowl, or the bowl of a free-standing mixer, and add the sugar. Whisk with a hand-held electric whisk, or the whisk attachment of the mixer, until the mixture is very pale and has reached the ribbon stage*. Add the sifted flour and cocoa and carefully fold* in with a large metal spoon or plastic spatula. Transfer the mixture to the prepared tins to fill equally and gently level the surfaces.

2. Bake in the heated oven for 25–30 minutes until the sponges are well risen and starting to shrink away from the side of the tin. Turn out on to a wire rack and leave to cool.

3. To make the filling, drain the cherries, reserving the juice, then chop them roughly into quarters. Spoon the cornflour into a small saucepan and stir in just enough of the reserved cherry juice to make a smooth paste. Gradually stir in the remaining juice. Set the pan over medium heat and

slowly bring to the boil, stirring constantly until thickened and smooth. Simmer for 2 minutes. Remove the pan from the heat and stir in the cherries. Leave to cool, then transfer to a bowl, cover tightly with clingfilm and chill until the mixture is quite firm.

4. For the decoration, melt* the white chocolate and the dark chocolate in 2 separate bowls. Dip 12 of the fresh cherries in the melted white chocolate and leave to set on a sheet of baking paper. Dip the remaining 12 cherries into the melted dark chocolate and leave to set on the paper. Spoon the rest of the melted dark chocolate into one small piping bag, and the white chocolate into the other piping bag.

5. Draw a rectangle the size of a credit card on a piece of paper, then draw a tree inside the rectangle – this will be the template for the piped decorations. Lay a large sheet of baking paper over the template. Snip the end off the dark chocolate-filled piping >>>

bag and pipe a chocolate tree shape on the paper, following the template beneath. Repeat, moving the template, so you pipe 12 good shapes – make a couple extra to allow for breakages. Leave until set and firm.

6. When the chocolate covering the cherries has set, snip the end off the white chocolate-filled piping bag and pipe thin lines of white chocolate over the dark chocolate-dipped cherries. Pipe thin lines of dark chocolate over the white chocolate-dipped cherries. Leave all the cherries to set on the baking paper.

7. Whip the chilled cream until it will stand in soft peaks*. Divide in half and set one portion aside for covering the cake. Divide the remaining cream into 3 portions.

8. Cut each sponge horizontally into 2 layers*. Divide the chilled thick cherry mixture into 3 equal portions, and spread one portion over one sponge layer. Cover with one portion of whipped cream. Top with another sponge layer, then spread with another portion of the cherry mixture followed by whipped cream. Repeat once more so you have 3 layers each of sponge, cherry mixture and cream. Top with the last sponge layer.

9. Spread half of the reserved whipped cream around the side of the cake and decorate with the piped chocolate trees. Spoon the rest of the cream into the piping bag fitted with the star nozzle and pipe rosettes around the top edge of the cake. Decorate with the chocolate-dipped cherries. Serve as soon as possible.

'I like to respect the classics: sponge, chocolate, cream, cherries and Kirsch in a Black Forest Gateau... It just works.'

ALVIN

TOASTED ALMOND & BITTER CHOCOLATE CAKE

Rich and glamorous, enrobed in melted chocolate and decorated with more chocolate and gold, this celebration cake is made with whole unblanched almonds, lightly toasted and then finely ground, rather than flour. The key to the richness is to use a good chocolate (70 per cent cocoa solids). For optimum flavour and texture, leave the cake to mature for a day after baking, and for extra drama, use chocolate transfer sheets to transfer edible gold patterns on to the top of the cake.

1. Heat your oven to 180°C/350°F/gas 4. Tip the whole almonds into a small baking dish or tin and toast in the oven for 7 minutes. Remove and cool; leave the oven on.

2. While the nuts are cooling, break up the chocolate for the sponge into even-sized pieces and melt* gently, stirring occasionally, until smooth. Set aside to cool until needed.

3. Tip the cooled nuts into a food processor and blitz until finely ground – take care not to go too far or the ground nuts will become a paste. Set aside.

4. Put the soft butter into a large mixing bowl, or the bowl of a large free-standing electric mixer, and beat well with a hand-held electric whisk, or the whisk attachment of the mixer, until creamy and mayonnaise-like. Set aside 1 tablespoon of the weighed sugar for the egg whites, then gradually beat the remaining sugar into the butter, adding a couple of tablespoons at a time.

Scrape down the side of the bowl and beat for a further 2 minutes until the mixture looks pale and fluffy. Scrape down the side of the bowl again, then add the egg yolks one at a time, beating well after each addition.

5. Put the egg whites and salt into another large mixing bowl (spotlessly clean and grease-free) and whisk (with a clean whisk) until soft peaks* form when the whisk is lifted out of the bowl. Sprinkle the reserved sugar over the whites, then whisk for another minute or so until the mixture stands in stiff peaks*.

6. Pour the melted chocolate into the butter and sugar mixture and gently fold in* using a large metal spoon or plastic spatula. Add the ground almonds and fold in. Add a quarter of the egg whites and gently stir in with the spoon or spatula to loosen the heavy mixture, then gently fold in the rest of the whites in 3 batches – take care not to knock out the air.

>>>

Serves 8–10

Kit you'll need: 1 x 20.5cm round springclip tin or round, deep cake tin, greased and base-lined*; a reusable silicone sheet or printed chocolate transfer sheet

FOR THE SPONGE
125g whole unblanched almonds
125g dark chocolate (about 70% cocoa solids)
125g unsalted butter, softened
100g caster sugar
4 medium eggs, at room temperature, separated
good pinch of salt

FOR THE CHOCOLATE COVERING
125g dark chocolate (about 70% cocoa solids)
1 tablespoon amaretto (almond liqueur) OR dark rum
100g unsalted butter, softened

TO DECORATE
75g dark chocolate (around 70% cocoa solids)
cocoa powder OR edible gold dust, for dusting (optional)

7. Spoon the mixture into the prepared tin and spread evenly. Bake in the heated oven for about 25 minutes until a skewer inserted into the cake halfway between the side of the tin and the centre comes out clean – the centre should remain a bit moist as you don't want to overcook this cake.

8. Remove the tin from the oven and set it on the worktop on top of a wet tea towel. Run a round-bladed knife around the inside of the tin to loosen the sponge, then leave to cool.

9. When the cake is cold, you can make the covering. Break up the chocolate and put into a heatproof bowl with the amaretto or rum, then melt gently over a pan of simmering water. Remove the bowl from the pan and stir in the butter a little at a time to make a smooth and glossy

mixture. If the chocolate starts to firm up before all the butter has been incorporated, set the bowl back over the hot water and stir until smooth again. Set aside.

10. Turn out the cake upside down on to a wire rack set over a baking sheet (to catch the drips). As soon as the chocolate mixture is starting to thicken but is still pourable, pour it over the cake and allow it to flow down the sides. Use a round-bladed knife or offset palette knife to neaten up and smooth the side. Transfer to a cake board or serving plate and leave until almost set.

11. Meanwhile, for the decoration, break up the chocolate and melt it. Stir until smooth, then pour on to the silicone sheet/chocolate transfer sheet (or on to a sheet of baking paper) and spread it out fairly thinly – work quickly so the chocolate doesn't firm up before

it is evenly spread. Leave in a cool spot but not the fridge (beads of moisture will appear when you bring it back into the kitchen).

12. Once set, carefully break the chocolate into shards and arrange on top of the cake – either gently pressed into the icing so the shards stand vertically like sails, or scattered over the icing to cover. Finish with cocoa powder or edible gold dust.

13. To cut neat slices it's best to use a warmed large, sharp knife – have a jug of very hot water and kitchen paper at hand so you can dip the knife in water and wipe it clean and dry between each slice. Store in an airtight container at cool room temperature – not in the fridge – and eat within 5 days.

ZINGY CITRUS MADEIRA CAKE

Fresh, vibrant and rich, this version of Madeira cake is made by carefully creaming butter and sugar, then gradually beating in eggs and folding in flour and grated orange and lemon zest to make a smooth batter. The baked cake is decorated with a citrus glacé icing and curls of candied citrus peel.

1. Heat the oven to 180°C/350°F/gas 4. Put the soft butter into a mixing bowl, or the bowl of a free-standing electric mixer, and beat with a wooden spoon or a hand-held electric whisk, or the mixer whisk attachment, until creamy. Add the sugar and beat until light and fluffy. Scrape down the side of the bowl, then gradually beat in the eggs, beating well after each addition, and adding a tablespoon of the weighed flour with each of the last 2 additions of egg.

2. Sift the rest of the flour and the salt into the bowl, then add the grated zests and carefully fold* in with a large metal spoon until thoroughly combined. Transfer the mixture to the prepared tin and spread evenly.

3. Bake in the heated oven for about 1 hour until the cake is a good golden brown and a skewer inserted into the centre comes out clean. Set the tin on a wire rack. Run a thin, round-bladed knife around the inside of the tin to loosen the cake, then leave to cool for 15 minutes before carefully removing the cake from the tin – use the ends of the lining paper to help you. Leave on the wire rack until completely cold.

4. Meanwhile, make the decoration. Put the sugar and water into a small pan, set over low heat and stir until the sugar has dissolved. Bring to the boil, then remove from the heat. Using a vegetable peeler, pare off long strips of peel from the orange and lemon and add it to the syrup. Return to low heat and simmer gently for about 5 minutes until the peel is very soft. Remove and cool, then drain. Leave the peel on a sheet of baking paper to dry.

5. To make the icing, sift the icing sugar into a small bowl and stir in the juices (squeezed from the orange and lemon) to make a smooth, runny icing – add a bit more juice, if necessary. Drizzle the icing over the top of the cake, letting it run down the sides.

6. Using a cocktail stick or skewer, carefully lift the candied peel on to the cake and arrange in curls. Transfer the cake to a plate.

Serves 8

Kit you'll need: 1 x 450g loaf tin, about 19 x 12.5 x 7.5cm, greased with butter, lined with a long strip of baking paper* and dusted with flour

FOR THE CAKE MIXTURE
150g unsalted butter, softened
150g caster sugar
4 medium eggs, at room temperature, beaten to mix
200g self-raising flour
pinch of salt
finely grated zest of 2 medium oranges
finely grated zest of 1 large unwaxed lemon

FOR THE CANDIED PEEL DECORATION
75g caster sugar
100ml water
1 medium orange
1 large unwaxed lemon

FOR THE ICING
150g icing sugar
about 1 tablespoon orange juice
about 1 tablespoon lemon juice

PURPLE FOREST GATEAU

A fun take on a classic theme: layers of very dark, purplish sponge, made with cocoa and grated beetroot, are sandwiched with a rich mascarpone cream and Kirsch-soaked, lightly cooked cherries. The cake is covered in a light and fluffy Italian meringue and decorated with small chocolate truffles and fresh cherries.

Serves 16

Kit you'll need: 3 x 18cm round, deep sandwich tins OR springclip tins, greased with butter, base-lined* and dusted with flour; an 18cm cake board or card; a kitchen blowtorch

FOR THE SPONGE LAYERS
250g plain flour
50g cocoa powder
1 teaspoon bicarbonate of soda
¼ teaspoon fine sea salt
175g lightly salted butter, softened
400g caster sugar
2 medium eggs, separated,
    at room temperature

250g cold cooked beetroot,
    grated
1 vanilla pod, split open
300ml hot water (from the tap)

FOR THE POACHED CHERRIES
400g large fresh, ripe cherries,
    pitted
100g caster sugar
120ml Kirsch

FOR THE CREAM FILLING
250g mascarpone, chilled
30g icing sugar, sifted
100ml double cream, well chilled

FOR THE TRUFFLES
75ml double cream
100g dark chocolate (about 70%
    cocoa solids), finely chopped
1 tablespoon cocoa powder

FOR THE ITALIAN MERINGUE FROSTING
3 medium egg whites,
    at room temperature
¼ teaspoon cream of tartar
160g caster sugar
4 tablespoons water

TO FINISH
150g frozen 'Fruits of the Forest'
    berries and currants mix
    OR 200g fresh cherries

1. Heat the oven to 170°C/325°F/ gas 3. Sift the flour, cocoa powder, bicarbonate of soda and salt into a bowl and set aside. Put the soft butter and sugar into the bowl of a free-standing electric mixer fitted with the whisk attachment and beat thoroughly for about 4 minutes until fluffy – scrape down the side of the bowl from time to time. Add the egg yolks one at a time, beating well after each addition. Scrape down the

side of the bowl, then beat on full speed for 3 minutes until the mixture is light.

2. Add the grated beetroot, then, using the tip of a small, sharp knife, scrape the seeds from the split vanilla pod into the bowl. Using low speed, whisk in until thoroughly combined. Add half of the flour mixture and mix in on low speed. Gradually add the hot water, still mixing on

low speed, then add the rest of the flour mixture and mix until thoroughly combined.

3. In another bowl, whisk the egg whites until they will stand in stiff peaks*, then fold* into the mixture with a large metal spoon.

4. Divide the mixture equally between the 3 prepared tins and spread evenly. Bake in the heated oven for about 30 minutes until >>>

the sponges are well risen, starting to shrink from the side of the tin and feel firm when gently pressed in the centre. Run a round-bladed knife around the inside of each tin to loosen the sponge, then cool and firm up for 10 minutes before turning out on to wire racks. Leave to cool completely.

5. Meanwhile, prepare the poached cherries. Put them in a medium pan with the sugar and Kirsch and set over low heat. Stir gently until the sugar has dissolved, then bring to the boil and simmer for about 10 minutes until the fruit is soft – time depends on ripeness. Leave to cool, then drain the cherries, reserving the juice. Put the cherries on a plate, cover and keep in the fridge, with the syrup, until needed.

6. To make the cream filling, put the mascarpone and icing sugar into the (clean) bowl of the electric mixer and beat with the whisk attachment on low speed until smooth and creamy. Add the double cream and beat on full speed until very thick. Cover and keep in the fridge until needed.

7. For the truffles, heat the cream until almost boiling. Put the chocolate into a heatproof bowl and pour over the hot cream, then leave for a couple of minutes until melted. Stir gently until this ganache is smooth, then cover and chill until firm. Put the cocoa powder into a shallow dish. Scoop up a rounded teaspoon of the firm ganache and roll it in your hands to a neat ball, then drop it into the cocoa. Repeat with the rest of the ganache. Jiggle the dish so the truffles become coated in cocoa. Cover and keep in the fridge until needed.

8. To make the Italian meringue frosting, put the egg whites and cream of tartar into the (clean and grease-free) bowl of the mixer and whisk on full speed until the mixture will stand in stiff peaks. Put the sugar and water into a small pan and heat gently, stirring frequently, until the sugar has completely dissolved (have a bowl of cold water and a pastry brush at hand to brush down the side of the pan, to prevent the sugar from crystallising on the side). Bring to the boil and boil until the syrup reaches 120°C on a sugar thermometer.

Working quickly, pour the hot syrup in a steady stream on to the egg whites while whisking at full speed, to make a thick, glossy meringue. Continue whisking until the meringue cools to room temperature.

9. To assemble the cake, set one sponge crust-side down on the cake board and lightly brush with cherry syrup. Spread half of the cream filling over the sponge and arrange half of the poached cherries on top. Repeat with a second sponge, cherry syrup and the rest of the cream filling and poached cherries. Top with the third sponge, crust-side up. Gently press the top so the layers stick together. Thickly spread and swirl the meringue over the top and side of the cake, using an offset palette knife to cover evenly. Quickly tinge the tips of the swirls brown with a kitchen blowtorch.

10. Decorate the cake with the truffles and frozen mixed berries and currants, or fresh cherries, then serve immediately.

SUGAR-FREE PINEAPPLE UPSIDE-DOWN CAKE

Good things in baking often start off upside down and then get turned the right way up for eating, especially those with sticky-sweet toppings: think tarte tatin. This upside-down cake is an interesting variation on the classic, being made without refined sugar. Instead the all-in-one sponge is sweetened with agave nectar, a golden-coloured syrup made from various species of the spiky Mexican agave plant (which also are used to make tequila).

1. Heat the oven to 170°C/325°F/ gas 3. First prepare the base, which will become the topping on the cake. Spoon half of the agave nectar into the tin and spread it out evenly. Place the pineapple rings on top and set a cherry in the centre of each; arrange the remaining cherries along the middle of the tin. Set aside while you make the sponge.

2. Sift the flour and salt into a mixing bowl and make a well in the centre. Pour the melted butter, agave nectar, eggs and vanilla into the well, then gradually mix in the flour, using a wooden spoon or wire whisk, to make a smooth, thick yet runny batter.

3. Carefully spoon the batter into the tin to cover the fruit – if you pour it in you might dislodge the fruit. Spread evenly so the corners are filled. Bake in the heated oven for about 30 minutes until the sponge is golden brown and a skewer inserted into the centre comes out clean.

4. Set the tin on a heatproof surface and leave the cake to cool and firm up for 5 minutes, then hold an upturned wire rack over the top of the tin and invert the whole thing. Lift off the tin and carefully peel off the lining paper. Drizzle the remaining agave syrup over the cake. Leave to cool.

5. Meanwhile, make the custard. Pour the milk into a medium pan. Using the tip of a small, sharp knife, scrape the vanilla seeds from the split pod into the milk. Add the maple syrup and bring almost to the boil. Remove from the heat and leave to infuse for 5 minutes. Meanwhile, put the egg yolks and cornflour into a heatproof mixing bowl and beat until smooth using a wooden spoon or wire whisk. Pour the warm milk into the bowl, whisking constantly, then pour the mixture back into the pan. Set over medium heat and stir until the mixture thickens enough to coat the back of the spoon. Pour into a jug and serve with the cake.

Serves 8–10

Kit you'll need: 1 baking tin, 32 × 22cm × 5cm, greased and lined*

FOR THE FRUIT TOPPING
120ml agave nectar
    (light amber mild variety)
1 × 425g tin pineapple rings
    in juice, drained
12 frozen pitted cherries

FOR THE SPONGE MIXTURE
300g self-raising flour
¼ teaspoon salt
300g unsalted butter,
    melted and cooled
200g agave nectar
    (light amber mild variety)
5 large eggs, at room
    temperature, beaten to mix
1 teaspoon vanilla extract

FOR THE MAPLE SYRUP CUSTARD
500ml full-fat
    or extra-creamy milk
1 vanilla pod, split open
75g maple syrup
6 medium egg yolks,
    at room temperature
15g cornflour

HONEY CAKE

A light-as-air honey cake is typical for Rosh Hashana, Jewish New Year. As this is an autumnal festival, apples dipped in honey are often added, but this one has nuts and brandy (or rum). Best baked a day or so in advance to allow the flavours to mature, the cake looks pretty baked in a ring, or you could use a loaf tin.

Serves 12–16

Kit you'll need: 1 x 20cm fluted cake ring tin, well greased with butter or sunflower oil, OR a 900g loaf tin, about 26 x 12.5 x 7.5cm, well greased with butter or oil and lined with a ready-made loaf tin liner or lined base and sides*, OR a 2-litre bundt tin, well greased with butter or oil

250g plain flour
100g walnut pieces
1 tablespoon cocoa powder
1 teaspoon ground cinnamon
½ teaspoon ground mixed spice
½ teaspoon baking powder
½ teaspoon bicarbonate of soda
175g clear honey
125ml sunflower oil
3 tablespoons brandy
   OR dark rum
1 tablespoon instant coffee
   (powder or granules), dissolved
   in 75ml boiling water
3 medium eggs,
   at room temperature
good pinch of salt
100g caster sugar
50g dark brown muscovado sugar
icing sugar, for dusting

1. Heat the oven to 180°C/350°F/gas 4. Put a tablespoon of the weighed flour into a small bowl. Chop the walnuts a bit finer – if the pieces are too big it will be difficult to slice the light sponge neatly – then add to the flour in the bowl and toss to combine. Set aside.

2. Sift the rest of the flour into another bowl with the cocoa powder, cinnamon, mixed spice, baking powder and bicarbonate of soda. Set aside.

3. Weigh the honey in a measuring jug, then add the oil, brandy or rum and coffee. Stir well.

4. Separate the eggs, putting the whites into a large mixing bowl, or the bowl of a free-standing electric mixer, and the yolks into another bowl. Add the salt to the whites and whisk with a hand-held electric whisk, or the whisk attachment of the mixer, until stiff peaks* form when the whisk is lifted. Set aside.

5. Add both sugars to the egg yolks and whisk (there's no need to wash the whisk) for about 3 minutes until the mixture is thick and looks much paler.

Give the honey mixture a stir, then slowly pour into the yolk mixture in a thin, steady stream, whisking on medium speed. The mixture will become thinner.

6. Sift the flour mixture into the bowl and gently stir in with a large metal spoon or plastic spatula, then stir in the flour-coated walnuts. Finally, fold* in the egg whites in 3 batches.

7. Pour the mixture into the prepared tin and spread evenly. Bake in the heated oven for about 40 minutes until well risen and a skewer inserted into the deepest part of the cake comes out clean. Check the cake after 25 minutes and cover lightly with a sheet of baking paper or foil if it seems to be browning too quickly – the honey will give the crust a good colour but it burns easily too.

8. Set the tin on a wire rack and leave the cake to cool before turning out. For the best flavour wrap the cake in baking paper or foil and store in an airtight container for 1–2 days before slicing. The cake looks very pretty dusted with icing sugar just before serving. Best eaten within 5 days.

HARVEST APPLE CAKE

Cakes made to celebrate every kind of harvest are part of a worldwide tradition. This light, crunchy-topped apple and nut sponge is perfect for using up windfall apples. For a short time in early autumn you might find fresh, sweet cobnuts (the cultivated variety of the hazelnut) at farmers' markets and in some greengrocers – otherwise choose hazlenuts, almonds or walnuts.

Serves 8–10

Kit you'll need: 1 x 20.5 round springclip tin, greased with butter and base-lined*; a baking sheet

FOR THE FRUIT MIXTURE
4–5 medium/large tart eating apples, such as Braeburns (about 650g)
40g cobnuts OR other nuts such as hazelnuts, almonds or walnuts, chopped
30g sultanas or raisins
2 tablespoons caster sugar
½ teaspoon ground cinnamon
25g unsalted butter, melted

FOR THE SPONGE MIXTURE
75g unsalted butter, softened
140g caster sugar
½ teaspoon vanilla extract
2 medium eggs, at room temperature, separated
140g self-raising flour
4 tablespoons milk, at room temperature

FOR THE TOPPING
1 tablespoon caster sugar
½ teaspoon ground cinnamon

1. Heat the oven to 180°C/350°F/gas 4. Peel, quarter and core the apples, then slice thinly into a mixing bowl (if you are using windfall or blemished apples you will need 400–425g prepared apples). Set aside 1 tablespoon of the chopped nuts for the topping, then add the rest of the nuts and the sultanas to the sliced apples.

2. Sprinkle the caster sugar and cinnamon over the mixture, then toss everything together with your hands or a wooden spoon. Drizzle the melted butter over the top and toss again until thoroughly combined. Tip the mixture into the prepared tin and gently spread out evenly – don't compact the apples as you want the sponge mixture to trickle down to fill the spaces between slices. The tin will be about half full.

3. To make the sponge, put the softened butter, sugar and vanilla into a mixing bowl, or the bowl of a large free-standing electric mixer, and beat with a wooden spoon or hand-held electric whisk, or the whisk attachment of the mixer, until light and fluffy. Scrape down the side of the bowl, then add the egg yolks one at a time, beating well after each addition.

4. Sift half the flour into the bowl and add half the milk. Mix in gently, using a large metal spoon or plastic spatula, or the mixer whisk on low speed. Add the rest of the flour and milk and mix in until everything is thoroughly combined to make a fairly stiff mixture.

5. Put the 2 egg whites into a very clean, grease-free bowl and whisk with a clean whisk until the mixture stands in stiff peaks*. Add a quarter of the whites to the yolk mixture and gently mix in with a large metal spoon or plastic spatula, then fold in* the rest of the whites gently but thoroughly.

6. Spoon the sponge mixture over the apples and gently spread it out. Give the tin a little shake to settle the mixture, then set the tin on the baking sheet (unless you know your tin is leak-proof).

7. To make the topping, combine the reserved chopped nuts with the sugar and cinnamon in a small bowl. Scatter evenly over the top of the sponge mixture. Bake in the heated oven for 40–45 minutes until the cake is risen and golden brown, and a skewer inserted into the centre comes out clean. Check the cake after 30 minutes and cover with a sheet of foil or baking paper if it is browning too quickly.

8. Transfer the tin to a wire rack. Run a thin, round-bladed knife around the inside of the tin to loosen the sponge, then unclip the side. Leave the cake to cool before transferring it to a serving plate (the apples on the base of the cake will be moist). Store in an airtight container and eat within 2 days.

FROSTED WALNUT LAYER CAKE

A pretty white-iced triple-layer cake to make in autumn, when walnuts are harvested, this looks glamorous enough for an anniversary or other important celebration. There are walnuts galore in the cake – the sponge is made with chopped nuts, and walnut halves coated in a rich caramel provide the decoration. The sponges are sandwiched with a vanilla buttercream and the cake is covered with a divine thick marshmallow-like icing.

Serves 8–10

Kit you'll need: 3 x 20cm round, deep sandwich tins, greased with butter and base-lined*; a silicone sheet OR oiled baking sheet

FOR THE SPONGES
225g self-raising flour
1 teaspoon baking powder
100g walnuts, finely chopped
225g unsalted butter, softened
225g caster sugar
4 large eggs, at room
 temperature, beaten to mix

FOR THE CARAMELISED WALNUTS
100g caster sugar
10 walnut halves

FOR THE BUTTERCREAM
125g unsalted butter, softened
½ teaspoon vanilla extract
2 tablespoons milk,
 at room temperature
250g icing sugar, sifted

FOR THE BOILED ICING
2 large egg whites
350g caster sugar
4 tablespoons water
¼ teaspoon cream of tartar

1. Heat the oven to 170°C/325°F/ gas 3. Combine the flour, baking powder and chopped walnuts in a mixing bowl.

2. In another large mixing bowl, or a free-standing electric mixer, beat the butter with the sugar until pale and fluffy using a wooden spoon or a hand-held electric whisk, or the mixer whisk attachment. Scrape down the side of the bowl, then gradually add the eggs, beating well after each addition. Add the flour mixture to the bowl and gently fold* in using a large metal spoon.

3. Divide the mixture equally between the 3 prepared tins and spread evenly, making sure the surfaces are level. Bake in the heated oven for 25–30 minutes until the sponges are golden and springy when lightly pressed in the centre. Cool in the tins for a few minutes, then turn out on to a wire rack* to finish cooling.

4. For the caramelised walnuts, tip the sugar into a pan and cook over low heat until the sugar is beginning to melt. Increase the heat so the sugar syrup boils and cook until it turns to a dark golden caramel. Remove from the heat, add the walnuts and swirl in the pan so the nuts are completely coated in caramel. Transfer to the silicone sheet, or oiled baking sheet, and leave to set.

5. To make the buttercream, put the soft butter, vanilla, half of the milk and half of the icing sugar into a bowl. Beat with a wooden spoon or hand-held electric whisk until smooth. Scrape down the bowl, then beat in the rest of the icing sugar, plus more milk, as needed, to make a smooth, spreadable buttercream.

6. Set one of the cold sponges, crust-side down, on a serving plate or cake board and spread half of the buttercream over the surface in an even layer. Place a second sponge on top, crust-side up, and spread the rest of the buttercream evenly over the surface. Place the third sponge on top, crust-side up.

7. To make the boiled icing, put the egg whites, sugar, water and cream of tartar into a large heatproof bowl. Set the bowl over a saucepan of hot water (the base of the bowl shouldn't touch the water) and whisk using a hand-held electric whisk for 8–10 minutes until the icing is very thick and white and will hold stiff peaks*. Remove the bowl from the pan and, working quickly as the icing will set rapidly, cover the top and sides of the cake, swirling the icing to form softened peaks.

8. While the icing is still soft, decorate with the caramelised walnuts, then leave to set in a cool place (not the fridge).

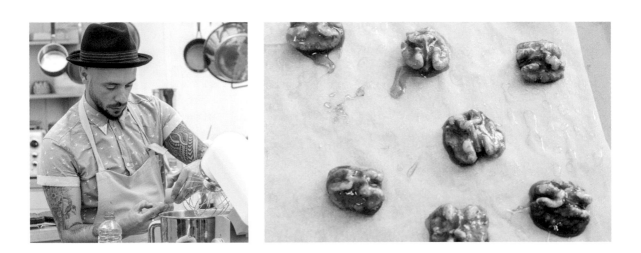

DOUBLE CHOCOLATE
SWIRLED CAKE

Ask the Bakers what kind of cake they make for a birthday or other special occasion and almost inevitably they say chocolate – the richer and more eye-catching the better. This one ticks all the boxes. Dark and white chocolate mixtures are swirled together in the tins to make the sponge layers and these are sandwiched with a rum truffle ganache. The final, spectacular touch is the icing: dark chocolate ganache marbled with white chocolate. The cake tastes even richer if left for a day before cutting.

Serves 12

Kit you'll need: 2 x 20.5cm round, deep sandwich tins, greased and base-lined*

FOR THE SPONGE
250g unsalted butter, softened
250g caster sugar
4 large eggs, at room temperature
1 teaspoon vanilla extract
250g self-raising flour
good pinch of salt

75g dark chocolate (about 70% cocoa solids), roughly chopped
75g white chocolate (about 30% cocoa solids), roughly chopped
1 tablespoon cocoa powder

FOR THE FILLING
100g dark chocolate (about 70% cocoa solids), broken up
1 tablespoon dark rum
125ml whipping cream

FOR THE DARK CHOCOLATE GANACHE
150g dark chocolate (about 70% cocoa solids), broken up
150ml whipping cream

FOR THE WHITE CHOCOLATE GANACHE
75g white chocolate (about 30% cocoa solids), broken up
75ml whipping cream

1. Heat the oven to 180°C/350°F/gas 4. Put the soft butter into a large mixing bowl, or the bowl of a free-standing electric mixer, and beat with a wooden spoon or a hand-held electric whisk, or using the whisk attachment of the mixer, for a few minutes until creamy and mayonnaise-like. Gradually beat in the sugar and continue beating until the mixture turns pale and fluffy, scraping down the side of the bowl from time to time.

2. Beat the eggs with the vanilla extract just until combined, then gradually add to the creamed

mixture, beating well after each addition. Add 1 tablespoon of the weighed flour with each of the last 2 portions of egg to prevent the mixture from curdling. Sift the rest of the flour and the salt into the bowl and gently fold in* with a large metal spoon. Transfer half of the mixture to another bowl.

3. Gently melt* the chopped dark chocolate. Leave to cool while you melt the white chocolate; cool this too.

4. Sift the cocoa into one bowl of cake mixture and add the cooled melted dark chocolate, then fold

them in gently until thoroughly combined. Carefully fold the cooled melted white chocolate into the other bowl of cake mixture.

5. You want to put roughly half of the dark chocolate mixture and half of the white chocolate mixture into each of the prepared tins. Spoon the 2 mixtures alternately into the tins – a heaped tablespoonful of the dark chocolate mixture into each tin and then a heaped tablespoonful of the white chocolate mix into both tins. When you've finished, gently bang each tin on the worktop several times to >>>

settle the mixtures and eliminate any pockets of air. Carefully swirl a chopstick or table knife through the 2 mixtures in each tin to marble them.

6. Bake in the heated oven for 25–30 minutes until the sponges feel springy when gently pressed in the centre. For best results check the cakes after 20 minutes and rotate the tins to be sure the sponges bake evenly. Remove from the oven and set on a heatproof surface. Run a round-bladed knife around the inside of the tins to loosen the sponges, then turn out on to a wire rack and leave to cool completely.

7. When the cakes are cold, make the filling. Put the chocolate into a food processor and blitz to chop fairly finely. Stop the machine and add the rum. Heat the cream in a saucepan until it just comes to the boil, then, with the machine running, pour the cream into the processor through the feed tube. When the mixture is thick and smooth, scrape down the side of the processor bowl, then run the machine for a couple of minutes until the mixture is no longer warm. Transfer the mixture to a mixing bowl, or the bowl of a free-standing mixer, and whisk to the ribbon stage*.

8. Place one sponge layer crust-side down on a wire rack set over a baking sheet. Spread over the chocolate filling. Set the second sponge on top, crust-side up. Leave to set and firm up.

9. To make the dark chocolate ganache, put the chocolate in the food processor bowl and chop finely. Heat the cream until just boiling, then, with the machine running, pour into the processor bowl through the feed tube. Blitz until smooth. Scrape down the side of the bowl, then run the machine until the ganache is barely warm but still very fluid. Pour the ganache over the cake to cover it completely, using a palette knife if necessary to help ease the ganache down the side of the cake.

10. Working quickly, before the dark ganache has time to set, wash out the processor bowl and make the white chocolate ganache in the same way. Pour it into a jug and, if necessary, leave until it has thickened up but is still pourable – like double cream. Then, working across from one side of the cake to the other, pour the white ganache in thick stripes over the cake surface, allowing it to trickle down the sides. Gently draw a skewer along the stripes (not across them) to give a marbled appearance. Leave until firm and set before transferring to a cake board or serving plate. Store in an airtight container in a cool place – not the fridge – and eat within 5 days.

'My family love anything chocolate-related. Our traditional Bangladeshi food for a celebration is savoury, but I will round it off with a classic centrepiece chocolate cake.'

NADIYA

GINGERBREAD CAKE HAUNTED HOUSES

These are great fun for young bakers to help make for a Hallowe'en party — a simple melt-and-mix gingerbread sponge to be baked, white fondant icing to be mixed, black ready-made icing to be rolled, squares measured and cut, and the houses assembled and decorated. For a spooky effect, put LED flickering tea lights amongst the haunted houses and turn off the other lights...

1. Heat the oven to 180°C/350°F/gas 4. Sift the flour, bicarbonate of soda, cinnamon, mixed spice, ginger and salt into a mixing bowl.

2. Gently melt the butter with the syrup, treacle and sugar in a small pan. Remove from the heat and leave to cool. Heat the milk in another small pan until lukewarm, then pour into the flour mixture, followed by the butter mixture and the beaten egg. Mix well with a wooden spoon to make a thick, sticky, lump-free mixture.

3. Scrape into the prepared tin and spread evenly so the corners are filled. Bake in the heated oven for 12–15 minutes until firm to the touch. Set the tin on a wire rack. Run a round-bladed knife around the inside of the tin to loosen the sponge, then leave to cool.

4. When the sponge is cold, turn it out on to a cutting board. Put the black ready-to-roll icing between 2 sheets of clingfilm and roll out to a thin rectangle just slightly larger than the base of the cake tin. Peel off the top sheet of clingfilm.

5. Put the fondant icing sugar into a bowl, add the cold water and stir to make a smooth icing with the consistency of double cream. Spread a thin layer of this white fondant icing over the top of the cake. Slip your hands under the clingfilm beneath the black icing and flip it over on to the cake. Peel off the clingfilm and gently press the black icing smoothly on to the top surface of the cake.

6. With a large knife and a ruler, neatly trim the sides of the cake to make a 20 x 25cm rectangle. Now cut into 20 equal squares, using the ruler to help. Cut 6 of the squares in half diagonally — these will be the 12 roofs. You need 12 squares for the houses (you will have 2 squares left over — cook's perk to enjoy).

>>>

Makes 12

Kit you'll need: 1 traybake tin or cake tin, 20.5 x 25.5 x 5cm, greased with butter and base-lined*

175g plain flour
1 teaspoon bicarbonate of soda
1 teaspoon ground cinnamon
1 teaspoon ground mixed spice
1 tablespoon ground ginger
good pinch of salt
100g unsalted butter
2 tablespoons golden syrup
2 tablespoons black treacle
100g light or dark brown muscovado sugar
100ml milk (whole or semi-skimmed)
1 large egg, beaten to mix

TO FINISH
250g black ready-to-roll fondant icing
200g fondant icing sugar
2 tablespoons cold water
liquorice sweets, such as All-sorts

7. Place one house square, black-iced-side up, on the worktop in front of you. Spread some white fondant icing thickly in a strip across one vertical side of the house square. Press the flat edge of the long side of a roof triangle on to this strip of white icing so the roof is attached to the house – be sure to place the triangle black-iced-side up, so the iced sides of the house and roof are facing in the same direction. The roof triangle will extend beyond the sides of the house square like eaves. Repeat with the other 11 houses and roofs. Leave the shapes flat on the board for now (don't try to stand them up).

8. Spoon the remaining white icing into the piping bag and snip off the tip to make a fine writing opening. Pipe a rectangular door and 2 windows on to the black-iced side of each house – save the remaining white fondant icing. Leave until set, then turn the houses upright and arrange on a board or large serving plate (if necessary, use a good dab of fondant icing to 'glue' the base of each house to the board or plate).

9. Fix a liquorice sweet 'chimney' on to each roof with a dab of icing. You could use the rest of the icing to pipe thin strands of 'cobwebs' between the houses. Leave to set. Best eaten the same or the next day.

Variation

If you're not having a Hallowe'en party, finish the cake with a lemon water-icing instead: sift 65g icing sugar into a bowl and stir in 1 tablespoon lemon juice to make a smooth, runny icing (like thin cream). Drizzle over the cake, then decorate with thin slices of stem ginger (from a jar) or crystallised ginger.

DATE & WALNUT CAKE

There is something wonderfully cosy about a date and walnut cake – imagine curling up by a log fire in the days after Christmas, tucking into a slice of this lovely melt-and-mix loaf made with the last of the dates in the box and the few remaining walnuts. The cake is fairly low in fat but the dates give it a rich sticky-toffee-pudding taste.

1. Put the dates, sugar, butter, milk and bicarbonate of soda in a large saucepan (it has to be big enough to hold all the ingredients). Set over low heat and stir gently with a wooden spoon until the butter has melted. Turn up the heat to medium so the mixture boils (it will turn foamy), then let it simmer for 30 seconds. Remove the pan from the heat and give the mixture a stir. Leave it cool for 20 minutes.

2. Heat the oven to 180°C/ 350°F/gas 4.

3. Stir the beaten egg into the date mixture. Sift the flour, salt and baking powder into the pan. Add the pieces of bran left in the sieve together with the walnuts and mix everything together until thoroughly combined.

4. Scrape the mixture into the prepared tin and spread evenly so the corners are well filled. Bake in the heated oven for about 40 minutes until the cake is golden and a skewer inserted into the centre comes out clean. Set the tin on a wire rack and leave until the loaf cake is cool before carefully lifting it out of the tin (use the lining paper to help you).

5. You can eat the cake straight away but it will be even better if you wrap it in foil or baking paper and keep it in an airtight container for a day before slicing. Consume within 5 days.

Serves 10

Kit you'll need: 1 x 900g loaf tin, about 26 x 12.5 x 7.5cm, greased with butter and lined with a long strip of baking paper*

175g pitted dates, chopped
100g light brown muscovado sugar
50g unsalted butter
250ml milk
½ teaspoon bicarbonate of soda
1 medium egg, beaten to mix
225g stoneground plain wholemeal flour
good pinch of salt
1½ teaspoons baking powder
50g walnut pieces

NUT-TOPPED CHRISTMAS CAKE

Here's a lovely rustic cake finished with glazed nuts and bursting with the flavours and fragrances of Christmas. For a rich cake it is fairly low in fat and it's very simple to make. All you need is a pan and wooden spoon – stir the dried fruit, spice, sugar, butter and cider together until the fruit becomes plump and richly aromatic, then mix in the eggs and flour.

Serves 12

Kit you'll need: 1 x 20.5cm square, deep cake tin, greased with butter and base-lined*

FOR THE CAKE MIXTURE
225g luxury dried fruit mix (including vine fruits plus cherries and pineapple pieces)
50g soft-dried apricots
50g soft-dried prunes
200g dark brown muscovado sugar
75g unsalted butter
1 teaspoon ground mixed spice
1 teaspoon ground cinnamon
1 teaspoon ground ginger
350ml dry cider
2 medium eggs, at room temperature, beaten to mix
225g plain flour
2 good pinches of salt
2 teaspoons baking powder

TO DECORATE
3 tablespoons apricot jam
1 tablespoon water
200g whole mixed nuts (brazils, almonds, pecans, walnut halves)

1. You need a saucepan large enough to hold all the ingredients. Tip the dried fruit mixture into the pan. Using kitchen scissors, snip the apricots and prunes into quarters and add to the pan together with the sugar, butter, mixed spice, cinnamon, ground ginger and cider.

2. Set the pan over medium heat and stir gently until the butter has melted, then bring it to the boil, stirring constantly. Turn down the heat and simmer gently for 5 minutes, stirring frequently. Remove the pan from the heat, cover and set aside to macerate for 2 hours.

3. Towards the end of this time, heat the oven to 170°C/325°F/gas 3. Stir the fruit mixture gently, then stir in the beaten eggs until thoroughly combined. Sift the flour, salt and baking powder into the pan and gently mix in.

4. Scrape the mixture into the prepared tin and spread evenly. Bake in the heated oven for about 45 minutes until the cake is a rich brown and a skewer inserted into the centre comes out clean. Set the tin on a wire rack and leave until the cake is completely cold before turning out. If you don't want to finish the cake immediately, wrap it in baking paper and store in an airtight container for up to 2 days.

5. To finish the cake, gently warm the jam with the water in a small pan until it liquefies (don't worry about small fragments of fruit in the melted jam, but if there are large lumps it is best to sieve the jam and then return it to the pan). Stir over low heat until the jam just comes to the boil. Remove from the heat.

6. Brush a layer of jam glaze over the cake. Arrange the nuts on top, either in neat rows or randomly – the sticky glaze will hold them in place. Reheat the remaining glaze and carefully brush it over the nuts. Tie a ribbon around the side of the cake. Leave until the glaze has set before cutting. Store in an airtight container and eat within a week.

WHISKY, FRUIT & NUT CAKE

In Scotland there is a long-standing tradition of baking a rich fruit cake – moistened with whisky, naturally – for Hogmanay. Often this would be in the form of Black Bun, in which the cake is encased in pastry. This lighter version is a rich creamed sponge, similar to Madeira cake, but it's still full of fruit and nuts and moistened with whisky. It would make a great centrepiece for a New Year's party.

Serves 12–16

Kit you'll need: 1 x 20cm fluted cake ring tin, well greased with butter, OR a 900g loaf tin, about 26 x 12.5 x 7.5cm, greased with butter and lined with a long strip of baking paper*, OR a 2-litre bundt tin, well greased with butter; a small disposable piping bag

FOR THE CAKE
225g unsalted butter, softened
225g caster sugar
4 medium eggs,
   at room temperature
3 tablespoons whisky (or milk)
225g self-raising flour
85g mixed vine fruit
   (raisins, sultanas, currants)
100g nuts (almonds,
   walnuts, pecans or a mix),
   coarsely chopped

¼ teaspoon freshly grated nutmeg
¼ teaspoon ground mace
good pinch of salt

FOR THE ICING
100g fondant icing sugar
about 1½ tablespoons water

1. Heat your oven to 180°C/350°F/gas 4. Put the softened butter in a mixing bowl, or the bowl of a free-standing electric mixer. Beat with a wooden spoon or hand-held electric whisk, or the whisk attachment of the mixer, until very creamy and mayonnaise-like. Gradually beat in the sugar, then continue beating until the mixture looks very light and fluffy, scraping down the side of the bowl from time to time.

2. Break the eggs into a jug, add the whisky and mix with a fork until just combined. Gradually add to the butter mixture, about a tablespoon at a time, beating well after each addition and scraping down the side of the bowl as before. Add a tablespoon of the weighed flour with each of the last 2 additions of egg to prevent the mixture from curdling.

3. Combine the fruit and nuts in another bowl. Add a tablespoon of the weighed flour and toss gently to coat – this will help to stop the fruit clumping together in the cake mixture. Set on one side for now. Sift the remaining flour, the nutmeg, mace and salt into the butter mixture and gently fold in* with a large metal spoon or plastic spatula. Add the fruit and nut mixture and carefully fold in until evenly distributed.

4. Spoon the mixture into the prepared ring tin and spread evenly. Bake in the heated oven for 40–45 minutes until a good golden brown and a skewer inserted into the deepest part of cake comes out clean. Set the tin on a wire rack and leave the cake until completely cold before turning it out on to the rack.

5. To make the fondant icing, sift the fondant icing sugar into a bowl and mix with 1–1½ tablespoons water using a wooden spoon, to make a smooth, fluid piping icing (it should almost have the consistency of double cream). Spoon into the piping bag and snip off the end to make a very small opening about 2mm across.

Pipe the icing in zigzags over the cake – it can be as neat and precise or as random and quirky as you choose. Leave to set. Store the cake in an airtight container for up to a week.

SUGAR-FREE GRAPEFRUIT POLENTA CAKE

British cooks have really embraced all things Italian. Polenta is one ingredient that has been happily adopted, here with ground almonds giving a lovely texture to a cake. Refined sugar is replaced by clear, mild acacia honey and there is more honey in the soaking syrup along with grapefruit and blood orange juices. The unusual topping is made from heavily reduced maple syrup mixed with creamy mascarpone.

Serves 8–10

Kit you'll need: 1 x 20.5cm round, deep cake tin (not loose-based), lined* and then brushed with melted butter; a baking sheet; a sugar thermometer

FOR THE CAKE MIXTURE
150g ground almonds
70g polenta
80g plain flour
1 teaspoon bicarbonate of soda

200g unsalted butter, softened
140g clear Acacia honey
finely grated zest
   of 1 large red grapefruit
2 large eggs, at room
   temperature, beaten to mix

FOR THE CITRUS
SOAKING SYRUP
200ml freshly squeezed
   red grapefruit juice
200ml blood orange juice
   (freshly squeezed if possible)

160g clear Acacia honey

FOR THE MASCARPONE
CREAM TOPPING
150g maple syrup
300g mascarpone, chilled

FOR THE CANDIED PEEL
DECORATION
1 red grapefruit
2 oranges
250g clear Acacia honey
125ml water

1. Heat the oven to 170°C/325°F/gas 3. To make the cake, weigh the ground almonds, polenta and flour into a bowl. Add the bicarbonate of soda and mix thoroughly. Set aside. Put the soft butter into a large mixing bowl, or the bowl of a free-standing electric mixer, and beat with a hand-held electric whisk, or the mixer whisk attachment, until creamy. Add the honey and grated grapefruit zest and beat thoroughly until the mixture is very light. Gradually

add the eggs, beating well after each addition. With the whisk on slow speed, gradually mix in the polenta mixture until it is all thoroughly combined.

2. Transfer the mixture to the prepared tin and spread evenly. Set the tin on the baking sheet and bake in the heated oven for about 40 minutes until the cake is a good golden brown and a skewer inserted into the centre comes out clean.

3. While the cake is baking, make the soaking syrup. Pour both fruit juices into a medium pan, add the honey and bring to the boil, stirring. Boil rapidly until the syrup reaches 105°C on a sugar thermometer. Remove from the heat and keep warm.

4. When the cake is done, set the tin on a wire rack, Prick the hot cake all over with a skewer, then spoon the syrup evenly over the surface and let it soak into >>>

the sponge – do this gradually until the cake will absorb no more syrup. Leave to soak in and cool for at least 30 minutes.

5. To make the topping, weigh the maple syrup into a small pan and set over medium heat. Bring to the boil, then leave the syrup to bubble away until it reaches 108°C. Leave the thick syrup to cool completely. Put the chilled mascarpone in a bowl and beat well with a wooden spoon until smooth and creamy. Add 60g of the cold, thick syrup and beat well. Cover and keep in the fridge until ready to assemble.

6. To make the candied peel decoration, peel very thin strips of zest (the coloured part of the peel) from the grapefruit and oranges, taking care to leave the white pith on the fruit. Put the peel into a medium pan and cover with boiling water from the kettle. Set over medium heat and simmer for 2 minutes. Drain, then return the peel to the pan and repeat this 'blanching' procedure two more times to remove any bitterness. Drain the peel.

7. Put the honey and water into a small pan and heat gently until liquefied, then bring to the boil and leave to bubble away (it will froth up so take care) until it reaches 115°C. Add the peel to the pan and cook gently for 5–7 minutes until the strips of peel turn translucent. Drain and leave to dry on kitchen paper.

8. To assemble, unmould the cake and set it on a serving plate. Spread and swirl the mascarpone mixture on top, then decorate with the strips of candied peel. Serve immediately. Any leftovers can be kept to enjoy the next day.

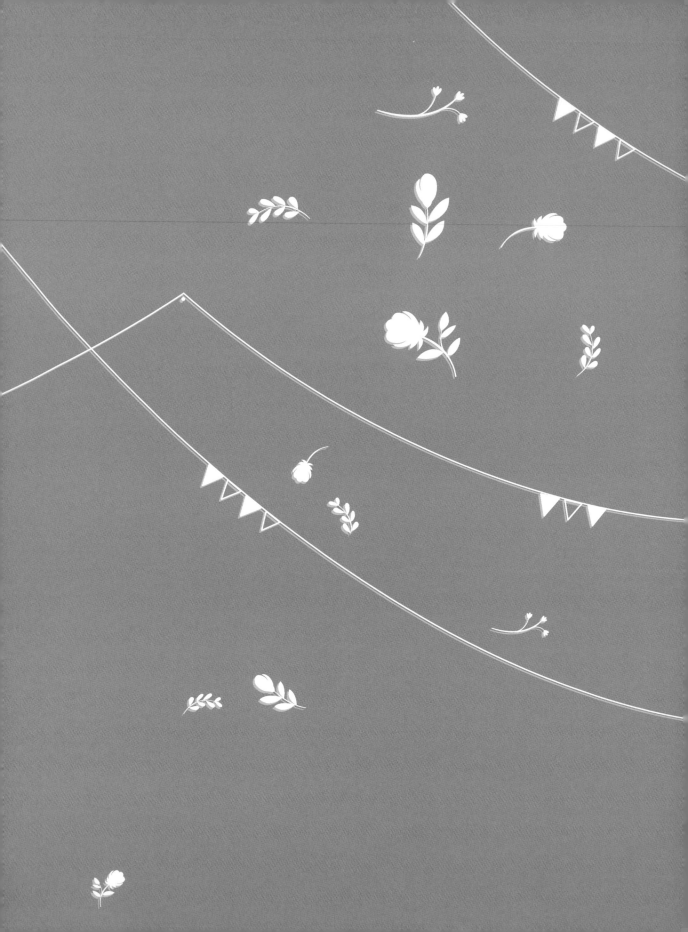

BISCUITS & SMALL BAKES

Snappy and crumbly or soft and chewy, baked in fun shapes, or beautifully wrapped as festive favours or presents, biscuits are the most versatile of bakes that can be adapted for any celebration. From traditional Sticky Gingerbread Traybake (page 78) for Bonfire Night or chocolate Coal Lump Cookies (page 100) for Hogmanay to biscotti cheekily infused with rosemary and studded with cranberries (page 94), there is something for every occasion.

And the bonus is that because they are usually quick to bake, biscuits are easy to make in large numbers. Bake an ovenful of Black Pepper Polenta Crackers (page 76) to put out with bowls of dips for parties, or take sweet inspiration from Sandy: 'For a big family get-together, I will often put out a platter of biscuits in a mixture of flavours and styles,' she says. She might include biscotti, adding almond

or hazelnut liqueur to the recipe, or Ricciarelli, the soft, almondy marcaroon-style Christmas biscuit from Siena, or her own Garibaldis, a traditional British biscuit that is enjoying something of a renaissance today amongst home bakers.

Many of our favourite recipes for biscuits and small bakes have similar relatives around the world that are associated with special celebrations. The buttery shortbread we link with Scotland has a distant cousin in Nankhatai (page 80), a sweet treat to celebrate Diwali, the Indian festival of lights – and its typical flavours of cardamom and vanilla can easily be adapted to your own biscuit-making.

Nadiya shows how to weave together different influences and family traditions to create something new and surprising. Although she grew up in Britain, her family are from Bangladesh

where few houses have ovens, so most sweet things are cooked on the stovetop or fried: 'My mum makes a snack that is a fried tapioca dumpling, with fennel seeds, coconut and sugar in it', she says, 'so I thought, why not take those flavours and incorporate them in a biscotti or shortbread – or a variation on Anzac biscuits [the classic from Australia and New Zealand made with coconut for Anzac Day; see page 67]?'

For the adventurous baker the possibilities of experimenting with flavours are endless. You could even follow Tamal's example and try substituting what you might think is the most crucial ingredient: he makes his gingerbread without any ginger! 'I use a similar recipe, but substitute orange zest and star anise. The aroma of star anise is incredible', he says, 'it just fills the kitchen when you are baking.'

The Bake Off Bakers love to experiment with unusual flavours, but whether you are inspired by their creativity, or prefer to stick to a classic recipe such as the one for Lemon Easter Biscuits (page 70), remember that a generous quantity, presented with a flourish, can elevate a biscuit from a small treat to have alongside a cup of tea to party status.

WHITE CHOCOLATE BUTTERSCOTCH BLONDIES

Scrumptuous little squares to make for Mother's Day, birthday parties or just for a treat, these are called blondies because they are made with white chocolate rather than the dark chocolate used in brownies. They're topped with fresh raspberries, which add a flash of flavour and colour. The mixture is very easy to make – everything combined in a saucepan. Be sure to use a good-quality white chocolate.

Makes 16

Kit you'll need: 1 x 20.5cm square cake tin or brownie tin, greased with butter and base-lined*

115g unsalted butter
115g dark brown
    muscovado sugar
1 medium egg,
    at room temperature
½ teaspoon vanilla extract
150g plain flour
2 good pinches of salt
½ teaspoon bicarbonate of soda
100g good-quality white
    chocolate (at least 30% cocoa
    solids), broken up
100g fresh raspberries

1. Heat the oven to 180°C/350°F/ gas 4. Put the butter in a medium pan and set over low heat. When the butter has melted, turn up the heat to medium and leave the butter to bubble until it is golden with darker speckles (don't stand too close as the butter may spit). Remove from the heat and add the sugar. Stir with a wooden spoon until thoroughly mixed and lump-free. The mixture will look a bit of a mess at this stage, but don't worry! Leave to cool for 5 minutes.

2. Meanwhile, break the egg into a small bowl or cup, add the vanilla extract and beat with a fork until combined.

3. Add the egg to the butter mixture and stir well with the wooden spoon. Sift the flour, salt and bicarbonate of soda into the pan and mix in. Finally, add the broken-up chocolate to the pan and mix until evenly distributed.

4. Transfer the mixture to the prepared tin and spread evenly, making sure the corners are evenly filled. Top with the raspberries, setting them pointed end up on top of the mixture.

5. Bake in the heated oven for about 25 minutes until a skewer inserted into the blondie cake halfway between one side and the centre comes out clean (the centre will still be soft but the mixture will continue cooking for a few minutes after it comes out of the oven).

6. Set the tin on a wire rack. Run a round-bladed knife around the inside of the tin to loosen the blondie cake, then leave until cold before cutting into squares and removing from the tin. Best eaten the same or the next day – store the blondies in an airtight container in a cool spot.

ARLETTES

These delicate puff pastry biscuits flavoured with cinnamon are similar to Palmiers but texturally quite different. They are much crunchier, thanks to being rolled out incredibly thinly and baked until the sugar is golden, almost caramelised. They make a perfect crunchy accompaniment to ice creams and sorbets or try serving them for a special afternoon tea.

1. To make the dough, put both flours, the salt, butter and water into a bowl and mix together gently with your fingers to make an even dough. Scoop out on to a lightly floured worktop and knead* for 5 minutes until smooth. Shape the dough into a 10cm square, then wrap in clingfilm and chill for 1 hour.

2. Meanwhile, make the butter layer. Put the butter and both flours into a mixing bowl and beat with a wooden spoon until smoothly combined. Scoop up the mixture and set it in the middle of a large sheet of clingfilm. Place a second sheet on top, then roll out the butter mixture to a rectangle about 30 × 10cm. Chill, wrapped in the clingfilm, for 25 minutes.

3. Unwrap the butter sheet and place it on the floured worktop, positioning it so the short ends are top and bottom. Set the square of dough in the centre of the butter sheet. Now lift up the top end of the butter sheet and

fold it down over the dough. Fold up the bottom end of the butter sheet so the dough is completely enclosed and you have a neat sandwiched square.

4. If necessary, lightly flour the worktop again, and the rolling pin if necessary, then roll out the square away from you into a 40cm long rectangle – make sure that the edges are as neat as possible. Measure and mark the central point of a long side. Fold the top quarter down and the bottom quarter up so they meet neatly in the centre, then fold the dough over in half along this centre line – this is called a 'book turn'. Wrap the dough in clingfilm and chill for 25 minutes.

5. Repeat the rolling out and 'book turn', then wrap and chill for another 25 minutes.

6. To make the filling, mix the granulated sugar with the cinnamon in a small bowl. Unwrap the chilled dough and roll out >>>

Makes 12

Kit you'll need: 2 baking sheets, lined with silicone sheets

FOR THE DOUGH
60g strong white bread flour
60g plain flour
1 teaspoon salt
40g unsalted butter, melted
50ml cold water

FOR THE BUTTER LAYER
125g unsalted butter,
    at room temperature
25g strong white bread flour
25g plain flour

FOR THE FILLING
50g granulated sugar
2 teaspoons ground cinnamon
icing sugar, for dusting

on the lightly floured worktop to a rectangle as before. Sprinkle the sugar mixture over the pastry, then make another 'book turn' to incorporate the sugar.

7. Now roll out the pastry to a 12 × 20cm rectangle and 1cm thick. Starting at one short end, roll up like a swiss roll. Wrap in

clingfilm and chill for 25 minutes. Towards the end of this time, heat your oven to 200°C/400°F/gas 6.

8. Trim the ends of the roll to neaten them, then cut across into 12 slices that are 1cm thick. Dust the worktop heavily with icing sugar. Lay one slice flat and carefully roll out very thinly to a

10cm disc, turning to coat it in sugar and prevent it from sticking. Set the biscuits slightly apart on the lined baking sheets.

9. Bake in the heated oven for 5 minutes, then carefully turn the biscuits over and bake for a further 3–4 minutes until golden and crisp. Cool on a wire rack.

ANZAC DAY BISCUITS

These chewy/crunchy biscuits are associated with Anzac Day (April 25th), which commemorates the anniversary of the ANZACS (Australian and New Zealand Army Corps) landing in Gallipoli in 1915. It is said that women baked biscuits like these and sent them to soldiers, to give them a taste of home. Eggs were scarce so they used golden syrup to bind the oat mixture. Coconut is thought to be a later addition.

1. Heat the oven to 180°C/350°F/gas 4. Put the butter and golden syrup into a medium pan and set over low heat. Leave to melt gently, stirring now and then with a wooden spoon, then remove the pan from the heat.

2. Put the boiling water in a small bowl or cup and stir in the bicarbonate of soda until dissolved. Pour into the melted mixture – it will turn foamy – and stir gently. Leave the mixture to cool for a couple of minutes.

3. Meanwhile, combine the oats, flour, sugar and coconut in a mixing bowl and mix together with your hand. Pour in the melted mixture and mix with the wooden spoon. When thoroughly combined, take a level tablespoon of the mixture (use a tablespoon measure) and roll it in your hands to a neat ball. Set it on a baking sheet. Repeat with the rest of the mixture, arranging the balls well apart on the baking sheets to allow for spreading.

4. Bake in the heated oven for 12–14 minutes until a rich golden brown – check after 10 minutes and rotate the sheets if necessary so the biscuits bake evenly. Remove from the oven and leave the biscuits on the sheets to firm up for a minute or so, then transfer them to a wire rack to cool. Store in an airtight container and eat within a week.

Makes 28

Kit you'll need: **2 baking sheets, lined with baking paper**

125g unsalted butter
2 tablespoons golden syrup
2 tablespoons boiling water
1 teaspoon bicarbonate of soda
100g porridge oats
100g plain flour
100g caster sugar
85g desiccated coconut

SYRNIKI

A treat for Easter morning, these are the festive version of the thick Russian breakfast pancakes that are also popular in Ukraine and Poland, made with home-made fresh 'pot', or sweet tvorog. This farmer's cheese is similar to the quark used in this recipe. The eggs are separated – the yolks enrich the mixture and the stiffly whisked whites are folded in to add lightness. The finished pancakes are pillowy-soft: lovely with fresh berries.

Makes about 16 to serve 4–6

Kit you'll need: a non-stick frying pan

400g quark (low-fat soft cheese)
4 tablespoons caster sugar,
    plus extra for dusting
finely grated zest of 1 large
    unwaxed lemon
100g plain flour
3 medium eggs,
    at room temperature
good pinch of salt
50g raisins
1–2 tablespoons sunflower oil,
    for frying

TO SERVE
your choice of fresh berries,
    soured cream OR yoghurt,
    honey OR maple syrup,
    conserve OR jam (see
    Blackberry and Apple Jam,
    page 11)

1. Put the quark into a large mixing bowl. Add the sugar and lemon zest, then sift the flour into the bowl. Stir everything together with a wooden spoon.

2. Separate the eggs, putting the whites into another mixing bowl (or the bowl of a free-standing electric mixer) and stirring the yolks into the quark mixture.

3. Add the salt to the egg whites, then whisk with a hand-held electric whisk, or the whisk attachment of the mixer, until stiff peaks* will form.

4. Sprinkle the raisins over the quark mixture, then carefully fold* in the whisked egg whites in 3 batches to make a thick but very light and fluffy batter.

5. Set a non-stick frying pan over medium heat and add a couple of teaspoons of oil, just enough to coat the base of the pan.

When it is hot, add a couple of tablespoons of the batter and gently ease it (using a palette knife) into a disc about 7.5cm across and 1cm thick. Make another disc of batter in the pan – depending on the size of the pan you can probably cook 3 or 4 pancakes at a time.

6. Leave the pancakes to cook for 2–3 minutes until puffed and the underside is a rich, deep golden brown. Carefully flip the pancakes over using the palette knife and cook the second side for about 2 minutes until a good golden brown. As the pancakes are cooked, remove them to a warm serving plate, quickly dust with caster sugar and serve immediately. Continue to cook the remaining batter in the same way, adding more oil to the frying pan as needed.

LEMON EASTER BISCUITS

Yellow is the colour of Easter, and lemon is one of the ingredients that is traditionally used in cakes and biscuits over the holiday. The very rich dough for these biscuits is cut into pretty shapes, which are glazed with egg white and sugar. For an Easter tea, you could thread ribbon through a hole made in each biscuit, then hang them from budding twigs.

Makes about 24

Kit you'll need: shaped biscuit cutters, about 7cm; 2 baking sheets, lined with baking paper

200g plain flour
pinch of salt
grated zest of 1 large unwaxed
    lemon, plus 1 teaspoon juice
150g unsalted butter,
    chilled and diced
60g caster sugar

TO FINISH
1 egg white
shimmer sugar, demerara sugar
    OR granulated sugar,
    for sprinkling
fine ribbon for hanging (optional)

1. Sift the flour and salt into a mixing bowl and mix in the lemon zest with your hand. Add the diced butter and cut into the flour with a round-bladed knife until the butter is reduced to rubble-like pieces. Now use your fingertips to rub* the butter into the flour until the mixture looks like coarse crumbs. Add the sugar and mix in with your hand. Sprinkle the lemon juice over the crumbs in the bowl, then gently work and press the dough together with your hand to make a ball.

2. Turn out the dough on to the worktop and form into a thick disc. Wrap tightly in clingfilm and chill for 15 minutes until firm.

3. Unwrap the dough and place it between 2 sheets of clingfilm. Roll out to about 5mm thickness (if thinner than this, the baked biscuits will be very fragile). Peel off the top layer of clingfilm, then stamp out shapes using floured cutters. Transfer the shapes to the baking sheets, spacing them apart to allow for spreading. Gather up the dough trimmings, re-roll and cut out more shapes. Cover the shapes lightly with clingfilm and chill for 20 minutes.

4. Towards the end of the chilling time, heat your oven to 190°C/375°F/gas 5.

5. Uncover the shapes. Lightly beat the egg white with a fork just until slightly frothy, then brush it lightly over the shapes. Sprinkle with the sugar of your choice. If you are going to use the biscuits as decorations, make a hole (large enough to thread ribbon through) about 1cm from the top of each biscuit using a skewer.

6. Bake in the heated oven for 12–15 minutes until lightly golden brown around the edges. Remove from the oven and very carefully use the skewer to enlarge and re-shape the hole (it will have closed up during baking) in each biscuit. Leave to firm up on the baking sheets for 3–4 minutes, then transfer to a wire rack to cool. Store in an airtight container and eat within 5 days.

TIFFIN

Another indulgent treat, this 'fridge' cake is made with good dark chocolate and home-baked biscuits spiked with chunks of spicy ginger and bright pistachios. If you make it at Easter, try decorating it with tiny sugar eggs. If you don't have a loose-based sandwich tin you can line a regular sandwich tin, or a springclip tin, with clingfilm to cover the base and side so the chilled cake can be easily lifted out.

1. Heat the oven to 180°C/350°F/gas 4. While the oven is heating put the pistachios in a small pan and add cold water just to cover. Set over medium heat and bring to the boil, then drain thoroughly. Tip the nuts on to kitchen paper and rub gently to remove the papery brown skin.

2. Transfer the nuts to a small baking dish or tin and toast in the heated oven for 5–6 minutes until lightly golden. Leave to cool. You can turn off the oven now.

3. Put the pieces of chocolate into a heatproof bowl large enough to hold all the ingredients. Add the diced butter and golden syrup and set the bowl over a pan of gently simmering water – the base of the bowl shouldn't touch the water. Leave to melt gently, stirring frequently with a wooden spoon.

4. As soon as the mixture is melted and smooth, remove the bowl from the pan. Chop the ginger as fine or as chunky as you like and add to the chocolate.

Set aside 20g of the best-looking pistachios (for the decoration) and add the rest to the chocolate. Stir gently to combine.

5. Break up the biscuits into thumbnail-sized pieces (use your hands, not a food processor as you don't want a heap of crumbs) and add to the chocolate. Stir until everything is thoroughly combined, then tip the mixture into the greased tin and spread it evenly – try not to compress the mixture but leave it looking a bit craggy rather than smooth and neat. Scatter the reserved pistachios over the top. Cover with clingfilm and chill for at least 3 hours – overnight if possible – until firm and set.

6. Gently push up the base of the tin to unmould the tiffin. Dust it with cocoa powder, then set it on a serving plate and decorate with tiny eggs. Leave it for 15 minutes to come to room temperature before cutting into wedges. Store in an airtight container in the fridge and eat within a week.

Makes 12

Kit you'll need: 1 x 20.5cm round, deep, loose-based sandwich tin, brushed with sunflower oil

100g pistachios
250g dark chocolate (about 70% cocoa solids), broken up
100g unsalted butter, diced
2 tablespoons golden syrup
75g stem ginger (about 3 lumps), well drained
200g Wholemeal Biscuits (see page 84) OR shop-bought digestive biscuits

TO FINISH
cocoa powder, for dusting
small chocolate or sugar Easter eggs, to decorate

BOX OF SAVOURY BISCUITS

There is something a little magical and Alice in Wonderland-ish about the idea of an edible box – you almost expect a tag that says 'eat me'. This particular box, crafted from savoury sun-dried tomato biscuit pastry, would make an intriguing centrepiece for a summer party. Open it and inside are wonderfully light, crisp Parmesan biscuits sandwiched in pairs around a filling of cream cheese and herbs.

Makes a large box plus 50 sandwiched biscuits

Kit you'll need: 3 large baking sheets, lined with baking paper; 2cm and 3cm plain round cutters; a 4cm fluted round cutter; disposable piping bag fitted with a large star nozzle

FOR THE BISCUIT BOX
750g plain flour
2 teaspoons sea salt flakes
1 teaspoon ground black pepper
4 medium eggs

2 x 80g tubes sun-dried
 tomato purée
1 teaspoon dried oregano
100ml cold water
beaten egg, for glazing

FOR THE PARMESAN CRISP BISCUITS
300g self-raising flour
175g Parmesan cheese, finely grated
240g slightly salted butter, chilled and diced
1½ teaspoons paprika, for sprinkling

FOR THE BISCUIT FILLING
300g full-fat cream cheese
1 tablespoon finely snipped
 fresh chives
1 rounded tablespoon
 finely chopped fresh parsley
ground black pepper, to taste

TO GARNISH
fresh flat-leaf parsley and chives

1. First make the box. Put the flour, salt and pepper in a food processor and 'pulse' a couple of times to combine. Break the eggs into a bowl and add the sun-dried tomato purée, oregano and water. Beat with a fork until thoroughly combined. With the machine running, pour the egg mixture into the processor bowl through the feed tube. Stop the machine as soon as the mixture comes together to form a firm dough. If it seems too dry to form a dough, add more water a tablespoon at a time.

2. Turn out the dough on to a lightly floured worktop and form into a ball. Flatten to a disc, then wrap and chill for 15 minutes.

3. Roll out the dough on the lightly floured worktop to 2.5mm thick. Cut into 6 pieces to form the box: 2 squares with 25cm sides (for the base and top) and 4 rectangles 9 x 22cm for the sides. Save all the trimmings.

4. Set the 2 squares on a lined baking sheet and the 4 rectangles on another sheet. Using your

fingers, flute* all the edges. Prick all the pieces with a fork, then chill for 15 minutes.

5. Meanwhile, heat the oven to 200°C/400°F/gas 6. Re-roll the dough trimmings, then stamp out about 12 discs with the 3cm cutter. Cut these in half – they will make the decorations for the top of the box.

6. Remove the baking sheet with the 2 squares on it from the fridge. Using the 2cm cutter, cut a circle out of the centre of >>>

one square. Decorate this square with the pastry semi-circles, attaching them with dabs of beaten egg. Bake for 5 minutes, then remove the sheet from the oven. Cover with another piece of baking paper and set another baking sheet on top. Bake for a further 5 minutes. Remove the baking sheet and baking paper, and lightly brush the squares with beaten egg to glaze. Bake for another 5 minutes until crisp and golden. Transfer to a wire rack and leave to cool.

7. Now you need to cut notches in the 4 rectangles (this will enable them to slot together to form the sides of the box): with a sharp knife, measure in 2cm from each short side and cut a slit 1cm wide and 5cm high.

8. Bake the rectangles in the same way as the squares. Leave to cool on a wire rack before assembling the box. (You can turn off the oven for now.)

9. Set the undecorated base square glazed-side up on a serving board. Place 2 rectangles opposite each other on top of the edges of the base (use small containers to support them), then carefully

slot together with the remaining 2 rectangles to make the sides of the box. If necessary, trim the pastry with a sharp knife so it all fits together neatly, with sides the same height. Put the box on one side until ready to fill.

10. To make the Parmesan crisp biscuits, put the flour and grated cheese in the (clean) food processor and 'pulse' several times until thoroughly combined. Add the diced butter and blitz until the mixture forms a ball of fairly soft dough. Remove the dough, flatten it to a thick disc and wrap in clingfilm. Chill for 20–25 minutes until firm but not hard.

11. Unwrap the dough and roll it out on the lightly floured worktop until 3mm thick. Flour the fluted cutter and stamp out discs. Gather up the trimmings, then re-roll and stamp out more discs. Set them slightly apart, to allow for expansion, on the lined baking sheets. Lightly sprinkle paprika over half of the discs, then chill for about 15 minutes.

12. Heat the oven to 200°C/ 400°F/gas 6 again. Bake the biscuits for 8–10 minutes until pale golden. Leave to cool and

firm up on the sheets for a couple of minutes (the biscuits are quite fragile), then transfer to a wire rack and leave until cold.

13. For the filling, beat the cream cheese with pepper to taste until creamy. Add the herbs and beat to mix. Transfer to the piping bag fitted with the star nozzle.

14. Turn the biscuits that weren't dusted with paprika upside down and pipe a star of filling on to each, then top with a paprika-dusted biscuit. You can cover the filled biscuits and keep in a cool place (preferably not the fridge) for up to an hour before assembling.

15. Fill the box with biscuits (serve the rest separately), then cover with the lid. Garnish with parsley and chives, inserting them into the hole in the top of the box.

BLACK PEPPER POLENTA CRACKERS

Everyone loves something crisp and crunchy to put out with dips or cheese at a party, and it is always more impressive if any savoury biscuits or crackers are home-baked. In this case the dough is dairy-free and vegan, being made with olive oil. The oil doesn't have to be a special one but a good peppery type would be ideal.

1. Put the polenta and flour into a mixing bowl. Smash the peppercorns fairly coarsely with a pestle and mortar, or grind coarsely, then add to the bowl with the salt. Mix well with your hand. Sprinkle the yeast into the bowl and mix in.

2. Make a well in the centre of the mixture and spoon in the olive oil. Pour in the water. Mix everything together with a round-bladed knife to make a fairly firm dough (if the mixture seems too dry and crumbly to come together, work in more water a teaspoon at a time) – it should feel like shortcrust pastry.

3. Turn out on to an unfloured worktop and knead gently with your hands just for a minute until the dough feels smooth. Shape into a ball and return to the bowl. Cover the bowl and leave to rest on the worktop for an hour (the dough will not rise or puff up).

4. Heat the oven to 190°C/375°F/ gas 5. Lightly flour the worktop and turn out the dough. Roll out very thinly to a square with 36cm sides. Cover lightly with clingfilm and leave to relax for 5 minutes.

5. Using a ruler and a pizza wheel-cutter or large sharp knife, trim the sides to make a neat 35cm square. Prick the dough square all over with a fork, then brush very lightly with cold water. Sprinkle lightly with salt or sesame seeds (if using), then cut into 5cm squares. Use a palette knife to transfer the squares to the baking sheets – they can be arranged quite close together as they won't spread.

6. Bake in the heated oven for about 12 minutes until golden brown – for the best results check the crackers after 8 minutes and rotate the sheets so the crackers bake evenly. Transfer to a wire rack and leave until completely cold. Store in an airtight container and eat within a week.

Makes 49

Kit you'll need: 2 baking sheets, lined with baking paper

25g polenta
200g plain flour
½ teaspoon black peppercorns, or to taste
½ teaspoon fine sea salt
¼ teaspoon fast-action dried yeast
3 tablespoons olive oil
100ml lukewarm water

TO FINISH (OPTIONAL)
sea salt flakes OR sesame seeds, for sprinkling

STICKY GINGERBREAD TRAYBAKE

Warm coats and scarves, fireworks, bonfires, and something rich and gingery to eat. November 5th is the time to bake this dark, almost black, sticky-toffee gingerbread with a crunchy topping. Dark muscovado sugar and black treacle give it a rich bitter-sweetness while stem ginger adds fire and heat. For a sweeter and less robust taste, replace the dark brown muscovado sugar with light brown.

1. Heat your oven to 180°C/350°F/gas 4. To make the base, put the butter, black treacle and dark muscovado sugar into a medium pan. Chop the stem ginger – not too finely – and add to the pan with the syrup from the ginger jar. Set over low heat and leave to melt gently, stirring occasionally. Remove from the heat and leave to cool for a couple of minutes.

2. In the meantime, sift the flour, ground ginger, mixed spice, salt and bicarbonate of soda into a mixing bowl. Break the eggs into a smaller bowl and beat lightly with a fork. Scrape the melted mixture into the flour, then add the eggs and mix everything together with a wooden spoon until thoroughly combined.

3. Pour the gingerbread mixture into the prepared tin and spread evenly, making sure the corners are well filled. Bake in the heated oven for 15 minutes.

4. While the base is baking, make the topping mixture. Mix together the flour, ground ginger and light muscovado sugar in a mixing bowl (check there are no clumps of sugar), then add the butter and rub in* with your fingertips until the mixture looks like very coarse crumbs. Add the chopped ginger and mix in with your fingers until it is evenly distributed.

5. When the base has been baked for 15 minutes, remove the tin from the oven. Scatter the topping mixture evenly over the base – it will have formed a thin 'skin' but will still be soft and not yet set, so don't press the topping down into it. Return to the oven and bake for a further 25 minutes until the topping is golden and a skewer inserted into the centre of the gingerbread comes out clean.

6. Set the tin on a wire rack. Run a round-bladed knife around the inside of the tin to loosen the gingerbread, then leave until cold before cutting into squares and removing from the tin. Store in an airtight container and eat within 5 days.

Cuts into 20 squares

Kit you'll need: I traybake tin or cake tin, 25.5 x 20.5 x 5cm, greased and base-lined*

FOR THE GINGERBREAD BASE
60g unsalted butter
85g black treacle
220g dark brown
    muscovado sugar
75g stem ginger (3–4 lumps), plus
    2 tablespoons syrup from the jar
150g plain flour
I tablespoon ground ginger
½ teaspoon ground mixed spice
pinch of salt
¼ teaspoon bicarbonate of soda
2 medium eggs,
    at room temperature

FOR THE GINGER TOPPING
150g plain flour
½ teaspoon ground ginger
100g light brown
    muscovado sugar
110g unsalted butter,
    chilled and diced
35g stem ginger (about 2 lumps),
    drained and finely chopped

NANKHATAI

Deliciously crisp and buttery, these easy-to-make cardamom biscuits are like an Indian shortbread. There are many variations to the basic recipe: some bakers add nutmeg or saffron instead of vanilla, for example. You can replace the pistachios with flaked almonds or leave off the nuts altogether.

Kit you'll need: 2 baking sheets, lined with baking paper

125g unsalted butter, softened
100g icing sugar
12 cardamom pods
¼ teaspoon vanilla extract
185g plain flour
¼ teaspoon baking powder
40g gram flour (chickpea flour)
1½–2 tablespoons
    natural yoghurt

TO FINISH
20g pistachios, chopped
    medium fine

1. Heat the oven to 170°C/325°F/ gas 3. Put the softened butter into a mixing bowl, or the bowl of a free-standing electric mixer. Beat with a wooden spoon or hand-held electric whisk, or the whisk attachment of the mixer, until creamy. Sift the icing sugar into the bowl and beat until the mixture is very light and fluffy – if you are using an electric whisk, start whisking on a slow speed, then gradually increase the speed to avoid sugary clouds.

2. Remove the seeds from the cardamom pods and finely crush or grind them. Add to the bowl with the vanilla extract, then beat for another minute. Add the flour, baking powder and gram flour and work in with your hand, a wooden spoon or a plastic spatula. Mix in 1½ tablespoons of the yoghurt to bring the dough together – add more yoghurt if the mixture is too dry or crumbly to come together to form a dough.

3. Using a tablespoon of dough for each biscuit, roll into balls and set them on the baking sheets, well apart to allow for spreading. Gently flatten the balls so they are about 5cm across. Sprinkle with the chopped pistachios.

4. Bake in the heated oven for 20–23 minutes until firm when gently pressed but still pale in colour. For the best results, rotate the sheets after 15 minutes so the biscuits bake evenly without colouring. Remove from the oven and leave to firm up on the baking sheets for 2 minutes, then transfer to a wire rack to cool. Store in an airtight container and eat within 5 days.

Variation

Rather than sprinkling the biscuits with pistachios before baking, simply mark a pattern with the back of a fork.

HAZELNUT & ORANGE BISCOTTI

Simple and festive, orange and hazelnuts make the perfect flavourings for Christmas biscotti.

1. Heat the oven to 170°C/325°F/ gas 3. Put the flour, sugar and baking powder into a large bowl and mix thoroughly. Slowly add the beaten eggs, mixing them in with a wooden spoon to make a firm dough. Sprinkle the nuts and orange zest into the bowl and work into the dough until thoroughly combined.

2. Turn out the dough on to a lightly floured worktop. Knead gently for a few seconds, then divide in half. Flour your hands, and shape and roll each piece of dough to a neat log about 25cm long.

3. Transfer both logs to the lined baking sheet, setting them well apart to allow for expansion. Bake in the heated oven for about 25 minutes until golden and just firm when pressed – the logs will

spread and flatten during baking. Remove the sheet from the oven, set it on a heatproof surface and leave to cool slightly.

4. Transfer one log to a chopping board and cut across, on a slight diagonal, into slices 1.5–2cm thick. Repeat with the second log, then lay the slices on the lined baking sheet.

5. Bake for a further 5–7 minutes until lightly golden and firm. Turn the slices over and bake for another 5–7 minutes until the second side is golden. Transfer to a wire rack and leave to cool. Store in an airtight container.

Makes 24–30

Kit you'll need: 1 large baking sheet, lined with baking paper

250g plain flour,
    plus extra for dusting
250g caster sugar
½ teaspoon baking powder
3 medium eggs, at room
    temperature, beaten to mix
200g blanched hazelnuts,
    chopped
finely grated zest
    of 1 large orange

'I like the flavours of orange, fruit, nuts and a little spice in biscotti.'

TAMAL

HALLOWE'EN HATS

Long-standing fans of the Great British Bake Off might remember the chocolate teacake challenge in series 3. These fun, sticky treats have all the same elements as the teacakes — biscuit base, marshmallow and chocolate — but are much simpler to make.

Makes 24

Kit you'll need: a 5cm plain round cutter; 1–2 baking sheets, lined with baking paper; a large disposable piping bag

FOR THE WHOLEMEAL BISCUITS
75g stoneground plain wholemeal flour
75g stoneground medium oatmeal
75g plain white flour
75g light brown muscovado sugar
¼ teaspoon bicarbonate of soda
¼ teaspoon ground ginger
¼ teaspoon fine sea salt
75g unsalted butter, chilled and diced
2–3 tablespoons milk, chilled

FOR THE MARSHMALLOW
5g (1 teaspoon) powdered gelatine
4 teaspoons cold water
3 medium egg whites, at room temperature
150g caster sugar
2 tablespoons golden syrup
¼ teaspoon fine sea salt
½ vanilla pod, split open

FOR THE CHOCOLATE COATING
250g dark chocolate (about 70% cocoa solids), broken up

1. To make the biscuits by hand: sift the wholemeal flour, oatmeal, white flour, sugar, bicarbonate of soda, ginger and salt into a mixing bowl. Add any coarse pieces left in the sieve to the bowl, then add the butter. Rub in* with your fingertips until the mixture looks like fine crumbs. Add 2 tablespoons of the milk and, using a round-bladed knife, mix to a firm dough, adding more milk as needed to bring the dough together — it should feel like shortcrust pastry.

2. To make the dough in a food processor, put all the ingredients except for the butter and milk in the processor bowl and 'pulse' a few times just to combine everything. Add the pieces of butter and blitz just until the mixture looks like fine crumbs. With the machine running slowly, add enough of the milk through the feed tube to bring the mixture together into a ball of fairly firm dough. Flatten the dough to a thick disc, then wrap in clingfilm and chill for 30 minutes.

3. Heat the oven to 190°C/375°F/ gas 5. Unwrap the dough and place it between 2 large sheets of clingfilm. Roll out to about 5mm thickness. Peel off the top sheet of clingfilm and stamp out discs with the round cutter. Transfer the discs to the baking sheet, setting them slightly apart to allow for expansion. Gather up the dough trimmings and gently knead them together, then re-roll as before and cut more discs. Prick the discs all over with a fork.

4. Bake in the heated oven for 13–15 minutes until golden with slightly darker edges — check after 10 minutes and rotate the baking sheets, if necessary, so the biscuits bake evenly. Remove from the oven and leave the biscuits on the baking sheet for a minute to firm up slightly, then transfer to a wire rack to cool. (The biscuits can be made up to 4 days in advance and stored in an airtight container.)

>>>

5. To make the marshmallow, sprinkle the gelatine over the cold water in a small heatproof bowl or cup. Leave to 'sponge' for 5 minutes, then set the bowl in a larger bowl or pan of very hot but not boiling water and leave the gelatine to dissolve.

6. Meanwhile, put the egg whites, caster sugar, golden syrup and salt in a large heatproof mixing bowl. Scrape the seeds from the vanilla pod (discard the pod) and add to the bowl. Set over a pan of simmering water (the base of the bowl shouldn't touch the water) and whisk with a hand-held electric whisk on full speed for 1 minute. Whisk in the gelatine mixture, then continue whisking for about 8 minutes until you have a glossy, silky-smooth and very stiff meringue-like mixture.

7. Remove the bowl from the pan and whisk for another 8 minutes until the mixture has cooled. Spoon the marshmallow mixture into the piping bag.

8. Arrange the biscuits, slightly apart, on a wire rack. Snip the end off the piping bag to make a 1.5cm opening. Holding the bag vertically above each biscuit, pipe a cone of marshmallow on top, about 5cm high and 4cm wide at its base; pull the bag up sharply to leave a peak that looks like a witch's pointy hat. There's enough marshmallow mixture to allow for some mistakes, so if the peaked cones lean to one side or you just don't like the way they look, scrape them off and start again. Leave the biscuits, uncovered, on the worktop for about 2 hours until the marshmallow has set.

9. When ready to finish, melt* the chocolate, then leave to cool for a minute. Place a baking sheet under the wire rack (to catch the drips) before carefully spooning the chocolate over the witches' hats to completely cover the marshmallow and the biscuit rim. Once you have coated all the hats, scoop up the drips underneath the rack and use to touch up any bare spots. Leave until set. Best eaten the same or the next day – store in an airtight container in a cool spot (not in the fridge).

Tip

You can make larger wholemeal biscuits to enjoy with coffee. Stamp out with a 7cm cutter and bake for 14–15 minutes.

CHOCOLATE STARS

The chocolate-hazelnut paste popularised by the chocolate-makers of Turin in the 19th century was the forerunner of Nutella, the spread that children all over the world know and love. The dark chocolate-hazelnut ganache that fills these rich chocolate shortbread biscuits is an adult version of that childhood treat. Make these for a special tea party – they can be baked and assembled a day or so in advance.

Makes 20 pairs

Kit you'll need: a 6–7cm star cutter; 2 baking sheets, lined with baking paper; a small disposable piping bag

FOR THE DOUGH
225g unsalted butter, softened
100g caster sugar
225g plain flour
65g cocoa powder
¼ teaspoon fine sea salt

FOR THE GANACHE FILLING
75g blanched hazelnuts
1 tablespoon caster sugar
75g dark chocolate (about 70% cocoa solids)
75ml double cream
25g unsalted butter
pinch of salt

TO FINISH
50g dark chocolate (about 70% cocoa solids)
icing sugar, for dusting

1. Make the dough first. Put the softened butter into a mixing bowl, or the bowl of a free-standing electric mixer. Beat with a wooden spoon or a hand-held electric whisk, or the whisk attachment of the mixer, until very creamy. Add the sugar and beat until the mixture is much lighter in colour and texture. Scrape down the side of the bowl.

2. Sift the flour, cocoa powder and salt into the bowl and mix in with a wooden spoon or plastic spatula, then use your hands to bring the mixture together into a firm dough.

3. Turn the dough out on to an unfloured worktop (flour will leave white marks on the dough) and gently knead to a flat disc. (In very warm weather, or if your dough feels soft, wrap it in clingfilm and chill for about 15 minutes until firm enough to roll out.) Place the disc between 2 large sheets of clingfilm and roll out to 5mm thickness. Peel off the top layer of clingfilm and stamp out stars with the cutter. Gather up the trimmings, then re-roll and stamp out more stars. You want an even number – the dough should make 40 stars – but a few extra will allow for breakages.

4. Set the stars, slightly apart to allow for expansion, on the baking sheets, then cover lightly with clingfilm and chill for 15 minutes. Meanwhile, heat your oven to 180°C/350°F/gas 4.

5. Uncover the stars and bake in the heated oven for about 12 minutes until just firm but not coloured – watch them carefully as the chocolate dough can quickly turn very dark around the tips (this would make the biscuits taste bitter). Remove from the oven and leave the stars to firm up on the baking sheets for 3 minutes before carefully >>>

transferring them to a wire rack to cool – the biscuits will be very fragile until completely cold. Leave the oven on.

6. While the biscuits are cooling, make the ganache filling. Tip the hazelnuts into a small baking dish or tin and toast in the oven for 7–10 minutes until a good golden brown. Remove 20 of the best-looking nuts and set aside for the decoration. Transfer the rest of the nuts to a food processor (there's no need to wait until they are cold). Add the sugar and process until ground to a fairly fine and slightly sticky powder.

7. Break or chop up the chocolate into even-sized pieces and put into a small, heavy-based pan

with the cream, butter and salt. Set over very low heat and stir gently with a wooden spoon until melted and smooth. Remove from the heat and stir in the ground hazelnuts. Leave the ganache on the worktop, stirring frequently, until firm enough to spread.

8. When you are ready to assemble the stars, give the ganache a good stir. Using about a rounded teaspoon of ganache for each, gently spread the ganache over the underside of 20 stars. The biscuits are quite fragile – a tip might break off, but you can 'glue' it back with a dab of ganache. Top each star with a second star, placing the biscuits underside to underside and matching up the points.

9. To finish the stars, gently melt* the chocolate. One at a time, dip the rounded base of each whole hazelnut in the melted chocolate, then set it in the centre of a star biscuit. Spoon the rest of the melted chocolate into the piping bag and snip off the end to make a small opening. Quickly pipe a fine zigzag of chocolate across each star. Leave until set, then very lightly dust with icing sugar. Store in an airtight container and eat within 5 days.

ALMOND CRESCENTS

Almonds are at the heart of many festive biscuits, sweets and cakes around the world. These snow-white almond biscuits are made to celebrate Channukah, Advent or Christmas in many Northern European countries. The secret to their 'more-ishness' is to use very fresh nuts and good butter, and to leave them for a day or so after baking for the almond flavours to deepen and become more intense.

1. Put the softened butter into a mixing bowl, or the bowl of a free-standing electric mixer. Add the almond extract and beat with a wooden spoon or hand-held electric whisk, or the whisk attachment of the mixer, until creamy.

2. Scrape down the side of the bowl, then sift the icing sugar into the bowl and beat well until the mixture is much paler in colour and very light and fluffy in texture. (If using an electric whisk, or a mixer, start off on the slowest speed and gradually increase once all the sugar has been incorporated.)

3. Sift the flour, salt and ground almonds into the bowl; add any nuts left in the sieve. Mix everything together with a wooden spoon or plastic spatula to make a firm dough.

4. Tip out the dough on to an unfloured worktop. Using a teaspoon measure, scoop up a heaped spoonful of the dough (about 15g) and roll it with your hands on the worktop to a sausage shape about 7.5cm long. Curve this into a crescent, then set it on a lined baking sheet. Continue making crescents with the rest of the dough, setting them slightly apart on the baking sheets to allow for expansion.

5. Cover the crescents lightly with clingfilm and chill for 10 minutes. In the meantime, heat the oven to 170°C/325°F/gas 3.

6. Uncover the crescents and bake in the heated oven for about 15 minutes until they are firm, but still pale with golden tips. Remove the sheets from the oven and dust the crescents with sifted icing sugar. Leave to cool and firm up on the sheets for 5 minutes before carefully transferring to a wire rack to finish cooling.

7. When cold, store in an airtight container and eat within a week. Dust again with icing sugar just before serving.

Makes 24

Kit you'll need: 2 baking sheets, lined with baking paper

110g unsalted butter, softened
2–3 drops of pure almond extract
60g icing sugar, plus extra
    for dusting
85g plain flour
pinch of salt
125g ground almonds

Variation

As a gift for chocolate lovers you can finish off the biscuits with a chocolate and pistachio decoration. After baking, leave the crescents to cool without dusting with icing sugar. Gently melt* 60g of your favourite dark chocolate. Dip one end of each crescent into the melted chocolate, then place on a sheet of baking paper. Sprinkle 25g finely chopped pistachios over the chocolate before it sets. Once it has set, dust the other end of each crescent with icing sugar, then gently arrange the crescents in a gift box.

LEBKUCHEN

At the Advent market at Nuremberg, the enticing spicy-sweet scent of Lebkuchen – the famous festive German gingerbread – fills the air and you can find the biscuits in almost any size or shape, plain, glazed or elaborately decorated. The first Lebkuchen, sweetened with honey, were made in Nuremburg in the middle ages. The spicy flavour of the biscuits will deepen, so they are best eaten a day or two after baking.

1. Measure the honey, muscovado sugar and butter into a medium pan. Add the lemon and orange zests, lemon juice and chopped ginger. Set over low heat and melt gently, stirring now and then.

2. While the mixture melts, sift the flour, ground almonds, baking powder, bicarbonate of soda and spices into a mixing bowl. Add 3 fine grinds of black pepper. Pour the melted mixture into the bowl and mix everything together with a wooden spoon to make a heavy and slightly sticky dough. Cover the bowl with clingfilm and leave on the worktop for an hour to firm up.

3. Towards the end of this time, heat the oven to 180°C/350°F/gas 4. Uncover the dough. Scoop up a rounded tablespoonful (use a measuring spoon) and roll it into a ball with your hands. Set the ball on a baking sheet and gently flatten it so it is about 5cm across and 1cm high. Repeat with the rest of dough, setting the biscuits well apart to allow for spreading.

4. Bake in the heated oven for 12–15 minutes until the biscuits are just firm when gently pressed in the centre – for the best results, rotate the baking sheets after 10 minutes so the lebkuchen bake evenly.

5. Meanwhile, make the glazes. For the white glaze, sift the icing sugar into a bowl and stir in the egg white with a wooden spoon to make a pourable, smooth icing (the consistency of double cream). For the chocolate glaze, put the chocolate, butter and water in a small heatproof bowl and set over a pan of steaming-hot water. Melt gently, stirring frequently. Remove the bowl from the pan.

6. As soon as the lebkuchen are ready, remove the baking sheets from the oven and set them on a heatproof surface. Using a pastry brush, quickly brush the white glaze over half of the lebkuchen to cover them all over. Leave to firm up and cool on the baking sheet.

7. Allow the rest of the lebkuchen to cool for 5 minutes before carefully spreading the chocolate glaze over them using a round-bladed knife. Leave to set and cool on the baking sheet. Store in an airtight container and eat within a week.

Makes 26

Kit you'll need: 2 baking sheets, lined with baking paper

FOR THE DOUGH
225g clear honey
50g dark brown muscovado sugar
85g unsalted butter
grated zest of 1 medium orange
grated zest of 1 medium unwaxed lemon, plus 1 tablespoon juice
50g crystallised ginger, finely chopped
250g plain flour
85g ground almonds
1 teaspoon baking powder
½ teaspoon bicarbonate of soda
2 teaspoons ground ginger
1 teaspoon ground cinnamon
¼ teaspoon grated nutmeg
¼ teaspoon ground cloves
½ teaspoon ground mixed spice
black pepper

FOR THE WHITE GLAZE
50g icing sugar
4 teaspoons egg white, at room temperature

FOR THE CHOCOLATE GLAZE
50g dark chocolate (about 70% cocoa solids), finely chopped
15g unsalted butter
1 tablespoon water

CRANBERRY, ROSEMARY & ALMOND BISCOTTI

Cranberries, almonds and an unusual twist of rosemary make these biscuits extra special.
For a Christmas party, the zabaglione dip, made with Marsala and Cointreau and a warm hint
of cinnamon, will add a touch of luxury.

1. Using a vegetable peeler, pare 1cm-wide strips of zest from the oranges, taking care to leave all the white pith on the fruit. Pile up the strips, then cut them across into shreds about 4mm wide. Put the shreds into a medium pan and add cold water to cover. Set over medium heat and bring to the boil, then simmer for 2 minutes. Drain in a sieve.

2. Return the shreds of zest to the pan, cover with fresh cold water, bring to the boil, simmer and drain. Repeat this 'blanching' process 2 more times.

3. Now return the softened strips of zest to the pan and add 300g of the sugar and the measured water. Set over medium/low heat and stir until the sugar has dissolved, then bring to the boil. Simmer gently for 5 minutes. Drain the strips of zest in the sieve set over a heatproof jug, to catch the syrup. Tip the zest on to a plate lined with kitchen paper and leave to cool.

4. Heat the oven to 180°C/350°F/ gas 4. Lightly oil a baking sheet, preferably one with a rim.

5. Return the syrup to the pan, set over medium heat and boil rapidly until the syrup turns to a good chestnut-coloured caramel. Quickly pour on to the oiled baking sheet (don't touch or move the baking sheet as the caramel is very fluid and will burn). Leave until cold and set.

6. Tip the almonds into a baking dish or tin and toast in the heated oven for 5–7 minutes until lightly golden. Set aside to cool (leave the oven on).

7. Break up the set caramel into large chunks and put into a food processor. Blitz to a coarse powder. Tip out the powder and weigh 200g (you won't need the rest), then return this to the processor bowl. Add 100g of the flour and blitz to make a fine, sandy powder. Tip this mixture into a large mixing bowl. >>>

Makes about 32

Kit you'll need: 2–3 baking sheets

4 large oranges
400g white caster sugar
150ml water
vegetable oil, for greasing
160g blanched almonds
500g plain flour
1 tablespoon baking powder
½ teaspoon finely chopped
   fresh rosemary
100g dried cranberries
4 medium eggs, at room
   temperature, beaten to mix

FOR THE ZABAGLIONE DIP
(OPTIONAL)
3 medium egg yolks
35g caster sugar
good pinch of ground cinnamon
3 tablespoons Marsala
3 tablespoons Cointreau
   OR orange juice
50ml whipping cream, chilled

8. Add the rest of the flour, the rest of the caster sugar, the baking powder, rosemary, cranberries and almonds. Mix thoroughly with your hand, then make a well in the centre. Add the eggs to the well and mix everything together with your hand, or a wooden spoon, until it all comes together to make a firm dough – if the mixture is very sticky, work in a little more flour.

9. Turn out the dough on to a floured worktop and knead it for a minute until even, then divide it into 2 equal portions. Flour your hands and form each portion into a neat loaf shape about 22 x 9cm and 5cm thick. Line 2 baking sheets with baking paper and set a loaf on each (they will expand quite a lot). Bake in the heated oven for 30–35 minutes until a good golden brown and just firm when gently pressed – check after 25 minutes and rotate the sheets, if necessary, to make sure the loaves bake evenly.

10. Remove the sheets from the oven and set them on a heatproof surface. Leave to cool for about 10 minutes. Reduce the oven temperature to 150°C/300°F/gas 2.

11. Transfer one loaf to a chopping board and, using a serrated bread knife, cut on a slight diagonal into 1cm-thick slices. Lay the slices, cut-side down, on the lined baking sheet. Repeat with the second loaf, then bake the biscotti for 30 minutes until lightly golden. Transfer them to a wire rack and leave to cool.

12. To make the zabaglione dip, if serving with the biscotti, put the egg yolks into a heatproof bowl, add the sugar and cinnamon, and whisk with a hand-held electric whisk for 30 seconds until frothy. Set the bowl over a pan of simmering water (the base of the bowl shouldn't touch the water). Add the Marsala and Cointreau and whisk until the mixture is very thick and mousse-like, and reaches the ribbon stage*. Remove the bowl from the pan and carry on whisking until the mixture cools to room temperature.

13. In another bowl, whip the cream until it is as thick as the whisked egg mixture, then carefully fold* in. Transfer the zabaglione to a serving dish and serve as soon as possible.

CHOCOLATE SHORTBREAD TWISTS

These twisted ropes of crisp, buttery shortbread studded with dark and white chocolate are a pretty adaptation of a much-loved recipe. Don't skip the chilling stage as the dough needs to be firm when it goes into the oven, to keep a good shape. For the best flavour, use really good chocolate.

1. Put the softened butter into a mixing bowl, or the bowl of a free-standing electric mixer, and beat until creamy with a wooden spoon or a hand-held electric whisk, or the whisk attachment of the mixer. Add the sugar and beat for a couple of minutes until the mixture is light and fluffy, scraping down the side of the bowl from time to time.

2. Break the egg into a small bowl, add the vanilla extract and beat with a fork just until combined. Gradually add the egg to the butter mixture, beating well after each addition and scraping down the side of the bowl as before.

3. Sift the flour, salt and cornflour into the bowl and mix in with a wooden spoon or plastic spatula. Use your hands to gently bring the mixture together into a ball of dough. Divide in half and transfer one portion to another bowl.

4. Grate or very finely chop the white chocolate – you can do this quickly in a food processor, but take care and use brief 'pulses' to avoid melting the chocolate. Add the chocolate to one portion of dough and mix in with a wooden spoon. Grate or finely chop the dark chocolate and mix into the second portion of dough.

5. Weigh the white chocolate dough and divide it into 4 equal portions. Using your hands, roll each portion back and forth on the worktop to a sausage 1cm thick and 40cm long. Move the white chocolate sausages to one side and repeat with the dark chocolate dough, to make a total of 8 sausages.

6. Lay one white chocolate sausage next to a dark chocolate sausage and gently twist them together – if the dough breaks just press it back together. Trim each end of the dough twist, then cut the twist >>>

Makes 24

Kit you'll need: 2 baking sheets, lined with baking paper

125g unsalted butter, softened
90g caster sugar
1 medium egg,
    at room temperature
½ teaspoon vanilla extract
225g plain flour
pinch of salt
1 tablespoon cornflour
50g good-quality white chocolate
    (at least 30% cocoa solids)
50g dark chocolate (about 70%
    cocoa solids)
icing sugar, for dusting

across into 6 equal pieces. Repeat with the remaining dough sausages to make 24 pieces in all.

7. Arrange the pieces on the lined baking sheets, setting them slightly apart to allow for expansion. Cover lightly with clingfilm and chill for 30 minutes.

8. Towards the end of the chilling time, heat the oven to 190°C/375°F/gas 5.

9. Bake the twists for 12–15 minutes until golden and firm – check after 10 minutes and rotate the sheets if necessary so the shortbreads bake evenly.

Remove from the oven and leave the biscuits to firm up on the baking sheets for a minute before transferring to a wire rack to cool. Once cold, dust with icing sugar. Store in an airtight container and eat within 5 days.

'Shortbread is a biscuit that never goes out of fashion. And of course millionaire's shortbread, made with a layer of caramel and chocolate, originated in Scotland – or at least we like to claim it!'

MARIE

COAL LUMP COOKIES

In Scotland, for 'first footing' on New Year's Eve, or Hogmanay, a dark-haired man enters the house after midnight, bringing gifts that signify good fortune for the coming year, including a piece of coal for a warm house. These rich, dark chocolate treats, made in the same way as brownies but baked like cookies, and shaped into 'coal lumps' as soon as they come out of the oven, hark back to that tradition.

Makes about 21

Kit you'll need: 2 baking sheets, lined with baking paper

200g dark chocolate (about 70% cocoa solids), broken up
50g unsalted butter, softened
2 medium eggs, at room temperature
150g light brown muscovado sugar
25g plain flour
10g cocoa powder, plus extra for dusting
¼ teaspoon baking powder
good pinch of salt
75g dark chocolate (about 70% cocoa solids), roughly chopped
75g walnut pieces or milk chocolate, roughly chopped

1. Heat the oven to 180°C/350°F/ gas 4. Melt* the 200g broken-up chocolate, then add the butter in small pieces and stir gently until smooth. Set aside to cool.

2. Put the eggs and sugar into a large mixing bowl, or the bowl of a free-standing electric mixer. Whisk with a hand-held electric whisk, or the whisk attachment of the mixer, for about 4 minutes to reach the ribbon stage*. Whisk in the chocolate mixture. Sift the flour, cocoa powder, baking powder and salt into the bowl. Add the pieces of chocolate and the nuts and fold* everything together with a large metal spoon or a plastic spatula until thoroughly combined.

3. The best way to shape the cookies is to use a tablespoon measure: take a rounded spoonful of the mixture for each cookie and drop it on to a lined baking sheet (use a round-bladed knife to ease the mixture out of the spoon) to make a craggy mound. Set the mounds slightly apart to allow for expansion. Bake in the heated oven for about 12 minutes until the cookies are puffed up, with a cracked surface that's just set – the centre will still be soft.

4. Remove from the oven and, working quickly, use 2 round-bladed knives to push in the sides of each cookie and mould into a rough lump shape – don't touch the cookies with your fingers as the chocolate will be molten-hot. Dust with plenty of cocoa powder, then leave to firm up on the baking sheets for about 5 minutes before transferring to a wire rack to finish cooling. Store the cookies in an airtight container and eat within 5 days.

BREADS

Every loaf you bake is a small celebration in itself. There's a reason that bread is often described as the staff of life: not only is it a staple of many diets, but there is something nurturing and miraculous about taking flour, salt, yeast and water, and allowing time, patience and science to do the rest. As Alvin says, "The first time you bake bread for your family is an amazing feeling. I still remember the first brioche that my daughter ate and the first baguette my son enjoyed.'

And if you are someone like Mat, with a demanding job, there is something very therapeutic about kneading and shaping a piece of dough. In Mat's case, nothing could be a sharper contrast to his shifts at the fire station. 'We are twelve guys, so it's loud, busy and energetic,' he says. 'Because of my shift patterns I am often home during the day and then I can go into the kitchen, put the radio on, make a cup of tea and bake.'

There is a wealth of festive breads here to try, from Panettone (page 147) and Cinnamon Sticky Buns (page 128), to the legendary Parker House Rolls (page 132), made first in the Boston hotel of the same name, famous for its association with John F. Kennedy.

Because of its simple core ingredients it is easy to adapt and transform even the simplest bread into something special. That might be by introducing exciting new flavours (like walnuts and Stilton in a soda bread; see page 142), or serving it with a tasty jam or dip (try your flatbreads with the roasted walnut, red pepper and pomegranate flavours of Muhammara, page 113). Or make your baking personal, as Ugne does for her children. 'I will make soft, white sweet-ish bread for them, with honey, butter and milk, and put in some dried fruit or nuts,' she says. 'Then I will shape it – rabbit shapes, or maybe flowers – and sometimes I will colour some caster sugar and dip the dough into it so that when it is baked it is

colourful and fun looking.' Today's bread baskets can be a rich and eclectic mix of influences and styles from all over the world. Why not take inspiration from Nadiya, who adds a Bangladeshi twist to her croissants, 'based on a flaky flatbread we eat for breakfast, filled with semolina, coconut, pistachios and currants', she explains. 'The texture is similar to the frangipane centre of an almond croissant, so I thought, why not bring the two ideas together?'

Tamal, too, likes to introduce Indian spicing to classic recipes, but he has also learned how to make Jewish challah bread, thanks to some help from the Jewish bakeries near his parents' home. Traditionally, challah is made for Shabbat, the day of rest, and for holidays, with different shapes for each occasion. Often the loaves are plaited, with each braid symbolising a particular quality. There are also chocolate versions, such as Babka, typical of Polish-Jewish baking: an elaborate, twisted creation including nuts as well as chocolate (see page 138 for the recipe). 'When I go to see the family I will always make a challah loaf', says Tamal, 'and we have it for breakfast on Sunday mornings.'

Baking your favourite bread is a potent way of celebrating tradition and cultural heritage – wherever you are.

IRISH WHEATEN BREAD WITH BACON

St Patrick's Day would be a good time to bake this loaf – but why wait, since it uses a quick bread dough that can be made in the time it takes to heat the oven. Thanks to the bacon, the smell of it baking is as enticing as the taste. In Ireland, this is traditionally made with a coarse brown wheaten flour, which is hard to find elsewhere, but using a stoneground wholemeal flour with a ready-made mix of wheatgerm and bran plus some plain flour will give you a good nutty-flavoured bread.

1. Heat the oven to 220°C/425°F/ gas 7. While the oven is heating, snip the bacon with kitchen scissors into 1cm chunks and put into a cold non-stick frying pan. Set over fairly low heat and cook, stirring occasionally, until the fat starts to run. Turn up the heat to medium and cook until the bacon starts to colour. Remove from the heat and leave to cool.

2. Put the wholemeal flour and wheatgerm into a large mixing bowl. Sift the white flour, bicarbonate of soda and salt into the bowl and mix all together with your hand. Cut up the butter into small flakes and add to the bowl. Toss the pieces of butter in the flour to coat them, then rub in* with your fingertips until they disappear.

3. Add the chives and mix in with your hand, then tip in the bacon along with any fat in the pan and mix in with a round-bladed knife. Make a well in the centre and pour in the buttermilk. Mix everything together with your

hands to make a soft and slightly sticky, shaggy-looking dough. If it feels dry, or if there are crumbs at the bottom of the bowl and the dough won't come together, work in some more buttermilk a tablespoon at a time.

4. Now you need to work more quickly*. Lightly dust the worktop and your hands with wholemeal flour, then turn out the dough and gently knead it for no more than a minute to make a ball of dough that's still a bit rough rather than smooth and neat. Set the ball of dough on the lined baking sheet and gently flatten with your fingers until it is about 19cm across and 3cm deep. Sprinkle with a little wholemeal flour, then cut a deep cross in the top with a table knife, to mark out four 'farls'.

5. Bake in the heated oven for about 35 minutes until the loaf is well browned and sounds hollow when tapped on the underside*. Transfer the loaf to a wire rack and leave to cool. Eat warm the same day or toasted the next.

Makes a medium loaf

Kit you'll need: 1 baking sheet, lined with baking paper

150g thick-cut smoked back bacon
300g stoneground plain wholemeal flour, plus extra for dusting
50g wheatgerm with bran
100g plain white flour
1 teaspoon bicarbonate of soda
5g fine sea salt
25g unsalted butter, at room temperature
small bunch of fresh chives
about 400ml buttermilk

Variation

For a breakfast loaf, make up the dough without the bacon and chives, and add 2 teaspoons light brown muscovado sugar with the white flour.

MILK & HONEY TIN LOAF

The very name conjures up a place of plenty, a 'land of milk and honey'. It's a loaf with a light but close crumb that slices neatly, so is perfect for sandwiches and toasties, charlottes and summer puddings (see page 184). You can buy special lidded tins to create the flat top on the bread, or improvise with a baking sheet.

Makes a medium loaf

Kit you'll need: 1 x 900g loaf tin, about 26 x 12.5 x 7.5cm, greased with butter; a baking sheet

500g strong white bread flour
8g fine sea salt
10g unsalted butter, at room temperature, plus extra for greasing
1 x 7g sachet fast-action dried yeast
10g clear honey
50ml lukewarm water
300ml lukewarm milk

1. Put the flour and salt in a large mixing bowl, or the bowl of a free-standing electric mixer fitted with the dough hook attachment, and mix well. Cut the butter into small flakes and add to the bowl. Rub* the butter into the flour using your fingertips, then sprinkle the yeast into the bowl and mix in, making sure it is thoroughly combined with the flour. Make a well in the centre.

2. Weigh the honey in a small bowl. Add the lukewarm water and stir until liquefied. Pour into the well in the flour mixture, followed by the lukewarm milk. Mix everything together with your hand, or the mixer on the lowest speed, to make a soft dough. If there are dry crumbs in the bowl, or if the dough feels dry and too firm to bring together, add more milk or water a tablespoon at a time. If the dough feels sticky, or clings to the side of the bowl, then work in a little more flour.

3. Turn out the dough on to a very lightly floured worktop and knead* thoroughly for 10 minutes, or for 5 minutes in the mixer on its lowest speed, until it feels silky smooth and stretchy. Return the dough to the bowl, if necessary, then cover with a snap-on lid or clingfilm and leave to rise on the worktop, at normal room temperature, for about 1 hour until doubled in size.

4. Punch down the risen dough with your knuckles, then turn it out on to the lightly floured worktop. Knead the dough for 2 minutes – this ensures all the larger air bubbles are deflated so the texture of the dough is very even. Shape into a ball, cover with the upturned bowl and leave to relax for 5 minutes.

5. Uncover the dough, then press out with floured fingers to an evenly thick rectangle about 26 x 30cm. Starting from one

short end, roll up the dough fairly tightly (like a swiss roll), pinching it together each time you roll it over. Pinch the seam firmly together, then tuck the ends under and set the loaf in the prepared tin. Gently press your hand flat on top of the dough roll to flatten its surface and push it into the corners of the tin. Grease the centre portion (about the size of your loaf tin) of the baking sheet with butter, then place it, buttered side down, over the top of the loaf tin to form a lid – this will ensure the loaf will have a flat top.

6. Leave the loaf to prove on the worktop for about an hour until it has risen to fill the tin – take a peek by lifting the baking sheet at one corner to check. Towards the end of the rising time, heat your oven to 220°C/425°F/gas 7.

7. The baking sheet needs to be weighted to prevent the loaf from pushing it off as the bread expands in the oven, so set an ovenproof weight (such as a heavy casserole or a heavy baking tin) on top of the sheet. Bake the loaf for 30 minutes, then carefully

remove the baking sheet and reduce the oven temperature to 180°C/350°F/gas 4. Bake for a further 5 minutes until the top is browned and the loaf is cooked – if tapped on the underside it should sound hollow*.

8. Transfer the loaf to a wire rack and leave to cool. Wait until it is completely cold before slicing. This loaf will freeze well if it is tightly wrapped.

FLATBREADS WITH LEMON & ZA'ATAR

Move over garlic bread! At once puffy and crisp, spicy and aromatic, these easy pitta-like flatbreads are perfect with dips and kebabs for a midsummer barbecue party. They can be made well in advance and then quickly finished on the barbecue (or a grill indoors). They're brushed with a savoury oil made with lemon and za'atar, an ancient Middle Eastern blend of herbs, spices and seeds. They're delicious with Muhammara, a walnut and red pepper dip.

Makes 6

Kit you'll need: **2 baking sheets; a ridged grill pan/griddle OR large, heavy-based frying pan**

100g stoneground wholemeal bread flour
300g strong white bread flour
6g fine sea salt
1 x 7g sachet fast-action dried yeast
2 tablespoons olive oil
about 250ml lukewarm water

TO FINISH
3 tablespoons olive oil
grated zest of 1 medium unwaxed lemon, plus about 1 tablespoon juice
4 tablespoons za'atar
salt and pepper (optional)
Muhammara (see page 113), for serving

Note

You can find jars of za'atar in larger supermarkets and Middle Eastern groceries. Any leftover za'atar topping can be used for dipping the flatbreads.

1. Put both flours and the salt into a mixing bowl, or the bowl of a free-standing electric mixer fitted with the dough hook attachment. Mix well with your hand, or the dough hook, then sprinkle the yeast into the bowl and mix in. Make a well in the centre.

2. Pour the olive oil and 250ml lukewarm water into the well and mix everything together with your hand, or the dough hook on the lowest speed, to make a fairly soft but not sticky dough. Flours vary, so if the dough feels stiff or dry, or there are dry crumbs at the bottom of the bowl, you may need to work in more water a tablespoon at a time. If the dough sticks to the side of the bowl, work in a little more flour.

3. Turn out the dough on to a very lightly oiled worktop and knead* thoroughly for 10 minutes, or for 5 minutes with the dough hook on the lowest speed, until the dough is smooth and stretchy. Return it to the bowl, if necessary, cover tightly with a snap-on lid or clingfilm and leave to rise in a warm spot for 50–60 minutes until doubled in size.

4. Turn out the dough on to the lightly floured worktop and gently knead into a ball. Weigh it, then divide into 6 equal portions. Shape each into a neat ball. Cover loosely with a sheet of clingfilm or a clean, dry tea towel and leave to rest for 15 minutes.

5. Using a lightly floured rolling pin, roll out each ball into a neat, thin disc about 22cm across and transfer to a sheet of baking paper. Cover the discs lightly with clingfilm or a dry tea towel and leave on the worktop for 15 minutes.

6. Meanwhile, heat the oven to 200°C/400°F/gas 6, and put the baking sheets into the oven to heat up.

7. Carefully slide a dough disc, on its baking paper, on to one of the hot baking sheets and quickly return to the oven; repeat with **>>>**

a second disc, then bake them for 4 minutes. The discs will puff up with bubbles of air. Remove the sheets from the oven and quickly and carefully flip the discs over using kitchen tongs. Return to the oven and bake for a further 3 minutes.

8. Use the tongs to remove the breads,wrap them in a clean, dry tea towel and leave to cool. Bake the rest of the breads, in 2 more batches, in the same way. They can be kept, well wrapped in the tea towel, for up to 8 hours before finishing.

9. When ready to serve the breads, heat a heavy ridged grill pan/griddle on the stove over medium/high heat (or prepare a fire in the barbecue). While you wait, make the topping: mix together the oil, lemon zest and juice, and za'atar in a small bowl. Taste and add a little more lemon juice or some salt and pepper.

10. Cook the breads one at a time. Using kitchen tongs, place the bread on the grill pan and cook for about 1 minute on each side until hot and puffed up once more, and browned with grill marks but not scorched. (If using a barbecue, you can cook the breads all at once; arrange them on the barbecue grill near the edge.) Remove to a heatproof plate or board, brush with the topping and serve immediately, with Muhammara.

MUHAMMARA

This roasted walnut and red pepper dip, flavoured with pomegranate, is very popular in the Middle East. Serve it at room temperature with warm flatbreads or with Cheese Beignets (see page 220).

1. Heat the oven to 220°C/425°F/gas 7. Put the peppers in an oiled roasting tin and roast in the oven for about 35 minutes, turning occasionally, until the skins are very dark brown. Transfer the peppers to a heatproof bowl and cover the top with a plate. Leave to steam for at least 20 minutes until cool enough to handle – this will loosen the skins.

2. While the peppers are cooling, tip the walnuts and peeled garlic clove into a small baking dish or tin and toast in the oven for 5–7 minutes until just turning golden – watch the nuts carefully so they don't get too dark. Set aside to cool. (You can turn the oven off now.)

3. When the peppers are cool, peel off the skins, then quarter and discard the cores, seeds and any thick white ribs. Leave to drain on kitchen paper.

4. Tear the bread into pieces and put them in a food processor. Blitz to make fairly fine breadcrumbs, then add the toasted garlic clove, cumin, lemon juice, pomegranate molasses, chilli flakes and oil, and blitz to make a thick paste.

5. Add the nuts and red peppers and 'pulse' to make a coarse, thick paste. Taste and season with salt and pepper, plus more chilli flakes or lemon juice as needed – the muhammara shouldn't be bland but the flavours should be balanced.

6. Transfer the dip to a serving bowl. Drizzle a little more oil over the top and serve at room temperature. The dip can be kept, tightly covered, overnight in the fridge; before serving, bring back to room temperature, then stir gently and drizzle a little oil over the surface.

Serves 6–8

3 red peppers
60g walnut pieces
1 large garlic clove, peeled
1 slice of bread, preferably wholemeal (about 50g), crusts trimmed off
1 teaspoon ground cumin
1 tablespoon lemon juice
1 tablespoon pomegranate molasses
2 pinches of chilli flakes, or to taste
2 tablespoons olive oil, plus extra for serving
salt and pepper, to taste

CHOCOLATE QUICK BREAD

Really rich and almost cake-like, this is the kind of treat that makes you want to revive the custom of an old-fashioned tea party. The bread is drizzled with a salted caramel sauce and decorated with caramelised pecans. Delicious at tea time instead of cake.

1. Heat the oven to 180°C/350°F/gas 4. Sift the flour, salt, baking powder, bicarbonate of soda and cocoa powder into a large mixing bowl. Add the chopped pecans and mix thoroughly, then make a well in the centre.

2. Put the butter and sugar in a medium pan and set over low heat. Heat gently, stirring occasionally, until the butter has melted. Remove the pan from the heat and stir in the buttermilk followed by the beaten eggs. Pour the mixture into the well in the flour mixture, then, using a wooden spoon, gradually work the flour into the egg mixture to make a heavy, slightly sticky, soft dough.

3. Lightly flour the worktop and your hands, then turn out the dough and knead it gently for a few seconds, just until smooth (it's important not to delay when making quick breads*). Divide the dough in half and quickly shape each piece into a neat ball. Set the balls on the lined baking sheet,

well apart to allow for expansion, then flatten them slightly with the palm of your hand so the loaves are about 15cm across.

4. With a large, sharp knife, cut a deep cross in the top of each loaf. Bake in the heated oven for 30–35 minutes until the loaves are firm and they sound hollow when tapped on the underside*. Transfer to a wire rack and leave to cool completely.

5. While the loaves are baking, make the sauce. Put the butter, cream and sea salt into a small pan and set over low heat. As soon as the butter has melted and the mixture is warm (but not hot), remove from the heat and set aside. Measure the sugar into a medium pan and heat gently, swirling the sugar in the pan until it has completely melted (if necessary, stir occasionally with a metal spoon). Bring to the boil and cook, without stirring, until the sugar syrup turns to a golden caramel. Quickly remove the pan from the heat and >>>

Makes 2 loaves

Kit you'll need: 1 large baking sheet, lined with baking paper; a baking sheet brushed with vegetable oil

FOR THE BREADS
450g plain flour
½ teaspoon fine sea salt
1 teaspoon baking powder
1 teaspoon bicarbonate of soda
80g cocoa powder
100g pecan halves, roughly chopped
115g unsalted butter, diced
200g caster sugar
200ml buttermilk
2 large eggs, at room temperature, beaten to mix

FOR THE SALTED CARAMEL SAUCE
15g unsalted butter
125ml whipping cream
½ teaspoon sea salt flakes
50g caster sugar

FOR THE CARAMELISED PECANS
20 pecan halves
200g caster sugar

immediately add a little of the cream mixture – it will froth up, so take care. Using a wooden spoon, gradually stir in the rest of the cream mixture. Return the pan to low heat and stir the sauce until smooth. Pour into a heatproof jug and leave to cool, then cover with clingfilm and keep in the fridge until needed.

6. To make the caramelised pecans, arrange the nuts, well apart, on the oiled baking sheet. Tip the sugar into a pan and melt gently, then cook to a golden caramel as before. Gently pour over the pecans to cover. Leave until set hard before breaking the caramel into small fragments, keeping the pecan halves intact.

7. To serve, decorate the loaves with the caramelised pecans, then trickle a little salted caramel sauce over the top and scatter the caramel pieces over the loaves. Serve with the rest of the sauce. Best eaten the same day.

PAINS AUX RAISINS

They may be part of every coffee shop or baker's display today, but there is still something very special about these butter-rich breads/pastries with their hearts of rum-soaked raisins and crème pâtissière. This is a recipe to show off your puff pastry skills. For the crispest, flakiest pains, bake until they turn a good golden colour.

Makes 18

Kit you'll need: 2 baking sheets, lined with baking paper

FOR THE DOUGH
35g caster sugar
10g fine sea salt
25g milk powder
325ml water,
    at room temperature
500g white bread flour,
    plus extra for dusting

1 x 7g sachet easy-blend
    dried yeast
250g unsalted butter, well chilled

FOR THE RAISIN FILLING
200g raisins
3 tablespoons dark rum

FOR THE CRÈME PÂTISSIÈRE
250ml creamy milk
1 vanilla pod, split open
3 medium egg yolks,
    at room temperature

50g caster sugar
15g cornflour
20g unsalted butter,
    at room temperature

TO FINISH
1 medium egg yolk, beaten
    with 1 tablespoon milk

1. Stir the sugar, salt and milk powder into the measured water and leave for a couple of minutes until completely dissolved. Put the flour into a large mixing bowl, or the bowl of a free-standing electric mixer fitted with the dough hook attachment. Add the yeast and mix it in with your hand. Pour the milky liquid into the flour and beat with your hand, or the dough hook on the lowest speed, for about 1 minute until the ingredients are thoroughly combined to make a soft, slightly sticky and shaggy-looking dough that comes away from the side of the bowl. Do not overwork or knead the dough at this point as you don't want to develop the gluten (this would make the dough stretchy but also tougher).

2. Cover the bowl with a snap-on lid or put it into a large plastic bag. Leave to rise in a warm spot for 30–45 minutes until the dough has doubled in size.

3. Gently punch down the dough to deflate it, then cover again and put the bowl into the fridge. Leave for at least 6 hours or overnight to firm up.

4. Put the raisins for the filling into a bowl with the rum and stir well. Cover and leave to soak until needed.

5. To make the crème pâtissière, heat the milk with the split vanilla pod in a medium saucepan until bubbles start to form around the edge. Remove the pan from the heat and leave the milk to infuse for about 10 minutes, then fish out the vanilla pod. Use the tip of a small sharp knife to scrape the tiny vanilla seeds into the milk (discard the pod).

>>>

6. While the milk is infusing, put the egg yolks, sugar and cornflour in a heatproof bowl set on a damp cloth on the worktop (the cloth will prevent the bowl from wobbling). Whisk together with a wire whisk for a couple of minutes until very smooth, then whisk in the hot milk. Tip the mixture back into the pan and whisk constantly over medium heat until the mixture boils and thickens – take care it doesn't catch on the bottom of the pan. Remove from the heat and whisk in the butter.

7. Transfer the mixture to a clean heatproof bowl and press a piece of clingfilm or dampened baking paper on to the surface to prevent a skin from forming. Cool, then cover the top of the bowl with clingfilm and chill for at least 6 hours or overnight.

8. Next day, place the block of chilled butter between 2 sheets of greaseproof paper and pound with a rolling pin to flatten it. Re-shape into a brick and repeat the process a few times until the butter is pliable but still cold and firm. Finally, shape the butter into a square with sides about 12cm.

9. Turn out the chilled dough on to a lightly floured worktop. Punch down to deflate it, then shape into a ball. Score a deep cross in the top. Using a floured rolling pin, roll out the dough 'flaps' from the scored cross in 4 directions – lift the dough and give it a quarter turn after each rolling. It should end up looking like a cross with a thick rough square in the centre. Place the butter on top of the rough central square, then fold the flaps of dough over the butter and tuck in the edges. Make sure the butter is completely enclosed so it doesn't ooze out during the rolling and folding processes that follow.

10. Lightly sprinkle the dough parcel with flour, then roll out away from you into a rectangle about 30 x 60cm. Fold the dough in thirds – fold up the bottom third to cover the centre third, then fold down the top third to cover the other 2 layers. Lightly press the open edges with the rolling pin to seal. Set the dough on a plate, cover tightly with clingfilm and chill for 30 minutes.

11. Set the dough on the floured worktop so that the folded edges are now to the left and right. Repeat the rolling out, folding and chilling. After this, repeat the whole process one more time.

12. Roll out the dough to a thin rectangle about 50 x 34cm. Using a pizza wheel-cutter or a floured large, sharp knife, trim the edges to make a neat 48 x 32cm rectangle. Spread the crème pâtissière evenly over the surface, leaving a 1.5cm border clear, then scatter the raisins on top. Starting from a short end, roll up the dough fairly firmly, like a swiss roll. Roll the rolled dough on to a sheet of baking paper, making sure the seam is underneath, then lift on to a baking sheet or board. Cover lightly with clingfilm and chill for an hour – this will make slicing easier.

13. Uncover the roll and, using a large, sharp knife, cut across into 18 slices – use a gentle sawing motion. Transfer the slices to the prepared baking sheets, arranging them cut side down and well apart to allow for expansion. Tuck the end of each spiral slice underneath, and gently push back into shape if necessary. Lightly cover with clingfilm and leave on the worktop to prove for 45 minutes until slightly puffy. If your kitchen is very warm, move the sheets to a cooler spot, or into the fridge.

14. Towards the end of the rising time, heat the oven to 190°C/375°F/gas 5.

15. Uncover the spirals and gently brush with beaten egg yolk to glaze. Bake in the heated oven for 18–22 minutes until a good golden brown. Check the pains after 15 minutes and rotate the baking sheets if necessary so they all bake evenly. Transfer to a wire rack to cool. Best eaten the same or the next day (gently warm through in a 180°C/350°F/gas 4 oven for 5–8 minutes before serving).

Note

Don't cut corners by skimping on the chilling and resting times. If the dough begins to feel soft, cover and chill it until it is firm enough to start work again.

GLUTEN-FREE PITTA BREADS

Pitta bread may have its roots in the Middle East, but it has long since been well and truly adopted in Britain. This is a tricky bread challenge: making twelve identical pitta breads using a rich gluten-free dough.

1. Mix the psyllium powder with 300ml of the water and set aside until needed – the mixture will swell and thicken.

2. Tip the flour and nigella seeds into a large mixing bowl. Add the sugar and salt to one side of the bowl and the yeast to the other side. Break the eggs into the centre of the flour and add the vinegar, oil and thickened psyllium mixture. Combine the ingredients with your hand to make a soft dough. Very gradually work in the remaining water – this flour absorbs water in a different way to wheat flour so you may not need it all – to make a dough that's soft and slightly sticky. If the dough is too dry it will crack when you try to shape it; if it is too wet you won't be able to form a neat shape.

3. Turn out the dough on to a floured worktop and knead it briefly just until smooth – as there's no gluten, the dough won't be stretchy and elastic. Return the dough to the bowl, cover tightly with clingfilm and leave to rest for 1½ hours until doubled in size.

4. Towards the end of the rising time, heat the oven to 220°C/425°F/gas 7 and put the 3 baking sheets in the oven to heat up.

5. Turn out the dough on to the floured worktop. Divide into 12 equal pieces and shape each into a ball. Roll or press out each ball to a neat oval shape about 4mm thick.

6. Remove the hot baking sheets from the oven and dust them lightly with flour. Arrange 4 pittas on each sheet, slightly apart. Bake for 10–12 minutes until puffed up and slightly golden, with no wet-looking patches – the tricky part is making sure the insides of the pittas are cooked and not doughy or sticky. Remove from the oven and immediately wrap in a clean, dry tea towel to keep the pittas soft. Eat as soon as possible.

Makes 12

Kit you'll need: 3 heavy-duty baking sheets (ungreased)

30g psyllium powder
600ml water
750g gluten-free strong
    flour blend
3 tablespoons nigella seeds
15g caster sugar
1 tablespoon salt
21g fast-action dried yeast
    (3 x 7g sachets)
3 large eggs, at room temperature
1 tablespoon white wine vinegar
90ml olive oil

Note

Psyllium powder is very useful in gluten-free baking as it binds with liquid to mimic the structure that gluten provides, enabling breads to rise. You can buy psyllium powder in wholefood and healthfood shops.

FLAOUNAS

A festive recipe from the island of Cyprus, these sweet cheese breads are baked both for Easter Sunday and Ramadan. There is yeast in the filling as well as the pastry, plus mastic powder, the dried sap of the mastic tree, which adds a slight pine flavour, and mahleb or mahlepi, the spice popular in Greece and the Middle East that has a bitter almond/cherry taste – it is one of Baker Tamal's favourite ingredients. Both mastic powder and mahleb are available from specialist shops and online.

Makes 12

Kit you'll need: a 15cm round cutter or saucer; 3 large baking sheets, lined with baking paper

FOR THE FILLING
500g pecorino romano, grated
250g halloumi, grated
75g plain flour
1 × 7g sachet fast-action
    dried yeast
90g fine semolina

2 teaspoons dried mint
100g sultanas
4 large eggs, at room temperature
4 tablespoons milk,
    at room temperature
1 teaspoon baking powder

FOR THE PASTRY
750g strong white bread flour
1 teaspoon mastic powder
2 teaspoons ground mahleb
1 teaspoon caster sugar

1 teaspoon salt
1 × 7g sachet fast-action
    dried yeast
60g unsalted butter, softened
450ml full-fat milk,
    at room temperature

FOR THE GLAZE
200g sesame seeds
1 teaspoon white wine vinegar
3 large egg yolks, at room
    temperature, beaten to mix

1. Make the filling first. Combine the grated cheeses in a large mixing bowl. Put the flour, yeast, semolina, dried mint and sultanas into another bowl and mix them together. Break the eggs into a jug, add the milk and beat with a fork just until combined. Tip the flour mixture over the cheeses, then add the egg mixture and mix everything together thoroughly with your hand. Cover the bowl with clingfilm and set aside while you make the pastry.

2. Tip the flour, mastic powder and mahleb into a large mixing bowl. Add the sugar and salt to

one side of the bowl and the dried yeast to the other side. Put the softened butter and 350ml of the milk in the middle. Using your hand, mix together all the ingredients to make a fairly soft dough, then gradually work in enough of the remaining 100ml milk to make a soft but not wet dough – if it is too wet it will be hard to shape, but if too stiff or firm it will crack as you try to shape it.

3. Turn out the dough on to a lightly floured worktop and knead* for 10 minutes until smooth. Shape the dough into

a ball, return it to the bowl and cover the bowl with clingfilm. Leave to rest on the worktop for about 1 hour until the dough has doubled in size.

4. Meanwhile, make the glaze. Put the sesame seeds and vinegar into a small pan and add enough water to cover. Bring to the boil, then drain the seeds thoroughly in a sieve. Spread out on a clean tea towel and leave to dry.

5. When the pastry dough is ready to be shaped, heat the oven to 200°C/400°F/gas 6.

>>>

6 Turn out the pastry dough on to the lightly floured worktop and divide into 12. Roll out each piece to a 20cm square. One at a time, pick up the pastry squares and press them on to the sesame seeds so one side of the pastry is coated in seeds. Set the pastry squares, seed-side down, back on the worktop.

7. Stir the filling well, then add the baking powder and mix thoroughly. Divide into 12 equal portions. Spoon one portion of filling into the centre of each pastry square, then lift up the 4 sides to shape a smaller square. You should still be able to see the filling in the centre. Press the corners firmly together to seal.

8. Arrange the flaounas well apart on the lined baking sheets. Carefully brush the pastry with beaten egg yolk. Bake in the heated oven for 15 minutes, then reduce the oven temperature to 180°C/350°F/gas 4. Bake for another 15 minutes until golden and puffed up. Cool on a rack. Eat warm or at room temperature.

BAGUETTES

The best baguettes are golden, crisp and crunchy on the outside, with an open, airy crumb inside. Characteristically, the thin crust bursts open slightly along the length of the bread, where the dough has been slashed before baking. A jugful of water poured into a hot baking tray in the oven creates steam and helps produce the crunchy crust. Producing four evenly sized baguettes is a difficult challenge, even for experienced bakers, so good luck!

1. Put the flour and salt in the bowl of a free-standing electric mixer fitted with the dough hook attachment. Add the yeast to the bowl, well away from the salt, and begin mixing on low speed, gradually adding three-quarters of the water. As the dough starts to come together, slowly add the remaining water, then continue mixing on medium speed for 5–7 minutes until the dough is very elastic and glossy. Scrape the dough into the oiled tub (it's important to use a square tub as it helps to shape the dough), cover and leave for 1 hour until at least doubled in size.

2. Dredge the linen cloth or couche with flour, and lightly dust the worktop with flour. Carefully tip the dough on to the worktop. Rather than knocking it back, handle it very gently to keep in as much air as possible: this helps to create the irregular, open texture of a really good baguette. The dough will feel wet and soft and will still seem lively.

3. Using a dough scraper, divide the dough into 4 equal pieces. Now for the trickiest part of this challenge – shaping. Do this one baguette at a time. First shape the piece of dough into an oblong by slightly flattening the dough and then folding the sides into the middle. Roll up into a neat sausage shape – the top should be very smooth and the seam underneath. Now, starting in the middle, roll the sausage backwards and forwards on the worktop with your hands – use the weight of your arms (rather than a lot of pressure) to roll the dough – until it is 30cm long.

4. Gently set the baguette on the cloth/couche, parallel to a short edge. Pleat up the cloth/couche against the edge of the baguette, to form a barrier and support. Shape the second baguette, then set it next to the pleat. Repeat the process until all 4 baguettes are lined up on the cloth with a pleat between them. Cover the baguettes with a clean tea >>>

Makes 4 loaves

Kit you'll need: a square plastic container, 2.4-litre capacity, greased with olive oil; a heavy linen cloth OR baker's couche, about 100 x 60cm; a roasting tin; 2 baking sheets, lined with baking paper

500g strong white bread flour, plus extra for dusting and dredging
10g salt
10g fast-action dried yeast
370ml cool water

towel and leave for about 1 hour until they have at least doubled in size and spring back instantly when gently prodded with the tip of your finger.

5. Towards the end of the rising time, heat the oven to 240°C/475°F/gas 9, and put the roasting tin in the bottom to heat.

6. Very gently roll the baguettes, one at a time, off the cloth/couche and on to the baking sheets — don't try to lift them. Make sure the seam side is still underneath and set them well apart. Dust the baguettes lightly with flour, then make 4 diagonal slashes across the top of each using a very sharp knife (or a razor blade).

7. Pour a jug of hot water into the heated roasting tin in the oven to create a good burst of steam, then quickly load the baking sheets into the oven. Bake the baguettes for 20–25 minutes until the crust has a slight sheen and has turned a rich golden brown. Take care when opening the oven door (because of all the hot steam inside), then transfer the baguettes to a wire rack to cool.

'I might make a simple white bloomer, with a spice mix of mustard seeds, fenugreek, fennel and cumin seeds, toasted in a dry pan, then crushed using a pestle and mortar, and added to the dough, so that the spices are flecked through it. It tastes delicious.'

MAT

CINNAMON STICKY BUNS

Loved in Scandinavia, fragrant cinnamon buns are great for the family to enjoy on a lazy weekend morning. These are sticky yet feather-light and warmly spiced, with a crunchy topping. They're made like Chelsea Buns, but instead of containing dried fruits and mixed spice, the brioche-like dough is flavoured with a touch of ground cardamom and then rolled up with the buttery, cinnamon-spiced filling.

Makes 9

Kit you'll need: 1 baking sheet, lined with baking paper

FOR THE DOUGH
425g strong white bread flour
1 x 7g sachet easy-blend
   dried yeast
50g light brown muscovado sugar
3g fine sea salt
8 cardamom pods
about 225ml lukewarm milk
1 medium egg,
   at room temperature
75g slightly salted butter, softened
   and cut into small pieces

FOR THE FILLING
100g slightly salted butter,
   softened
75g light brown muscovado sugar
2 teaspoons ground cinnamon

FOR THE TOPPING
50g walnut pieces, chopped finer
1 tablespoon demerara sugar

1. Put the flour and yeast into a mixing bowl, or the bowl of a free-standing electric mixer fitted with the dough hook attachment, and combine with your hand, or the dough hook. Add the sugar and salt and mix in. Roughly crush the cardamom pods and remove the seeds, then finely grind the seeds or crush in a mortar and pestle. Mix them into the flour. Make a well in the centre.

2. Beat the milk with the egg using a fork, just until combined, then add to the well. Gradually work the flour mixture into the liquid with your hand, or the dough hook on its lowest speed, to make a very soft dough. If the dough feels stiff and dry, or there are dry crumbs at the bottom of the bowl, work in more milk a tablespoon at a time. Add the butter and work into the dough – it will feel soft and slightly sticky.

3. Turn the dough on to a lightly floured worktop and knead* very thoroughly for 10 minutes, or for 5 minutes with the dough hook on low speed. The dough will firm up as it is stretched and worked, and will end up feeling

silky smooth and much less sticky. Shape the dough into a ball and return to the bowl, if necessary, then cover with a snap-on lid or clingfilm and leave to rise on the worktop for 1–1½ hours until doubled in size (if the dough is left in a warm spot it will become too soft and difficult to shape).

4. Punch down the risen dough with your knuckles to deflate, then turn it out on to the lightly floured worktop and knead it gently for a few seconds to form a neat smooth ball. Cover with the upturned bowl and leave to relax for 5 minutes while you make the filling.

5. Put the softened butter, muscovado sugar and cinnamon into a bowl and beat well with a wooden spoon until smooth and thoroughly combined. The filling should have a spreadable consistency.

6. Uncover the dough and roll it out with a floured rolling pin to a neat 28 x 38cm rectangle. Spread the filling evenly over the dough using a palette knife. Starting at a long edge, roll it up fairly tightly,

like a swiss roll, and pinch the seam together firmly to seal. Using a floured large, sharp knife, cut the roll across into 9 thick slices.

7. Arrange the slices cut-side down in 3 rows of 3 on the lined baking sheet, spacing the slices about 1.5cm apart (they will spread and join up during baking).

Cover the slices very lightly with clingfilm and leave to rise on the worktop for 40–50 minutes until almost doubled in size.

8. Towards the end of the rising time, heat your oven to 190°C/375°F/gas 5, and make the topping by mixing the chopped walnuts with the demerara sugar.

9. Remove the clingfilm and sprinkle some of the topping over each bun. Bake in the heated oven for about 25 minutes until a good golden brown. Transfer the buns to a wire rack and leave to cool before pulling apart. Eat warm the same or the next day.

SODA BREAD

Ireland's favourite bread, with its craggy good looks and nutty flavour, always feels special. There's no kneading and no proving since soda bread relies on the chemical reaction between tangy buttermilk and bicarbonate of soda for its lovely light texture.

1. Heat the oven to 200°C/400°F/gas 6. Put both the flours into a large mixing bowl. Add the salt and bicarbonate of soda and mix well with your hand. Make a well in the centre and pour in half of the buttermilk. Using your fingers or a round-bladed knife, gradually draw the flour into the buttermilk, then add more buttermilk as needed to make a soft, sticky dough. (Flours vary so you may not need all the buttermilk.)

2. Once the dough has been mixed, it's important not to delay*. Lightly flour the worktop and turn out the dough. Divide it in half and shape each piece into a ball. Flatten the balls slightly with the palm of your hand.

3. Set each loaf on a baking sheet and quickly cut a large, deep cross in the dough (almost but not quite through to the base) with a large, sharp knife. Dust the tops of the loaves with flour, then bake immediately in the heated oven for about 40 minutes until the loaves are golden brown and sound hollow when tapped on the underside*.

4. Transfer to a wire rack and leave to cool. Eat the same day, or toasted the following day.

Makes 2 loaves

Kit you'll need: 2 baking sheets, dusted with flour

500g plain white flour
500g plain wholemeal flour
2 teaspoons salt
2 teaspoons bicarbonate of soda
about 800ml buttermilk

PARKER HOUSE ROLLS

If a bread roll can achieve iconic status, this is it. Created in the 1870s at The Parker House in Boston, a glamorous gem of a hotel where the future President Kennedy proposed to Jacqueline Lee Bouvier, these rolls are very rich, thanks to lashings of butter, with a fine soft and light crumb. They owe their distinctive shape to being brushed with butter and then folded in half, so that as they puff up in the oven they open out slightly. The rolls are still served on many American tables alongside the turkey and ham at Thanksgiving, always the fourth Thursday of November.

Makes 24

Kit you'll need: a 7cm plain round cutter; 2 rimmed baking sheets OR a roasting tin/baking tin, well greased with butter (see recipe)

600g strong white bread flour
1 x 7g sachet easy-blend
   dried yeast
10g caster sugar
10g fine sea salt
300ml lukewarm water
1 medium egg,
   at room temperature
100g unsalted butter, softened
   and cut into flakes

TO FINISH
75g unsalted butter, melted

Note

Once cold, the rolls can be frozen, tightly wrapped, for up to a month; gently heat them from frozen in the oven before serving.

1. Put the flour and yeast into a large mixing bowl, or the bowl of a free-standing electric mixer fitted with the dough hook attachment, and mix well with your hand or the dough hook. Add the sugar and salt and mix in, then make a well in the centre.

2. Measure the water in a jug, add the egg and beat with a fork until combined. Pour into the well. Add the butter, then slowly work everything together, using your hand or the dough hook on the lowest speed, to make a soft dough. If there are crumbs on the bottom of the bowl, or if the dough feels hard and dry and difficult to bring together, work in more water a tablespoon at a time; if dough sticks to the side of the bowl, or feels sticky and wet, work in a little more flour.

3. Turn out the dough on to a lightly floured worktop and knead* for 5 minutes, or for 3 minutes using the dough hook on lowest speed, until the dough feels smooth and slightly pliable

– it will have a second kneading later on. Shape the dough into a ball and return it to the bowl, if necessary, then cover with a snap-on lid or clingfilm. Leave the dough to rise on the worktop for 1–1½ hours until doubled in size.

4. Punch down the dough to deflate it. Turn it out on to the lightly floured worktop and knead for 3 minutes, or 1 minute in the mixer, until silky smooth, satiny and more pliable. Shape the dough into a ball, cover it with the upturned bowl and leave to relax for 15 minutes.

5. With a lightly floured rolling pin, roll out the dough to an oblong about 1.25cm thick. Dip the round cutter in flour, then stamp out discs. Gather up the dough trimmings, re-roll and stamp out more discs. Because of the butter content (the rolls are not greasy, by the way), you will need to use baking sheets with a slight rim, or a roasting or baking tin.

>>>

6. To shape each roll, lay a disc on the worktop and firmly press it in the centre with your fingers to make the centre slightly thinner than the edges. Brush the disc liberally with melted butter, then fold it over in half and gently press the edges together. Place on the baking sheets, setting the rolls well apart to allow for expansion.

Brush the rolls with more melted butter, then cover very loosely with clingfilm and leave to rise for 30–45 minutes (depending on how warm your kitchen is) until almost doubled in size.

7. Towards the end of the rising time, heat your oven to 200°C/400°F/gas 6.

8. Remove the clingfilm and bake the rolls in the heated oven for 18–20 minutes until golden brown – check after 12 minutes and rotate the sheets, if necessary, so the rolls bake evenly. Transfer them to a wire rack and leave to cool. Best eaten the same or the next day.

FRESH CORN LOAF

A sheaf of corn or plaited 'corn dolly' have always been connected with the Harvest Festival, and now that sweetcorn is such a popular crop around the sunnier spots of the country, a loaf that combines yellow cornmeal (easy to find in the form of polenta) and fresh sweetcorn, sliced from the raw cobs, is just perfect for a celebration supper.

1. Put the flour and yeast into a large mixing bowl, or the bowl of a free-standing electric mixer fitted with the dough hook attachment, and combine with your hand or the dough hook. Add the cornmeal or polenta, sweetcorn kernels and salt and mix thoroughly. Make a well in the centre.

2. Measure the 300ml lukewarm water in a jug, then add the egg, honey and oil and mix thoroughly. Pour into the well, then work in the flour mixture with your hand, or the dough hook on the lowest speed, just until everything comes together to make a soft and slightly sticky dough. If there are dry crumbs in the bottom of the bowl, or the dough feels stiff and is difficult to bind, work in more water a tablespoon at a time.

3. Leave the dough, uncovered, for 5 minutes to hydrate*. This dough is quite heavy, and the sweetcorn makes it stickier than a regular white dough. After the hydrating, you will be able to judge whether or not to add more water if the dough feels dry.

4. Turn out the dough on to a lightly floured worktop and knead* for about 5 minutes, or 3 minutes with the dough hook on lowest speed. Cover the dough with the upturned bowl, or cover the mixer bowl with clingfilm, and leave to rest for 10 minutes.

5. Uncover the dough and knead it for another 5 minutes by hand, or 3 minutes in the mixer. The dough should now feel more pliable. Return it to the bowl, if necessary, then cover with a snap-on lid or clingfilm and leave to rise in a slightly warm spot for 1–1½ hours until doubled in size.

6. Punch down the risen dough to deflate it, then turn it out on to the lightly floured worktop. Knead just for a few seconds, then, using your hands, press out the dough into a rectangle about 26 x 30cm. Starting from a short end, roll up fairly tightly, like a swiss roll, pinching the edges together each time you roll it. Pinch the seam firmly and tuck the ends under.

>>>

Makes a large loaf

Kit you'll need: 1 x 900g loaf tin, about 26 x 12.5 x 7.5cm, greased with butter

500g strong white bread flour
1 x 7g sachet fast-action
    dried yeast
100g medium/fine yellow
    cornmeal OR polenta,
    plus extra for sprinkling
100g fresh sweetcorn kernels cut
    off the cob (about 1 large ear
    of sweetcorn)
10g fine sea salt
about 300ml lukewarm water
1 medium egg,
    at room temperature
45g clear honey
1 tablespoon corn oil

Note

The dough starts off feeling heavy and sticky but kneading in batches helps turn it light and lively.

7. Sprinkle the inside of the buttered loaf tin with a little cornmeal or polenta, then place the loaf in the tin, seam side down. Sprinkle the top with a little more cornmeal or polenta. Slip the tin into a large plastic bag and inflate it slightly so the plastic doesn't stick to the dough, then fasten the ends. Leave to rise on the worktop for about 1 hour until doubled in size.

8. Towards the end of the rising time, heat the oven to 200°C/400°F/gas 6.

9. Uncover the loaf and bake in the heated oven for about 40 minutes until it is a good golden brown and sounds hollow when tapped on the underside*. Transfer to a wire rack and leave until cold before slicing. Best eaten within 3 days or toasted.

'I love really interesting breads, whether artisan or sophisticated – every time I come across a gorgeous light brioche, or a malty, treacley or cheesey bread, I think, "I need to be baking this".'

DORRET

CHOCOLATE BABKA

Illustrating the power of family tradition in baking, the name of this Polish-Jewish bread means 'grandmother'. Babka is often simply spiced with cinnamon, but this version, which is popular at Channukah, the Jewish festival of lights, is an elaborate, richly swirled chocolate loaf. The recipe is an old one in which the rich, buttery yeast dough known as challah meets cake. It's fairly complicated to make, but well worth it for chocolate fiends.

1. Put the flour into a large mixing bowl, or the bowl of a free-standing electric mixer fitted with the dough hook attachment. Add the sugar and salt and mix in with your hand, or the dough hook. Sprinkle the yeast into the bowl and mix in. Make a well in the centre.

2. Break the eggs into a measuring jug and break them up with a fork without making them frothy, then add enough milk to make the eggs up to 265ml. Pour into the well, then gradually work the flour into the liquid using your hand, or the dough hook on the lowest speed, to make a soft and very sticky dough. If there are dry crumbs or the dough feels dry and tough, work in more milk a tablespoon at a time.

3. Using a dough scraper to help, turn out the dough on to a lightly floured worktop and knead* thoroughly for 10 minutes, or for about 6 minutes using the dough hook on lowest speed. The dough will feel slightly firmer and more elastic. Gradually work in the butter, a few pieces at a time, to

make a silky smooth, soft but still sticky dough. As soon as all the butter has been added, and you can no longer see any streaks, scrape the dough back into the bowl, if necessary. Cover tightly with clingfilm or a snap-on lid, or slip the bowl into a large plastic bag and close securely. Put the bowl into the fridge and leave the dough to rise slowly for about 2 hours until doubled in size.

4. Flour your knuckles and punch down the dough to deflate it. Re-shape it into a ball, then cover it tightly once more and return to the fridge to rise for another hour.

5. Turn out the dough on to the floured worktop and knead gently for a minute to make a neat ball. Cover with the upturned bowl. Now make the filling.

6. Break up the chocolate and put it into a food processor with the sugar. Blitz to a fine rubble. Add the walnuts or pecans and 'pulse' several times so the nut pieces are chopped slightly smaller.

>>>

Makes a large loaf

Kit you'll need: 1 x 900g loaf tin, about 26 x 12.5 x 7.5cm, greased with butter and lined with a long strip of baking paper*

FOR THE DOUGH
400g strong white bread flour
70g caster sugar
5g fine sea salt
1 x 7g sachet fast-action dried yeast
4 medium eggs, chilled
about 5 tablespoons milk, chilled
150g unsalted butter, diced

FOR THE FILLING
150g dark chocolate (about 70% cocoa solids)
50g light brown muscovado sugar
75g walnut pieces OR chopped pecans
90g unsalted butter, melted

TO FINISH
1 medium egg, beaten with a pinch of salt

7. Using a lightly floured rolling pin, roll out the dough away from you to an evenly thick 30 x 40cm rectangle. Brush with two-thirds of the melted butter in a thick, even layer. Scatter the chocolate mixture over the top and gently press it on to the buttery surface with the flat of your hand. Sprinkle the rest of the melted butter on top.

8. Lightly score a line across the centre (to divide the dough into two 30 x 20cm halves). Starting from the 30cm edge nearest to you, roll up the dough, fairly tightly, to the centre line. Repeat from the other end, so the 2 rolls meet in the middle. With a long, very sharp knife, cut along the scored line between the rolls. Pinch the cut edge of each roll to seal the seam, then pinch the 2 rolls together at one end.

9. Now, starting from the pinched-together end, twist the 2 rolls together. Tuck the ends under and lift the twist into the prepared tin. It doesn't have to look neat. Scoop up any filling that has escaped and sprinkle it around the twist. Don't pat or prod the twist – as it rises it will fill out the tin. Slip the tin into a large plastic bag, slightly inflated to prevent the dough from sticking to the plastic, and secure the ends. Leave to rise in a warm but not hot place (you don't want the butter to melt) for 1–1½ hours until almost doubled in size.

10. Towards the end of the rising time, heat your oven to 190°C/375°F/gas 5. Uncover the risen loaf and carefully brush it with beaten egg to glaze. Bake in the heated oven for 45–50 minutes until a skewer inserted into the centre of the loaf comes out clean.

11. Set the tin on a wire rack and run a round-bladed knife around the inside of the tin to loosen the loaf, then leave it for 10 minutes before gently removing it from the tin on to the rack – use the lining paper to help lift out the loaf as it is quite delicate until it cools and firms up. Leave until completely cold before slicing. Best eaten within 4 days. Use any leftover slices to make a sublime bread and butter pudding.

Tip

Coolness is the key to preventing the butter oozing out of the soft dough, so it is left in the fridge to rise slowly and firm up. This makes shaping easier too.

WALNUT & STILTON SODA BREAD

Flavoured with the classic combination of blue cheese and walnuts, it's very hard to resist this loaf – the aroma as it bakes is superb, and it emerges from the oven textured and golden. It's almost a meal in itself, but is great with soups and salads.

1. Heat the oven to 200°C/400°F/gas 6. Trim the rind from the Stilton, then crumble the cheese fairly coarsely into a medium bowl. Add the walnut pieces and sultanas and mix well.

2. Tip the white and wholemeal flours into a very large mixing bowl. Add the bicarbonate of soda and salt and mix thoroughly. Make a well in the centre and pour in 800ml buttermilk. You need to work quickly from now on*. Using your hand, or a wooden spoon, mix everything together to make a slightly soft, shaggy-looking dough. Flours vary, and if the mixture feels very dry, or there are crumbs at the bottom of the bowl and it's difficult to bring the dough together, work in more buttermilk (or milk) a tablespoon at a time.

3. Lightly dust the worktop with wholemeal flour and turn out the dough. Divide it into 2 equal portions, by weight or by eye. Gently knead one portion, just for a few seconds, to form a ball about 17cm across. Set it on a lined baking sheet and cut a deep cross into the ball. Sprinkle with flour. Repeat with the second portion of dough.

4. Bake the loaves in the heated oven for 30–35 minutes until they are a good golden brown and sound hollow when tapped on the underside* – check the loaves after 25 minutes and rotate the baking sheets, if necessary, so the loaves bake evenly. Transfer to a wire rack and leave to cool.

Makes 2 medium loaves

Kit you'll need: **2 baking sheets, lined with baking paper**

200g Stilton
150g walnut pieces
100g sultanas
600g plain white flour
400g plain wholemeal flour, plus extra for dusting
2 teaspoons bicarbonate of soda
2 teaspoons salt
about 800ml buttermilk

LUSSEKATTS

These sweet saffron buns, shaped to represent curled-up 'Lucia cats', are essential to the Swedish festival of St Lucia on 13th December. The saint is associated with light and celebrated with a procession of children in white gowns, led by a fair-haired girl wearing a crown of candles. The feline association is less clear, but one legend is that the buns ward off the devil who disguised himself as a cat.

Makes 15

Kit you'll need: 2 baking sheets, lined with baking paper

0.4g sachet (1 teaspoon)
    saffron strands
225ml single cream
    OR very creamy milk
1 medium egg,
    at room temperature
100g slightly salted butter,
    melted and cooled
70g caster sugar
5g fine sea salt
45g raisins
about 450g strong white
    bread flour
10g fast-action dried yeast
    (from 2 x 7g sachets)
1 medium egg, beaten, to glaze

Note

This dough is much heavier and richer than regular doughs, so be patient while it is rising.

1. Heat the oven to 180°C/350°F/gas 4. Tip the saffron strands into a ramekin and toast in the heated oven for about 10 minutes until slightly darker. Meanwhile, warm the cream until steaming hot but not quite boiling. Remove from the heat and crumble in the toasted saffron. Stir well, then leave to infuse for 2 hours.

2. When ready to make the dough, break the egg into a large mixing bowl and add the butter, sugar, salt, raisins and saffron cream. Mix thoroughly with a wooden spoon. In another bowl combine 400g of the flour with the yeast. Gradually work the flour into the saffron mixture with your hand to make a smooth, soft and slightly sticky dough. Gently knead the dough in the bowl for 2 minutes only, then cover the bowl with clingfilm, or slip it into a large plastic bag and fasten the end. Leave on the worktop to rise for 1½–1¾ hours until the dough has doubled in size.

3. Lightly flour the worktop, then turn out the dough and knead* it thoroughly for 10 minutes, working in more of the remaining flour as

you need to make a dough that's soft but not sticky, stretchy and satiny smooth. Cover the dough with the upturned bowl and leave it to relax for 15 minutes.

4. Weigh the dough and divide it into 15 equal portions. Shape each into a ball, then roll with your hands on the unfloured worktop into a sausage 21cm long. Form each sausage into a neat, tight S shape. Arrange on the prepared baking sheets, setting the buns well apart to allow for expansion. Loosely cover with clingfilm and leave to rise for 1–1½ hours until doubled in size.

5. Towards the end of the rising time, heat the oven to 200°C/400°F/gas 6.

6. Carefully brush the buns with beaten egg – take care not to 'glue' them to the lining paper. Bake in the heated oven for 15–18 minutes until a good golden brown; check after 10 minutes and rotate the sheets if necessary so the buns bake evenly. Transfer to a wire rack to cool. Eat warm the same day, or leave until cold, then wrap and freeze for up to a month.

PANETTONE

There are all sorts of stories about the origins of this 'Italian Christmas Cake', many of them involving a baker or his daughter called Toni, hence 'pan de toni'. Whichever legend you prefer, panettone has become a festive favourite far beyond its home in Milan. Home bakers now vie with the professionals to make the tallest, lightest, most delicate, buttery, egg-rich loaf.

1. Make the marrons glacés 4 or 5 days before you want to bake the panettone. Put the sugar, water and vanilla pod into a small pan and set over low heat. Stir occasionally until the sugar has dissolved, then bring to the boil and boil gently for 10 minutes to make a light syrup. Add the chestnuts and bring the syrup back to the boil, then simmer gently, without stirring, for 10 minutes. Remove from the heat and leave to cool. Once cold, cover the pan with a lid or saucer and leave on the worktop for 8 hours or overnight.

2. Uncover the pan and bring the chestnuts in syrup back to the boil. Reduce the heat and simmer for 1 minute. Remove from the heat and cool, then cover and leave again for 8 hours or overnight. Repeat this step once more the next day, then leave the chestnuts to cool.

3. Using a slotted spoon, lift the chestnuts out of any remaining syrup and set them in a single layer on a large plate lined with baking paper. Leave to dry out slightly on the worktop for about 12 hours. Before using, break the marrons glacés into large chunks, if necessary.

4. Put 250g of the weighed flour, the yeast and sugar in a large mixing bowl, or the bowl of a free-standing electric mixer fitted with the dough hook attachment, and mix together with your hand, or the dough hook. Make a well in the centre. Beat the whole eggs with the lukewarm water and pour into the well. With your hand, or the dough hook on the lowest speed, mix the flour into the liquid to make a thick, smooth batter. Sprinkle a little of the remaining weighed flour over the top of the batter to prevent a skin from forming, then leave the bowl in a warm spot for about 1 hour until the batter is very bubbly.

5. Stir the egg yolks, vanilla extract and grated zests into the batter using your hand, or the dough hook on the lowest speed, then gradually work in 350g of the remaining flour plus the salt to make a soft and very sticky dough. Add the butter >>>

Makes a very large loaf

Kit you'll need: 1 x 18cm (4.5-litre) loose-based panettone pan OR 18cm round, very deep cake tin

FOR THE MARRONS GLACÉS
200g caster sugar
200ml water
½ vanilla pod, split open
250g peeled chestnuts from
    a vacuum-pack tin or pouch

FOR THE PANETTONE
800g strong white bread flour
2 x 7g sachets fast-action
    dried yeast
150g caster sugar
4 medium eggs, plus 4 yolks,
    at room temperature
100ml lukewarm water
1 teaspoon vanilla extract
finely grated zest of
    1 large orange
finely grated zest of
    1 large unwaxed lemon
10g fine sea salt
350g unsalted butter, softened
    and cut into small pieces
150g large sultanas
about 30g unsalted butter,
    to finish

pieces and work them in by squeezing the dough through your fingers, or mixing with the dough hook on low speed, until the butter is thoroughly incorporated and there are no streaks.

6. Turn out the dough on to a floured worktop and knead* thoroughly for 10 minutes, or 3–4 minutes with the dough hook, gradually working in the rest of the weighed flour to make a dough that's satiny smooth, pliable and quite soft, not wet or sticky. Depending on the flour, you may not need it all or you may need a little more. Return the dough to the bowl, if necessary, and cover with a snap-on lid or clingfilm, or slip the bowl into a slightly inflated, large plastic bag. Leave to rise on the worktop for 2–2½ hours until doubled in size (don't leave in a sunny or very warm spot or the butter will begin to melt).

7. Uncover the dough and punch down with your knuckles to deflate it, then cover the bowl again and leave to rise on the worktop for about 1½ hours until doubled in size again.

8. Meanwhile, prepare the tin: brush the inside with a little melted butter and line* the base and side with a double layer of baking paper. If you are using a deep cake tin rather than a special tall panettone pan you will need to make sure that the paper lining the side of the tin extends 8cm above the rim. Wrap a folded newspaper around the outside of the pan or tin (again coming 8cm above the rim of the cake tin) and tie in place with string. The long baking time can make the crust hard and dry if the tin isn't well prepared, so don't skip this bit.

9. Put the sultanas and marrons glacés pieces in a small bowl, add a teaspoon of flour and toss to coat (this will prevent them from clumping together in the dough). Set aside for now.

10. Punch down the risen dough with your knuckles, then turn it out on to the floured worktop. Sprinkle the fruit and marrons mixture over the dough and work in very gently with floured hands until evenly distributed. Shape the dough into a ball and gently drop it into the prepared pan or tin. With the tip of a long, sharp knife, cut a cross in the top of the dough ball. Lay a sheet of clingfilm lightly across the top of the tin and leave to rise on the worktop for about 1½ hours until doubled in size.

11. Towards the end of the rising time, preheat the oven to 200°C/400°F/gas 6.

12. Set aside 10g of the butter for finishing and melt the rest. Uncover the tin. Brush half of the melted butter over the risen dough and put the remaining knob of butter in the centre of the scored cross. Bake in the heated oven for 20 minutes until just starting to colour, then brush again with the melted butter. Reduce the oven temperature to 180°C/350°F/gas 4 and bake for a further 60–70 minutes until the loaf is a good golden brown and a skewer inserted into the centre comes out clean.

13. Remove the tin from the oven and set it on a wire rack. Cool for 15 minutes to allow the crust of the panettone to firm up, then very gently unmould the loaf. Remove the lining paper and place the panettone on its side on the rack. Leave to cool completely before slicing. Best eaten within 3 days or toasted.

Variation

For a more traditional version, omit the marrons glacés and use 200g chopped candied peel (or a mix of candied citrus peel and candied fruit).

CHRISTMAS WREATH

This is a lighter version of stollen, the German Christmas bread. This loaf is flavoured, as is usual, with cardamom and nutmeg, studded with almonds and raisins, filled with creamy marzipan and finished with melted butter and icing sugar, and the dough is then shaped into a pretty centrepiece wreath, rather than the traditional hump-backed loaf.

1. Put the raisins, chopped peel and lemon zest and juice into a small bowl. Stir well, then cover tightly and leave to soak overnight.

2. Next day, uncover the bowl and stir again. Gently heat the milk with the butter, honey, cardamom and about 6 gratings of nutmeg. As soon as the butter has melted, remove the pan from the heat and leave to infuse for 15 minutes.

3. Combine the flour and salt in a large mixing bowl, or the bowl of a free-standing electric mixer fitted with the dough hook attachment, and mix in the dried yeast. Make a well in the centre. Add the egg yolks to the lukewarm milk mixture and mix briefly, then pour into the well. Work the flour into the liquid with your hand, or the dough hook on low speed, to make a very soft and slightly sticky dough that holds its shape. If the dough feels dry and firm, work in more milk a tablespoon at a time; if the dough seems sloppy, work in more flour.

4. Turn out the dough on to a lightly floured worktop and knead* thoroughly for 10 minutes, or for 5 minutes in the mixer on the lowest speed, until the dough feels firmer and very elastic. Flour your fingers and pat out the dough on the worktop to a rectangle about 1cm thick. Scatter the flaked almonds and fruit mixture (drain off any excess liquid, if necessary) all over the dough rectangle except around the edges. Fold in the two long edges so they meet in the centre, then fold in the two short ends to meet in the centre. Now fold the dough parcel over in half.

5. Lightly flour your hands and the worktop. Pat out the dough to a 1cm-thick rectangle again and fold up as before 2 or 3 more times until the fruit and nuts are evenly distributed. The dough will feel very soft and sticky.

6. Return the dough to the bowl, cover tightly with a snap-on lid or clingfilm and leave to rise on the worktop, at normal room >>>

Makes a large bread ring

Kit you'll need: 1 baking sheet, lined with baking paper

100g raisins
25g chopped mixed peel, chopped finer
finely grated zest and juice of 1 medium unwaxed lemon
150ml milk
60g unsalted butter
50g clear honey
seeds from 2 cardamom pods, finely crushed
freshly grated nutmeg
325g strong white bread flour
5g fine sea salt
1 x 7g sachet fast-action dried yeast
2 medium egg yolks, at room temperature
45g toasted flaked almonds

FOR THE FILLING
100g white/natural marzipan
30g ground almonds
40g full-fat cream cheese
1 tablespoon icing sugar

TO FINISH
30g unsalted butter, melted
icing sugar, for dusting

temperature, for 1½–2 hours until doubled in size (if the room is too warm the butter will start to ooze out).

7. Meanwhile, make the filling. Cut the marzipan into small pieces and put into a food processor with the ground almonds, cream cheese and sugar. Blitz to make a smooth paste, scraping down the side of the bowl from time to time to be sure everything is combined thoroughly.

8. Turn out the dough on to the lightly floured worktop. With a floured rolling pin, gently roll out the dough to a rectangle about 22 × 44cm. Check to be sure the dough is not sticking to the worktop, and lightly flour it if necessary. Spoon the marzipan filling on to the dough along its

length, about 3cm from one long edge, in a 3cm-wide line. Fold the 3cm dough border over the filling to cover it, then gently roll up the dough like a swiss roll, in the same direction, and pinch the seam together to seal.

9. Lift the roll (seam-side down) on to the lined baking sheet and form into a neat ring, pinching the ends together to seal. With a sharp knife, make 12 equally spaced cuts or slices around the edge of the ring, leaving the dough attached in the centre. Gently turn and twist each slice so one cut side is facing up. Cover the shaped wreath lightly with a sheet of clingfilm and leave to rise on the worktop for 1–1½ hours until doubled in size.

10. Towards the end of the rising time, preheat the oven to 180°C/350°F/gas 4.

11. Remove the clingfilm and bake the wreath in the heated oven for about 35 minutes until a good golden brown. Transfer to a wire rack and brush all over with the melted butter. Dust with a thick layer of sifted icing sugar, then leave to cool slightly. Best eaten warm, within 3 days (if necessary, reheat gently in a 150°C/300°F/gas 2 oven before serving).

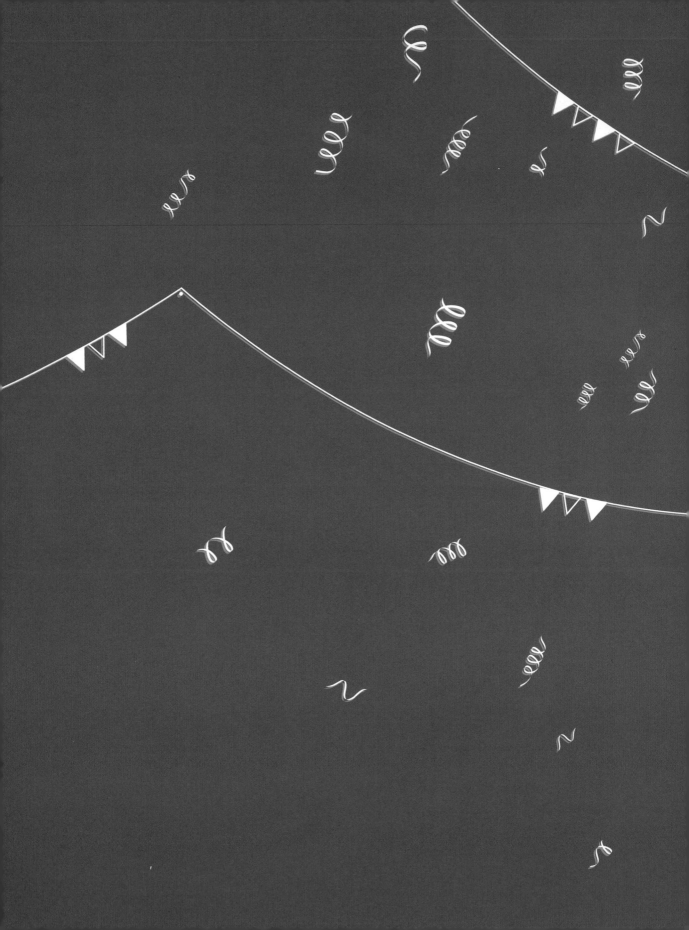

DESSERTS & PUDDINGS

This is where the fun really begins. Desserts and puddings offer the chance to indulge yourself, and though there are some wonderful, comforting puddings such as the plum Kaiserschmarrn (page 156) or the Cherry Clafoutis (page 159), there are also confections such as a multi-layered Mocha Torte (page 193) to challenge you and encourage you to celebrate your most creative and flamboyant side – follow Flora's example: 'I'm not one for restraint!' she says.

You might think of a cheescake as something to make in a single tier, such as the one made with white chocolate, rhubarb and stem ginger on page 167, but layer up several, perhaps in different sizes and flavours (see pages 179 and 187), and you have a very special centrepiece indeed.

Gorgeous meringue and whipped cream creations, such as the Spanish Windtorte (page 170), also look glamorous enough to serve at a wedding. This one is classically decorated with violets fashioned from sugar paste/ fondant icing – a skill that is Paul's speciality. 'I first got involved in sugarcraft when I made a friend's wedding cake – he wanted a really elaborate floral design,' he says.

For Nadiya, baking the likes of imaginative cheesecakes and impressive tiers of chocolate is a real joy, since the only dessert she grew up with was ice cream, as ovens are not traditional in Bangladesh where her parents are from. 'We didn't have an oven at home, but I had a lovely home economics teacher at school who would bake with me at lunchtimes. When I got married I was the first person in our family to have an oven!' she says.

Of course ice cream has long been associated with a party, but combining it with a baked sponge allows you to develop a stunning creation – see the Chocolate, Strawberry & Lime Ice-cream Roll (page 173) and the Passionfruit & Pineapple Ice-cream Roll (page 198).

The big advantage of a dessert like this is that it can be ready in the freezer, and then decorated just before serving – something that is invaluable if you are serving lots of people, or if you just want to know that there is a special dessert on hand for unexpected guests.

Ugne knows the value of thinking ahead like this. She bakes thin rounds of the cookie-like honey cake traditionally enjoyed in Lithuania for Christmas, Easter and other celebrations, and keeps them in the freezer. 'I can bring them out any time and then assemble them in layers with crème fraîche in between – this is the typical filling, but like most people nowadays I might add lemon juice to it, and maybe fresh fruit or little pieces of jelly for the children.'

Whichever recipe you choose, be sure to make plenty, as these puddings and desserts are dangerously more-ish and likely to disappear in the blink of an eye!

KAISERSCHMARRN

For a change from traditional lacy pancakes on Shrove Tuesday, try this classic Viennese dessert, a frivolous cross between a pancake and a soufflé ('schmarrn' means fluff) that is torn into shreds with forks and then caramelised. It's also known as 'the Emperor's Trifle' as it was named after Kaiser Franz Joseph I who apparently loved it. Viennese specialities are often complex, but this one is quite easy to make. Serve with spiced plums in port or with a bowl of fresh berries.

1. Heat the oven to 180°C/350°F/gas 4. Put the port, honey, sugar, lemon zest and star anise into a medium-sized flameproof baking dish. Bring to the boil, stirring to dissolve the sugar, then adjust the heat so the syrup is just simmering. Leave to simmer gently for 5 minutes.

2. Meanwhile, halve the plums and remove the stones. Add to the syrup, then remove from the heat. Cover the dish and place in the heated oven. Bake for 15–25 minutes until the plums are tender – check by prodding with the tip of a small sharp knife. Leave to cool (turn the oven off now). The plums can be served at room temperature or chilled. (Any leftover cooking syrup can be stored in a screw-topped jar in the fridge for up to 2 weeks, and used for baking more fruit.)

3. Put the sultanas and rum into a small bowl, cover and leave to soak for at least 30 minutes, or up to 4 hours.

4. When ready to cook, heat the oven to 180°C/350°F/gas 4 again. Separate the eggs, putting the yolks into one large mixing bowl and the whites into another, or into the bowl of a free-standing electric mixer. Using a hand-held electric whisk, or the whisk attachment of the mixer, whisk the egg whites until they will stand in stiff peaks*. Set aside for now (if using a mixer, transfer the whites to another bowl and tip the yolks into the mixer bowl).

5. Add the sugar, lemon zest and salt to the egg yolks and whisk (no need to wash the whisk) until the mixture is pale and mousse-like, and reaches the ribbon stage*. Using the slowest speed, gradually whisk in the milk followed by the flour. When everything is combined to make a smooth batter, stir in the sultanas and rum. Gently fold* in the egg whites using a large metal spoon.
>>>

Serves 4

Kit you'll need: **a large cast-iron or other ovenproof frying pan OR a flameproof baking dish**

FOR THE BAKED
SPICED PLUMS
450ml ruby port
3 tablespoons clear honey
75g caster sugar
2 strips of lemon zest
2 star anise
8 medium/large plums

FOR THE PANCAKE
2 tablespoons sultanas
2 tablespoons dark rum
4 medium eggs,
    at room temperature
3 tablespoons caster sugar
finely grated zest of
    1 medium unwaxed lemon
good pinch of salt
275ml milk
125g plain flour
30g unsalted butter, for frying

TO FINISH
15g unsalted butter
icing sugar, for dusting

6. Melt the butter in the frying pan or baking dish over medium-low heat, then pour in the batter. Cook for 5–6 minutes until the pancake has puffed up and the underside is golden (slide a palette knife under an edge to check). Transfer the pan to the heated oven and bake for 8–10 minutes until the top of the pancake is golden brown. Remove from the oven Heat the grill to its hottest setting.

7. Quickly tear the pancake, still in the pan, into small pieces using 2 forks. Dot with flakes of butter and dust with icing sugar, then briefly flash under the grill to caramelise the sugar. Dust with a little more icing sugar and serve immediately, with the plums.

CHERRY CLAFOUTIS

A summertime treat to celebrate Kentish cherries: our pride and joy for the last 500 years and in season for a glorious five weeks from July. They are perfect in this French clafoutis – a cross between an egg custard and a Yorkshire pudding, famous in the Limousin region, where it is made with the prized local morello cherries.

1. Heat the oven to 180°C/350°F/gas 4. Use the soft butter to grease the base and sides of the baking dish, then sprinkle with the sugar to coat evenly.

2. Arrange the cherries in the dish, packing them tightly together in a single layer – exactly how many you need depends on your dish and the size of the cherries.

3. To make the batter, put the eggs, cream, ground almonds, sugar, salt, melted butter and liqueur (if using) into a mixing bowl. Using a wire whisk, whisk everything together to make a smooth batter. Pour it evenly over the cherries.

4. Bake the clafoutis in the heated oven for about 30 minutes until the tip of a slim-bladed sharp knife inserted into the middle of the pudding comes out clean. Sprinkle with a little caster sugar and serve the clafoutis warm, rather than piping hot.

Serves 4

Kit you'll need: 1 × 20–22cm round baking dish

25g unsalted butter, softened
1 tablespoon caster sugar
450–500g cherries,
    stems removed

FOR THE BATTER
2 medium eggs,
    at room temperature
125g single or whipping cream
25g ground almonds
60g caster sugar, plus extra
    for sprinkling
pinch of salt
20g unsalted butter, melted
1 tablespoon cherry brandy
    OR Kirsch (optional)

RASPBERRY MERINGUE TRIFLE

A guaranteed crowd-pleaser for a summer party and yet one of the easiest and most foolproof of recipes! It simply involves layering crunchy hazelnut meringues, fresh raspberries in raspberry purée and heavenly clotted cream. You do need plenty of perfectly ripe, sweet, juicy berries, so take advantage of a late-summer glut. The trifle is impressive in a big glass bowl, but you could also use pretty individual glasses.

Serves 4–6

Kit you'll need: **2 baking sheets, lined with baking paper; a large disposable piping bag fitted with a large star nozzle (optional)**

FOR THE MERINGUES
2 medium egg whites,
   at room temperature
2 good pinches of cream of tartar
110g caster sugar
50g ground toasted hazelnuts

FOR THE COULIS
250g fresh raspberries
3 tablespoons caster sugar,
   or to taste
1 tablespoon framboise (optional)

TO ASSEMBLE
350g fresh raspberries
250g clotted cream
30g chopped toasted hazelnuts

Note

The quantitities can easily be doubled or trebled for a large party, and the meringues can be baked up to a week ahead.

1. Heat your oven to 120°C/250°F/ gas ½. Put the egg whites and cream of tartar into a spotlessly clean and grease-free mixing bowl, or the bowl of a free-standing electric mixer, and whisk using a hand-held electric whisk, or the whisk attachment of the mixer, until soft peaks* form. Gradually whisk in the sugar, then continue whisking until the meringue stands in stiff peaks*. Sprinkle the ground hazelnuts over the meringue and gently fold* in using a large metal spoon.

2. Transfer the meringue to the piping bag fitted with the star nozzle, if using (you can also spoon the meringue on to the sheets, using a heaped teaspoon for each). Pipe about 40 small meringue stars, 3–4cm across, on the lined baking sheets, placing them slightly apart.

3. Bake in the heated oven for about 1½ hours until crisp and dry. Turn off the oven and leave the meringues inside to cool. (Once cold, they can be packed into an airtight container and kept in a dry spot for up to a week.)

4. To make the raspberry coulis, put the raspberries and sugar into a food processor and blitz to a thick purée. Press through a large sieve into a bowl, to remove the seeds. Stir in the framboise, if using, then taste the coulis and add more sugar, if necessary. Cover and keep in the fridge until needed (up to 48 hours).

5. When you are ready to assemble the trifle, arrange half of the meringues in the base of a large glass serving bowl or in individual dessert glasses. Stir the rapsberries into the coulis, then spoon over the meringues. Arrange the rest of the meringues on top. Using a teaspoon, dot the clotted cream in small blobs on the meringues – avoid stirring the cream as it looks best if its unique golden crust is visible. Scatter the chopped toasted hazelnuts over the top and serve immediately, or cover and keep in the fridge for up to 2 hours.

RHUBARB & GINGER CRÈME BRÛLÉES

If there is one thing the Bakers love, it is a chance to add some drama and decoration to a classic recipe and turn it into a showpiece. Here the favourite creamy baked custard dessert includes a classic combination – rhubarb and stem ginger – enhanced by rhubarb crisps and elegant ginger tuile curls.

Makes 6

Kit you'll need: **6 x 175ml** ramekins, greased with butter; a roasting tin; a baking sheet, lined with a silicone sheet; 3 rings or moulds 10–11cm across

FOR THE STEWED RHUBARB
250g pink rhubarb, cut into 1cm-thick slices
100ml cloudy apple juice
40g caster sugar
1 lump stem ginger (about 20g), drained and finely chopped, plus 1 tablespoon syrup from the jar

FOR THE CRÈME BRÛLÉES
450ml double cream
50ml syrup from the jar of stem ginger
6 large egg yolks, at room temperature
180g caster sugar

FOR THE GINGER TUILE CURLS
40g plain flour
50g caster sugar
1 teaspoon ground ginger
1 large egg white, at room temperature

FOR THE RHUBARB CRISPS
1 large stick rhubarb
30g caster sugar
1 tablespoon grenadine syrup

TO DECORATE
about 40g (2 lumps) stem ginger, cut into small cubes
pink rose petals

1. Start by making the stewed rhubarb. Put the rhubarb in a medium pan with the apple juice, sugar, chopped ginger and ginger syrup. Set over medium heat and bring to the boil, stirring frequently. Reduce the heat and simmer gently for 3–5 minutes until the rhubarb is just tender. Drain the rhubarb in a sieve set over a large measuring jug. Leave the rhubarb and cooking liquid to cool completely.

2. Heat the oven to 180°C/350°F/gas 4. Divide the stewed rhubarb among the 6 ramekins, then set them, slightly apart, in the roasting tin.

3. Pour the cream and ginger syrup into a medium pan and bring to the boil, then remove from the heat. Put the egg yolks and 90g sugar in a heatproof bowl and whisk using a wire whisk for a minute until very smooth and light. Slowly whisk in the hot cream. Pour the mixture back into the pan and whisk over very low heat for a couple of minutes until the mixture feels warm and is slightly thicker. Transfer to a large jug, then slowly pour into the ramekins on top of the rhubarb, dividing equally.

4. Pour enough hot water into the roasting tin to come halfway up the sides of the ramekins. >>>

Bake in the heated oven for 35–40 minutes until the custards are almost set, with just a slight wobble when jiggled. Lift the ramekins out of the roasting tin (leave the oven on) and discard the hot water. Rinse the roasting tin under the cold tap to cool it quickly, then set the ramekins back in the tin. Add cold water to the tin to come halfway up the sides of the ramekins – this stops the custards from cooking further and helps cool them quickly. Once cold, cover the custards and chill for at least 3 hours, preferably overnight.

5. Now make the ginger tuile curls. Sift the flour, sugar and ground ginger into a mixing bowl. Add the egg white and mix thoroughly with a wooden spoon until very smooth. Spoon on to the silicone sheet and spread very thinly to a 28cm square. Bake for 7–10 minutes until just turning a light gold colour. Working quickly, cut the mixture into 2cm-wide strips with a large, sharp knife, then wrap the strips (one at a

time) around the outside of the rings or moulds to curl them. If the mixture on the baking sheet starts to firm up, return it to the oven for a minute to soften. You will need 6 good-looking tuile curls; make a few extra in case of breakages. Leave the curls to cool and set. (Keep the baking sheet lined with the silicone sheet for the rhubarb crisps.)

6. Reduce the oven temperature to 100°C/225°F/gas ¼. Using a very sharp vegetable peeler, peel or shave the rhubarb into long, very thin slices. You will need 12 crisps, so if necessary cut the slices across in half. Put 100ml of the reserved rhubarb cooking liquid, the sugar and grenadine syrup into a pan and bring to the boil, stirring to dissolve the sugar. Remove from the heat and add the rhubarb slices. Leave to soak for 5 minutes, then drain thoroughly. Carefully arrange the slices on the silicone sheet so they lay flat and straight, then bake for 25–30 minutes until dry and crisp. Set aside to cool.

7. When ready to serve, heat the grill to its highest setting. Sprinkle the remaining 90g caster sugar over the top of the chilled custards so they are evenly covered. Place them under the grill, as close as possible to the heat, and grill for 4–5 minutes until the sugar has melted and caramelised to a rich brown.

8. Set each ramekin on a serving plate and decorate with the cubes of stem ginger, a tuile curl, 2 strips of rhubarb crisp and rose petals.

Note

You can also use a kitchen blowtorch to caramelise the sugar on the custards.

WHITE CHOCOLATE & RHUBARB CHEESECAKE

The appearance of the first delicately pink and tender 'forced' rhubarb in early spring is a cause for celebration in itself. A speciality of Yorkshire, where the rhubarb is brought on in special pitch-dark forcing sheds and tended by candlelight, it is only in season briefly before the more sturdy outdoor-grown rhubarb takes over. Make the most of it, mingling it with stem ginger to crown this elegant cheesecake made with the best white chocolate you can find.

Serves 10

Kit you'll need: 1 x 20.5cm round springclip tin, greased with butter; a baking sheet

FOR THE BISCUIT CRUST
150g Wholemeal Biscuits
  (see page 84) OR digestive
  biscuits
50g unsalted butter

FOR THE FILLING
100g good-quality white
  chocolate (at least 30% cocoa
  solids), broken up
600g full-fat cream cheese
150ml soured cream
3 medium eggs, plus 1 yolk
100g caster sugar
finely grated zest of
  1 unwaxed lemon

FOR THE TOPPING
350g trimmed young,
  pink rhubarb
50g light brown muscovado sugar
35g stem ginger (about 2 lumps),
  finely chopped, plus
  3 tablespoons syrup
  from the jar

1. Heat the oven to 180°C/350°F/gas 4. Crush the biscuits to crumbs either in a food processor or by putting them into a plastic bag and bashing with a rolling pin. Tip them into a large mixing bowl. Melt the butter in a small pan (or in a bowl in the microwave). Add to the biscuit crumbs and mix in thoroughly with a wooden spoon.

2. Tip into the greased tin set on the baking sheet. The crumbs need to be compressed into a case for the filling – you will need about a third of them for the side and the rest for the base. First push the crumbs for the side towards the edge of the tin, then spread the crumbs remaining on the base to distribute them evenly. Press them down with the back of a spoon to make a firm layer. Next use the back of the spoon to ease and gently press the crumbs at the edge halfway up the side of the tin. Once the side looks fairly even in height and thickness, press the crumbs firmly, making sure that the angle

between the base and the side is 90 degrees. Cover with clingfilm and chill for 5 minutes.

3. Uncover the biscuit crust, then bake in the heated oven for about 5 minutes. Transfer the tin, still on the baking sheet, to a heatproof surface and leave to cool. (Don't turn off the oven.)

4. For the filling, melt* the chocolate, then leave to cool. Put the remaining filling ingredients into a large mixing bowl, or the bowl of a free-standing electric mixer. Beat everything together with a hand-held electric whisk, or the mixer whisk attachment, on low speed to soften the cream cheese and break up the eggs. Scrape down the side of the bowl, then whisk on medium speed until the mixture is very smooth and creamy – don't be tempted to use high speed to save time as you don't want a frothy mixture. Add the melted chocolate and mix in on medium/low speed.

>>>

5. Pour and scrape the filling into the tin and spread evenly — it will come slightly above the biscuit crust rim. Place the tin, still on the baking sheet, in the oven and bake for 45–50 minutes until the surface of the filling looks set and no longer damp — it will still have a slight wobble when you gently move the baking sheet. Turn off the oven and leave the cheesecake to cool inside, with the oven door ajar, for 10 minutes.

6. Set the tin on a heatproof surface. Slip a round-bladed knife (or palette knife) around inside the tin to loosen the cheesecake (this helps to stop it cracking as it cools and contracts). Leave until cold, then cover the tin with clingfilm and chill for 6 hours — overnight if possible.

7. While the cheesecake is baking, make the topping. Slice the rhubarb, on a slight diagonal, into 3cm pieces. Put into a baking dish in a single layer and sprinkle with the sugar. Scatter the ginger over the rhubarb, then drizzle over the ginger syrup. Cover the dish and bake in the oven alongside the cheesecake for about 20 minutes until just tender when tested with the tip of a small sharp knife. Leave to cool, then cover and keep in the fridge until needed.

8. When ready to serve, unclip the sides of the tin and set the cheescake on a serving plate. Using a slotted spoon, spoon the drained rhubarb on top of the cheesecake in a single layer. Put any remaining rhubarb and all the syrup into a bowl to serve separately. The cheesecake can be kept in a covered container in the fridge for up to 5 days.

SPANISH WINDTORTE

Magnificent enough for a summer wedding or anniversary, this glamorous and complex Viennese confection of meringue, whipped cream and summer berries, finished with fondant violets, dates back to the Baroque period of the Austro-Hungarian Empire. At this time (the end of the 17th century), the House of Hapsburg ruled in both Austria and Spain; architecture, music and culture flourished; and Spanish influences were fashionable. Piping skills are put to the test here!

Serves 12

Kit you'll need: **3 large baking sheets, lined with baking paper; 2 large disposable piping bags; 1.5cm plain nozzle; a large star nozzle; a small paintbrush**

FOR THE FRENCH MERINGUE SHELL
8 large egg whites,
   at room temperature
½ teaspoon cream of tartar
475g white caster sugar

FOR THE FONDANT VIOLETS
25g lavender-coloured ready-to-roll sugar paste/fondant icing
25g purple-coloured ready-to-roll sugar paste/fondant icing
icing sugar, for dusting
10g yellow-coloured ready-to-roll sugar paste/fondant icing

FOR THE SWISS MERINGUE DECORATION
4 large egg whites,
   at room temperature
250g white caster sugar

FOR THE FILLING
600ml double cream (pourable, not extra-thick), well chilled
50g icing sugar, sifted
1 teaspoon orange blossom water
400g strawberries, roughly chopped
200g raspberries

1. Heat the oven to 120°C/250°F/gas ½. Using the base of a 20cm cake tin as a guide, draw 2 circles on the baking paper lining on 2 of the baking sheets and one circle on the paper lining the third sheet. Turn the paper over on the baking sheets so the marks are on the underside.

2. To make the meringue for the shell, put the egg whites into a large and spotlessly clean, grease-free bowl, or the bowl of a free-standing electric mixer. Add the cream of tartar and whisk with a hand-held electric whisk, or the mixer whisk attachment, on high speed until the whites will form stiff peaks*. Whisk in the sugar, a tablespoon at a time, to make a thick, glossy meringue.

3. Spoon two-thirds of the meringue into a piping bag fitted with the 1.5cm plain nozzle. Cover the rest of the meringue and save for assembly. Pipe a thick ring of meringue just inside one of the 2 circles drawn on one baking sheet and continue piping in a spiral until the whole circle is filled to make a neat disc of meringue. Repeat to make a second disc: these 2 discs will form the base and the lid of the meringue torte.

4. To make the sides of the shell, pipe a thick ring just inside each of the 3 remaining drawn circles – don't fill in the circles as you only want neat hoops of meringue. Bake all 5 piped shapes in the heated oven for about 45 minutes until crisp and dry.

5. While the meringues are baking you can make the 13 violets to decorate the torte. For each one, take 2 little pieces of lavender sugar paste/fondant and 3 little pieces of purple sugar paste/fondant – each piece about the size of an orange pip – and roll them into small balls. Dust >>>

2 sheets of baking paper with icing sugar. Set the balls, well apart, on the paper and gently press with your fingers to flatten them out into thin 1cm discs; these will be the petals. Then roll 3 very tiny balls of yellow sugar paste/fondant for each flower; these will form the stamens.

6. To assemble each flower, lightly moisten a small paintbrush, then use to dampen the edges of the petals. Arrange them into the shape of a violet, with 2 lavender petals at the top, 2 purple petals below them and the remaining third purple petal set in the middle at the bottom. Press gently together. Dampen the 3 yellow stamens and press them carefully into the centre. Leave the violets to dry on the baking paper.

7. When the meringue shapes are ready, remove from the oven (leave the oven on). Gently slide one of the discs on to a heatproof serving plate. Spoon the reserved meringue into the previously used piping bag that is fitted with the plain nozzle and pipe 8 small blobs, evenly spaced, around the top edge of the disc. Set one of the baked meringue hoops on the blobs and gently press it in place. Repeat the process to stack up the remaining 2 meringue hoops.

8. Pipe the rest of the meringue around the outside of the assembled shell to fill in the gaps between the hoops, then, using an offset palette knife or a regular palette knife, smooth out the meringue to make the side completely straight and even (like the side of a cake).

9. Set the shell, on the serving plate, in the oven and bake for about 45 minutes until crisp and dry. Remove from the oven and set aside to cool (leave the oven on).

10. While the shell is baking, make the Swiss meringue for the decoration. Put the egg whites into a large heatproof mixing bowl and add the sugar. Set the bowl over a pan of gently simmering water (the base of the bowl shouldn't touch the water) and whisk with a hand-held electric whisk on full speed until the sugar has completely dissolved and the meringue reaches 70°C on a sugar thermometer. Remove the bowl from the pan and continue whisking until the meringue is very stiff and has cooled to room temperature.

11. Spoon the meringue into the second piping bag fitted with the star nozzle: you are going to decorate the meringue shell as

well as the second meringue disc to make an attractive lid. Pipe a pretty border around the base of the shell, around the middle and then around the top edge. Pipe a border around the edge of the disc for the lid, then pipe a ring inside this and a shape in the centre. (Cover any leftover meringue and save for assembly.) Bake the shell and the lid (on its baking sheet) for about 30 minutes until crisp and dry. Leave to cool (you can turn off the oven now).

12. For the filling, whip the cream with the icing sugar until it will form soft peaks*. Whisk in the orange blossom water, then gently fold* in the strawberries and raspberries. Spoon into the cooled meringue shell and set the meringue lid in place. Use tiny blobs of the saved meringue to attach the fondant violets to the side and top of the torte. Serve immediately.

Note

Ready-coloured sugar paste and fondant for modelling can be found in specialist cake-decorating shops and online.

CHOCOLATE, STRAWBERRY & LIME ICE-CREAM ROLL

What an elegant and spectacular dessert! With coconut cream–based ice creams, decorated sponge and strawberry-lime jam, and finished with chocolate-dipped strawberries, it definitely has the 'wow' factor for a summer party. Time to get out the ice-cream maker.

Serves 6

Kit you'll need: a sugar thermometer; an ice-cream machine; 2 large disposable piping bags; 2 baking sheets; a piping bag fitted with a No. 2 fine writing nozzle; a 23 x 33cm swiss roll tin, greased with dairy-free spread and lined* (see recipe)

FOR THE STRAWBERRY-LIME JAM
300g fresh strawberries, hulled
300g jam sugar (sugar with added pectin)
finely grated zest of 1 small lime, plus 1 tablespoon juice

FOR THE STRAWBERRY-LIME ICE CREAM
1 x 400g tin full-fat coconut cream

5 tablespoons agave nectar (light amber mild variety)
16g freeze-dried strawberry pieces
85g strawberries, hulled and mashed
2 teaspoons agar agar flakes
finely grated zest of 2 small limes

FOR THE CHOCOLATE ICE CREAM
2 x 400g tins full-fat coconut cream
2½ tablespoons instant coffee granules
115g caster sugar
40g cocoa powder
¼ teaspoon salt
2 teaspoons agar agar flakes
3 large eggs, at room temperature, beaten to mix

FOR THE DECORATIVE PASTE
1 large egg white, at room temperature
40g plain flour
30g caster sugar
30g dairy-free spread
rose-pink food colouring gel

FOR THE SPONGE
4 large eggs, at room temperature
100g caster sugar, plus extra for sprinkling
100g self-raising flour

FOR THE DIPPED STRAWBERRIES
100g dark chocolate (dairy-free), melted*
50g white chocolate (dairy-free), melted
200g fresh strawberries (with stalks)

1. Make the jam first so it has time to set. Put the strawberries into a medium pan and crush well with a potato masher. Add the sugar and lime juice, then set over medium/low heat and stir until the sugar has completely dissolved. Turn up the heat and boil rapidly until the jam reaches setting point (see Blackberry and Apple Jam on page 11) or 105°C on a sugar thermometer. Remove from the heat and stir in the lime zest, then transfer to a heatproof bowl and leave until cold and set. Spoon into a food processor and 'pulse' a few times to make a thick purée. Set aside until needed.

2. To make the strawberry ice cream, put the coconut cream into a mixing bowl and whisk until frothy using a hand-held electric whisk. Add the remaining ingredients with 2 tablespoons of the jam. Whisk on medium speed until thoroughly combined. Transfer to the ice-cream >>>

maker and churn until frozen but not set hard. Spoon the ice cream into a large disposable piping bag and cut off the tip to make a 3.5cm aperture. Line a baking sheet with clingfilm and pipe a sausage shape, 33cm long and 3.5cm thick, down the centre. Wrap the clingfilm around it to maintain the sausage shape and pop it in the freezer.

3. For the chocolate ice cream, gently warm the coconut milk in a medium pan over low heat. Remove from the heat, add the coffee and stir until dissolved. Put the sugar, cocoa powder, salt and agar agar into a heatproof bowl and mix well together. Mix in the eggs until thoroughly combined, then gradually stir in the warm coconut milk. Pour the mixture back into the pan and stir over medium/low heat until it thickens enough to coat the back of the spoon. Pour into a heatproof bowl and set in a sink of icy water to cool. Transfer to the (clean) ice-cream maker and churn until frozen but not set hard.

4. Spoon the chocolate ice cream into a disposable piping bag and snip off the end to make a 1cm aperture. Line a baking sheet with clingfilm, then pipe the ice cream in 33cm-long lines down the centre of the clingfilm to make a strip 14cm wide. Freeze for a couple of minutes to firm up.

5. Gently roll the strawberry ice cream sausage out of its clingfilm and on to the centre of the chocolate ice cream strip. Lift up the clingfilm on the baking sheet to wrap the chocolate ice cream around the strawberry ice cream and completely enclose it. Wrap the clingfilm tightly around this sausage to maintain the shape and keep in the freezer until needed.

6. Heat the oven to 200°C/400°F/gas 6. To make the decorative paste, put the egg white, flour, sugar and dairy-free spread in a mixing bowl and beat well with a hand-held electric whisk until very smooth. Add a tiny amount of colouring gel – scoop out with the end of a cocktail stick – then whisk well until streak-free. If necessary, add more gel until you have a vibrant pink colour. Transfer to the piping bag fitted with a fine writing nozzle. Set your template for the design on the base of the swiss roll tin before lining it with baking paper and lightly greasing with dairy-free spread. Following the template, pipe the pink paste on to the lining paper. Freeze for about 10 minutes until firm.

7. Meanwhile, make the sponge. Put the eggs and sugar into a free-standing electric mixer and whisk on high speed to the ribbon stage*. Sift the flour into the bowl and carefully fold in*. Gently spoon the mixture on top of the frozen pink pattern in the tin and spread evenly. Bake in the heated oven for 10–12 minutes until golden and springy when pressed in the centre.

8. While the sponge is baking, cover a chopping board with a sheet of baking paper, then lightly grease it with dairy-free spread and sprinkle with sugar. Turn out the sponge on to the paper, then lift off the tin and peel off the lining paper. Set a clean sheet of baking paper on top of the sponge, then top with an upturned wire rack. Hold together and invert the whole thing. Remove the board, but leave the baking paper in place. Gently roll a rolling pin over the sponge to slightly compress it. Starting from one long side, roll the sponge around the rolling pin – the patterned side will be facing out. Cover with a tea towel and leave to cool.

9. For the dipped strawberries, stir the melted dark chocolate until smooth, then drop the melted white chocolate in small dots into the bowl and 'feather' through the dark chocolate with a skewer. Holding the strawberries by their stalks, dip them briefly in the melted chocolate so they are half-coated. Leave to set on baking paper.

10. To assemble the roll, carefully unroll the sponge and spread with a thin, even layer of jam. Unwrap the ice cream sausage and set it down the centre of the sponge, then gently roll the sponge around it and press it all together. Wrap the roll tightly in clingfilm and freeze until very firm. To serve, trim the ends off the roll, then cut across into 6. Arrange the slices on a chilled serving plate with the dipped strawberries and serve immediately.

GLORIOUS HIGH SUMMER SPONGE FLAN

Red and gold are the colours of high summer fruit: think soft slices of apricot, peach or nectarine, whole strawberries, raspberries and cherries. You can decorate this flan as festively as you like with your favourite fruit. The flan case is made from a light orange genoise, a delicate but buttery whisked sponge, and this is filled with an orange crème pâtissière lightened with whipped cream. Heavenly with ripe, sweet fruit atop.

Serves 8

Kit you'll need: 1 x 25cm round, deep, loose-based sponge flan tin with a sponge insert, greased with butter and base-lined*

FOR THE GENOISE SPONGE
90g plain flour
good pinch of salt
20g cornflour
4 medium eggs,
   at room temperature
finely grated zest
   of 1 medium orange
100g caster sugar

50g unsalted butter,
   melted and cooled

FOR THE SOAKING SYRUP
50g caster sugar
4 tablespoons orange juice, plus
   1 tablespoon orange liqueur
   OR 5 tablespoons orange juice

FOR THE CRÈME MOUSSELINE
400ml creamy milk
finely grated zest
   of 1 medium orange
4 medium egg yolks,
   at room temperature

75g caster sugar
30g cornflour
30g unsalted butter,
   at room temperature
1 tablespoon orange liqueur
   OR orange juice
200ml double cream, well chilled

TO FINISH
about 400g mixed fresh
   fruit: sliced apricots, peaches
   or nectarines; strawberries,
   raspberries, blackberries,
   blueberries, redcurrants;
   halved grapes; cherries

1. Heat the oven to 180°C/350°F/gas 4. To make the genoise sponge, sift the flour, salt and cornflour on to a large sheet of baking paper. Put the eggs and orange zest into a large heatproof bowl (the mixture will increase five-fold) and whisk with a hand-held electric whisk until frothy. Add the sugar.

2. Set the bowl over a pan of gently simmering water (the base of the bowl shouldn't touch the water) and whisk on full speed until the mixture is very pale, thick and mousse-like, and reaches the ribbon stage*. Remove the bowl from the pan and whisk for a few more minutes until the mixture cools to room temperature.

3. Sift half of the (sifted) flour mixture on to the egg mixture and delicately fold* in using a large metal spoon. Trickle half of the cooled melted butter into the bowl and fold in. Repeat to fold in the rest of the flour and then the remaining butter. When you can no longer see any specks of flour or streaks of butter, gently pour the mixture into the prepared tin.

4. Bake in the heated oven for 15–20 minutes until the sponge is golden and springs back when gently pressed in the centre. Set the tin on a wire rack and leave the sponge until cold before turning out.

5. Meanwhile, make the soaking syrup. Put the sugar, orange juice and liqueur (if using) into >>>

a small pan and heat gently, stirring until the sugar dissolves. Bring to the boil and simmer for a minute to make a light syrup. Set aside until needed.

6. For the crème mousseline filling, warm the milk with the orange zest in a medium-sized pan, then remove from the heat and set aside to infuse. Put the egg yolks, sugar and cornflour into a heatproof bowl set on a damp cloth (to prevent wobbling) and mix together with a wire whisk for a couple of minutes until very smooth and lighter in colour. Whisk in the warm milk, then pour the mixture back into the pan and whisk over medium heat until the crème boils and thickens.

Set the pan on a heatproof surface and whisk the crème for a minute to make sure it is very smooth. Whisk in the butter and the orange liqueur or juice. Transfer the mixture to a clean bowl and press a piece of clingfilm on to the surface to prevent a skin from forming. Leave to cool, then chill the crème for at least 4 hours.

7. Whip the cream until it stands in soft peaks*, then cover and keep in the fridge until needed.

8. When ready to assemble, set the sponge flan on a serving plate or board. Reheat the orange syrup, then brush over the inside of the case. Leave it to soak in for

10 minutes. Meanwhile, stir the chilled crème well until smooth, then carefully fold in the whipped cream. Spoon this filling into the sponge case and spread evenly. Decorate with the fruit and serve immediately, or keep in the fridge for up to an hour.

TIERED RASPBERRY & WHITE CHOCOLATE CHEESECAKE

A centrepiece glamorous enough for a summer wedding or other celebration. The baked cheesecakes are flavoured with white chocolate and studded with fresh raspberries, and there are more raspberries and whipped cream in the decoration. All the preparation can be done well ahead (though you will need plenty of fridge space) and then the tower is assembled at the last minute.

Makes a 3-tier cake to serve 24–30

Kit you'll need: **3 round, deep, loose-based or springclip cake tins: 1 x 13cm, 1 x 18cm and 1 x 23cm, greased with butter and lined*; a large serving plate or board; 2 silver cake boards 3mm thick: 1 x 13cm and 1 x 18cm; 6 cake dowels; a piping bag fitted with a medium star nozzle**

FOR THE BASES
150g unsalted butter, diced
75g dark chocolate (about 46% cocoa solids), broken up
700g shortbread biscuits, finely crushed

FOR THE FILLING
900g good-quality white chocolate, broken up
1.2kg full-fat cream cheese
6 medium eggs, beaten to mix

450ml soured cream
1 tablespoon vanilla extract
450g fresh raspberries

TO DECORATE
200g fresh raspberries
1 teaspoon icing sugar
300ml double cream, well chilled
50g good-quality white chocolate bar
icing sugar, for dusting

1. Heat the oven to 170°C/325°F/gas 3. To make the biscuit bases, put the butter and chocolate in a large pan, set over very low heat and stir until melted and smooth. Remove from the heat and stir in the crushed biscuits until thoroughly combined. Divide the crumb mixture among the prepared tins and press evenly on to the bottom with the back of a spoon to make a 1.5cm layer. Chill while you make the filling.

2. Melt* the white chocolate, then set aside. Put the cream cheese and eggs into the bowl of a free-standing electric mixer fitted with the whisk attachment and whisk until smooth. Add the soured cream and vanilla extract and whisk again until completely smooth. Stir the melted white chocolate, then stir it into the cream cheese mixture until it is all evenly combined.

3. Divide half of the cream cheese mixture among the 3 tins, pouring it evenly over the chilled bases and filling the tins to the same height. Scatter the raspberries over the filling in each tin, then cover with the rest of the mixture – again filling the tins to the same height. Spread the filling so the surface is smooth and even.

4. Bake the cheesecakes in the heated oven until they are firm around the edge and just set in the middle: 30–35 minutes for the 13cm cheesecake, 35–40 minutes for the 18cm cheesecake and 40–45 minutes for the 23cm cheesecake. Remove the cheesecakes as soon as they are ready and leave to cool in the tins. Once cold, cover and chill for at least 6 hours or overnight.

>>>

5. To make the decoration, put 50g of the raspberries and the icing sugar into a food processor and blitz to make a purée. Press the purée through a sieve into a bowl, to remove the seeds. Cover and keep in the fridge until needed.

6. Carefully remove the chilled cheesecakes from their tins. Set the largest cheesecake on the serving plate and set the other 2 cheesecakes on their silver cake boards. Cut 3 of the cake dowels to 2cm longer than the height of the largest cheesecake, then gently press them down, spaced apart, in a triangle around the centre of the cheesecake, all the way to the bottom. Repeat this process with the 18cm cheesecake – these dowels will support the weight of the cheesecake tiers and prevent them from touching and sinking into one another.

7. To assemble the tiers, set the 18cm cheesecake on top of the largest cheesecake, then place the smallest cheesecake on top of the 18cm cheesecake.

8. Whip the chilled cream until it will stand in soft peaks*. Spoon it into the piping bag fitted with the star nozzle. Carefully pipe rosettes around the edge of all 3 cheesecakes, and top each rosette with a raspberry. Spoon the raspberry purée into the centre of the top tier to 'flood' – the border of piped cream will prevent the purée from dripping down the side.

9. To make the white chocolate curls, place the bar of chocolate upside down (so the flat side is uppermost), then drag the blade of a long, sharp knife, held at a slight angle, towards you. Carefully arrange the curls on the top tier. Dust with icing sugar.

STRAWBERRY 'PIZZA'

A summer party dessert to have some real fun with. The 'pizza' base is a large, thick biscuit, which is spread with creamy lemon curd and then generously topped with ripe strawberries and basil leaves. You could choose a mixture of fresh fruit instead – grapes, cherries, blueberries, sliced plums or peaches, bananas, kiwi fruit – and arrange them in triangular wedge patterns to resemble real pizza slices.

Serves 6–8

Kit you'll need: **1 baking sheet**

FOR THE BISCUIT BASE
225g plain flour
good pinch of salt
70g icing sugar
175g unsalted butter,
   chilled and diced
2 medium egg yolks
¼ teaspoon vanilla extract

FOR THE LEMON TOPPING
3 medium eggs, plus 1 yolk,
   at room temperature
75g caster sugar
grated zest and juice
   of 2 medium unwaxed lemons
60g unsalted butter,
   chilled and diced

TO FINISH
450g ripe strawberries
a few small, fresh basil sprigs

1. Make the biscuit dough using a food processor: put the flour, salt and icing sugar into the bowl and 'pulse' a few times just to combine. Add the pieces of butter and blitz until the mixture looks like fine crumbs. With the machine running, add the yolks and vanilla extract through the feed tube. As soon as the dough comes together in a ball, stop the machine and remove the dough. Shape it into a thick disc, wrap in clingfilm and chill for 25 minutes until firm but not hard.

2. Unwrap the dough and place it on the worktop between 2 sheets of baking paper. Roll it out to a disc 25cm across. To keep the shape neat, keep rotating the disc between rolls. Slide the paper-enclosed disc on to the baking sheet and peel off the top piece of paper. With floured fingers, carefully flute* the edge of the disc. Prick well with a fork, then chill for 15 minutes.

3. Towards the end of this time, heat the oven to 180°C/350°F/ gas 4. Bake the base for about 20 minutes until golden and just firm – check after 15 minutes and, if necessary, rotate the baking sheet so the base bakes evenly. Remove the baking sheet from the oven, set it on a wire rack and leave the base to cool on the sheet.

4. Meanwhile, make the lemon topping. Break the eggs into a heatproof bowl. Add the yolk and sugar and whisk with a wire whisk for a minute until frothy. Add the lemon zest and juice. Switch to a wooden spoon and stir well. Set the bowl over a pan of simmering water (the base of the bowl shouldn't touch the water) and stir the mixture as it thickens. It is ready when you can draw a finger through the mixture on the wooden spoon and leave a clear path. Remove the bowl from the pan and immediately add the

pieces of butter – they will quickly cool the mixture and prevent it from over-cooking. As soon as the butter has been incorporated, press a disc of dampened baking paper, or a piece of clingfilm, directly on to the surface of the lemon mixture to prevent a skin from forming. Leave to cool, then cover the bowl and chill for at least 4 hours, or up to 12 hours.

5. When ready to finish the dessert, hull and quarter the strawberries. Set the biscuit base on a large serving plate or board and spread the lemon mixture evenly over the top. Arrange the strawberries, cut side up, on the filling and decorate with small basil sprigs. Serve immediately, or keep in the fridge for up to 2 hours.

SUMMER PUDDING

The quintessential pudding to celebrate the glorious fruits of summer, to be served straight from the fridge, icy-cold, with a jug of thick cream. The juice-soaked bread slices that encase the filling are a low-fat foil to the intense fruitiness – in the mid-19th century the dessert was associated with spas and known as hydropathic pudding (it only acquired its more seasonal name early in the 20th century).

Serves 6–8

Kit you'll need: a pudding basin, about 1.25-litre capacity

1kg mixed fresh berries, such as 500g raspberries, 300g small strawberries, 100g stemmed redcurrants and 100g blackberries, plus extra to decorate
200g caster sugar
2 tablespoons Kirsch OR crème de cassis (optional)
about 8 x 5mm slices Milk & Honey Tin Loaf (page 108), crusts removed
sunflower oil, for the basin

Note

The bread used needs to have a close, slightly firm texture so it holds up when it becomes saturated. Choose a good mix of berries and currants for the best flavour, making sure you include plenty of raspberries.

1. Put the berries into a large saucepan and add the sugar and Kirsch, if using. Toss everything together gently so the berries are coated in sugar. Cover the pan and leave to macerate at room temperature for 4–6 hours.

2. Set the pan over medium heat and bring to the boil, gently stirring occasionally. Adjust the heat so the juices simmer gently and cook for 3–4 minutes to soften the fruit. Remove from the heat and leave to cool while you make the bread lining.

3. Before you prepare the basin, work out how the lining will fit together. First cut a disc of bread to fit the base of the basin, then cut fingers of bread about 10 x 5cm to line the side. These should be slightly overlapping towards the bottom of the basin so it is completely lined (cut wedges to fit in any gaps towards the top). Once you have fitted all the bread, take it out. Brush the basin with oil and fit a disc of baking paper on the base. Now you can re-assemble the bread lining.

4. Spoon in the fruit and juices right to the top of the basin, pressing the fruit down firmly to compact it. (Save any leftover fruit in a covered container.) Cut another slice of bread to cover the top, filling in the gaps with small pieces of bread, like a jigsaw. If any of the lining slices stick up above the bread lid, trim them so the top is level. Set the basin on a plate with a deep rim (to catch any drips), then place a small plate or saucer on top – this should just fit inside the rim of the basin – and weight it down with tins of food to compress the pudding. Chill for at least 12 hours, and up to 24 hours.

5. To serve the pudding, hold an upturned deep serving plate or dish on top of the basin and quickly invert the whole thing. Bang on the base of the basin and lift it off. Remove the paper disc. If necessary, use juices in the reserved fruit mixture to 'paint' any unstained patches of bread. Decorate the top with some extra berries and serve immediately, with cream.

CHEESECAKE TOWER

Are you a peanut butter and chocolate person, or perhaps you prefer coconut, or honeycomb? Whichever your taste, there is something for you in this three-in-one celebration dessert, where each shortbread-based cheesecake is flavoured differently. Of course you could serve them separately, but they are most eye-catching arranged in a tower. If you are going to present them this way it is easiest to bake and complete the decoration of each cheesecake in advance and then assemble.

Serves about 36 (see Note)

Kit you'll need: 3 round springclip tins, greased with butter: 1 × 24cm, 1 × 21cm and 1 × 19cm; a baking sheet; 3 small disposable piping bags: a baking sheet, brushed with sunflower oil; a large serving plate or board; 2 silver cake boards 3mm thick: 1 × 21cm and 1 × 19cm; 6 cake dowels

FOR THE PEANUT BUTTER & CHOCOLATE CHEESECAKE
200g plain flour
245g golden caster sugar
140g unsalted butter,
  chilled and diced
125g salted roasted peanuts,
  finely chopped

500g full-fat cream cheese
300g smooth peanut butter
  (unsweetened)
125ml soured cream
4 medium eggs, plus 3 yolks,
  beaten to mix
100g milk chocolate chips
50g milk chocolate, melted*

FOR THE COCONUT & VANILLA CHEESECAKE
150g plain flour, plus
  2 tablespoons
185g golden caster sugar
100g unsalted butter,
  chilled and diced
75g desiccated coconut
600g full-fat cream cheese
140ml soured cream
1 teaspoon vanilla paste

2 medium eggs, plus 1 yolk
3 tablespoons coconut cream
  (from a 160ml tin)
50g milk chocolate, melted*

FOR THE HONEYCOMB & VANILLA CHEESECAKE
225g golden caster sugar
4 tablespoons golden syrup
1½ teaspoons bicarbonate
  of soda
110g plus 1½ tablespoons
  plain flour
75g unsalted butter,
  chilled and diced
450g full-fat cream cheese
100ml soured cream
¾ teaspoon vanilla paste
2 medium eggs, beaten to mix
40g milk chocolate, melted*

1. Start with the **peanut butter and chocolate cheesecake**. Heat the oven to 180°C/350°F/gas 4. To make the base by hand, combine the flour and 70g of the sugar in a bowl and rub in* the butter until the mixture looks like coarse crumbs. Add 25g of the peanuts and mix thoroughly. To make the base in a food processor 'pulse' the flour with the sugar to

combine, then add the butter and blitz to make coarse crumbs. Add the peanuts and 'pulse' a couple of times just until combined.

2. Tip the crumbs into the prepared 24cm tin and spread evenly, then press on to the base with the back of a spoon to make a flat, even layer. Bake in the heated oven for 15–20 minutes

until set and lightly coloured. Set the biscuit base aside to cool. Leave the oven on.

3. To make the filling, put the cream cheese, remaining 175g sugar, 250g of the peanut butter, the soured cream and eggs in a large mixing bowl, or a bowl of free-standing electric mixer. Whisk everything together >>>

until smooth and creamy using a hand-held electric whisk, or the mixer whisk attachment, starting on slow speed and gradually increasing it.

4. Pour the mixture on to the biscuit base, then set the tin on the baking sheet. Sprinkle the chocolate chips evenly over the filling – they will slowly sink. Bake for 55–65 minutes until just set when you jiggle the baking sheet – check after 45 minutes and cover the top of the cheesecake with foil if it is starting to turn brown. Remove from the oven and run a thin round-bladed knife around the inside of the tin to loosen the cheesecake (this will help prevent it from cracking as it cools). Leave to cool, then cover and chill for at least 6 hours, preferably overnight, before turning out.

5. To decorate the cheesecake, gently warm the remaining 50g peanut butter in a pan over low heat, or for 10 seconds in the microwave, then lightly brush or spread around the side of the cheesecake. Press the remaining 100g chopped peanuts on to the side to coat evenly. Spoon the melted chocolate into the piping bag and snip off the very tip, then pipe a delicate lattice across the top of the cheesecake. Return the cheesecake to the fridge to firm up, then store in an airtight container in the fridge until ready to serve or assemble the tower.

6. For the **coconut and vanilla cheesecake**, heat the oven to 180°C/350°F/gas 4. Make the biscuit base in the same way as for the peanut butter cheesecake, with 150g of the flour, 50g of the sugar and the butter, and mixing in 25g coconut in place of the peanuts. Bake in the 21cm tin until set and lightly coloured. Set aside to cool, leaving the oven on.

7. Make the filling in the same way as the peanut butter cheesecake, with the cream cheese, remaining 135g sugar, the soured cream, remaining 2 tablespoons flour, vanilla paste and eggs. When the mixture is smooth and creamy, stir in 20g of the remaining coconut. Pour on to the base in the tin (omit the chocolate chips), set on the baking sheet and bake in the heated oven for 40–45 minutes until just firm when you jiggle the sheet. Loosen in the tin, then leave to cool. Cover and chill for 6 hours, preferably overnight, before turning out.

8. To decorate, stir the coconut cream until very smooth, then brush around the side of the cheesecake. Press the remaining 30g desiccated coconut around the side to cover evenly. Finish with a piped chocolate lattice as for the peanut butter cheesecake. Return to the fridge to firm up, then store in an airtight container in the fridge until ready to serve or assemble.

9. For the **honeycomb and vanilla cheesecake**, you need to make some honeycomb first. To do this, put 100g of the sugar and 2 tablespoons of the golden syrup in a medium saucepan and heat gently over low heat for about 10 minutes, stirring frequently until the sugar has dissolved. Bring to the boil and cook just until the mixture turns to a golden caramel. Immediately remove from the heat, add the bicarbonate of soda and whisk well with a wire whisk (take care as the mixture will foam up alarmingly). Quickly pour the frothy mixture on to the oiled baking sheet. Leave until cold and set.

10. Once the honeycomb has set hard, lightly crush 80g of it; break the rest into large shards. Heat the oven to 180°C/350°F/gas 4. Make the biscuit base in the same way as for the peanut butter cheesecake, with 110g of the flour, 25g of the remaining sugar and the butter, and mixing in 25g of the crushed honeycomb in place of the peanuts. Bake in the 19cm tin until set and lightly coloured. Set aside to cool, leaving the oven on.

11. Make the filling in the same way as for the peanut butter cheesecake, with the cream cheese, remaining 100g sugar, the soured cream, remaining 1½ tablespoons flour, vanilla paste and eggs. When the mixture is smooth and creamy, pour a third

of it into a jug and set aside. Stir 30g of the crushed honeycomb into the remaining filling mixture, then pour this on to the base in the tin (omit the chocolate chips). Slowly and carefully pour the reserved mixture on top. Set the tin on the baking sheet and bake in the heated oven for 35–40 minutes until just firm when you jiggle the sheet. Loosen in the tin, then leave to cool. Cover and chill for 6 hours, preferably overnight, before turning out.

12. To decorate, warm the remaining 2 tablespoons golden syrup, then brush over the side of the cheesecake. Gently press the remaining 25g crushed honeycomb around the side to cover evenly. Finish with a piped chocolate lattice as for the peanut butter cheesecake. Return to the fridge to firm up, then store in an airtight container in the fridge until ready to serve or assemble.

13. To **assemble the tower**, place the peanut butter cheesecake on a serving plate or board, and the other cheesecakes on the cake boards. Cut 3 of the cake dowels to 2cm longer than the height of the largest cheesecake, then gently press the dowels down, spaced apart, in a triangle around the centre of the cheesecake, all the way to the bottom. Repeat the process with the 21cm cheesecake – these dowels will support the weight of the cheesecakes and prevent them from touching or sinking into one another. Place the 21cm cheesecake on top of the largest cheesecake, then set the smallest cheesecake on top of the 21cm cheesecake.

Note

If you want to make just one cheesecake, the peanut butter and chocolate cheesecake will serve 16; the coconut and vanilla cheesecake will serve 12; and the honeycomb and vanilla cheesecake will serve 8.

PASSIONFRUIT & LIME CHARLOTTE RUSSE

One of the prettiest of desserts, this confection of light, crisp sponge finger biscuits and a set creamy, fruit–flavoured custard is said to have been conjured up at the beginning of the 19th century by the French chef Marie-Antoine Carême, chef to the Prince Regent and celebrity cook of his day. Carême is said to have made this elegant dessert for a banquet to honour the visit to Britain of Tsar Alexander I of Russia.

Serves 10

Kit you'll need: 2 baking sheets, lined with baking paper; a large piping bag fitted with 1.25cm plain nozzle; a 20cm round springclip tin, greased with butter and lined*

FOR THE SAVOIARDI
3 medium eggs,
    at room temperature
70g caster sugar
½ teaspoon vanilla extract
60g plain flour
1 tablespoon cornflour

pinch of salt
pinch of cream of tartar
25g icing sugar

FOR THE BAVAROIS
7 leaves gelatine
450ml full-fat milk
6 medium egg yolks,
    at room temperature
75g caster sugar
200ml passionfruit juice (sieved
    from about 17 passionfruit)
350ml double cream (not extra-
    thick or spoonable), chilled

FOR THE LIME JELLY
3 leaves gelatine
finely grated zest and juice
    of 2 limes
125g caster sugar
150ml water
green food colouring

TO FINISH (OPTIONAL)
450g ripe strawberries
    or other seasonal fruit

1. First make the savoiardi. Heat the oven to 190°C/375°F/gas 5. Draw 10 lines, 11cm long and 2.5cm apart, on both sheets of baking paper lining the baking sheets, then turn the paper over so the drawn lines are underneath (but still visible).

2. Separate the eggs, putting the egg yolks into one mixing bowl and the whites into another. Add half the caster sugar (35g) to the yolks and whisk with a hand-held electric whisk until the mixture is very light and mousse-like and

reaches the ribbon stage*. Whisk in the vanilla extract. Sift the flour, cornflour and salt into the bowl and fold in gently. Set aside.

3. Add the cream of tartar to the egg whites and whisk (with a clean whisk) until they stand in soft peaks*. Whisk in the remaining 35g caster sugar a tablespoon at a time, then continue whisking to make a stiff, glossy meringue. Gently fold* the meringue into the yolk mixture in 3 batches, taking great care not to knock out all the air that was whisked in.

4. As soon as everything has been thoroughly combined, with no streaks of flour or blobs of meringue, spoon the mixture into the piping bag fitted with the 1.25cm plain nozzle. Pipe the mixture in straight lines on the baking paper, following the drawn lines, to make 20 fingers. Sift the icing sugar over the fingers, then bake in the heated oven for 10–12 minutes until fairly firm but still slightly spongy when gently pressed – the savoiardi will firm up as they cool. Set the baking sheets on wire racks and cool for >>>

2–3 minutes, then carefully transfer the savoiardi from the baking sheets to the racks using a palette knife. Leave until completely cooled.

5. Meanwhile, make the bavarois. Drop the leaves of gelatine into a bowl of cold water and leave to soak for about 5 minutes until soft. Pour the milk into a medium pan and heat until almost boiling; remove from the heat. Whisk the egg yolks with the caster sugar in a heatproof bowl until pale and creamy, then gradually whisk in the hot milk. Pour the mixture back into the pan and stir constantly with a wooden spoon over medium/low heat until the custard thickens enough to coat the back of the spoon – don't let the custard come to the boil. Remove from the heat.

6. Drain the gelatine and squeeze out the excess water (it will feel like damp clingfilm), then add it to the hot custard and stir until completely melted. Pour into a clean heatproof bowl. Cool slightly, then fold in the passionfuit juice. Leave to cool for at least 30 minutes until the custard is at room temperature.

7. Whip the cream in another bowl until it will stand in soft peaks*. Carefully fold into the passionfruit mixture. Cover the bowl and keep in the fridge while you line the tin.

8. Stand the savoiardi vertically around the inside of the tin, close to each other and with the upper or crust side facing the tin. They need to fit tightly together to form a seal (to prevent the filling from leaking). Spoon the passionfruit bavarois mixture into the lined tin. The tips of the savoiardi will extend slightly above the level of the bavarois filling. Cover with clingfilm and chill for 3–4 hours until set.

9. To make the lime jelly for the topping, soak the gelatine as before. Put the lime zest and juice, sugar and measured water in a small pan. Heat gently, stirring until the sugar has dissolved, then bring to the boil. Remove from the heat. Drain and squeeze out the gelatine as before, then add to the hot syrup and stir until melted. Strain through a fine sieve into a heatproof jug. Stir in enough food colouring to make a vibrant lime-green jelly. Leave

to cool until the jelly is starting to set, then carefully pour it over the surface of the set bavarois. Return the tin to the fridge to chill for another 3–4 hours until set.

10. When ready to serve, unclip the tin and transfer the charlotte to a serving plate or cake stand. Gently peel off the lining paper. Tie a ribbon around the outside of the charlotte, if you like.

MOCHA TORTE

There is something about an exquisite, indulgent, multi-layered (sixteen!) chocolate torte that evokes images of Viennese waltzes in elaborate ballrooms. A satisfying challenge to make, this torte consists of thin layers of chocolate joconde sponge (the almondy confection typical of such multi-layered gateaux) sandwiched with a very rich mocha mousseline, and finished with a shiny chocolate glaze. You can leave the torte looking simply elegant, or add candles for a birthday celebration.

Serves 20

Kit you'll need: **4 sheets of parchment-lined foil; 2–4 baking sheets; a 14 x 28cm piece of thin card**

FOR THE SPONGE
8 medium eggs,
   at room temperature
good pinch of salt
120g icing sugar, sifted
200g caster sugar
55g plain flour
35g ground almonds
35g cocoa powder

FOR THE COFFEE SYRUP
65g caster sugar
125ml water
1½ tablespoons instant coffee
   (granules or powder)
1 tablespoon coffee liqueur,
   such as Kahlua, OR dark rum

FOR THE CHOCOLATE MOUSSELINE
325ml double cream, chilled
300g dark chocolate (about 70%
   cocoa solids), chopped
6 medium egg yolks,
   at room temperature

1 tablespoon coffee liqueur,
   such as Kahlua, OR dark rum
150g caster sugar
150ml water

FOR THE CHOCOLATE GLAZE
150g unsalted butter
225g dark chocolate (about 70%
   cocoa solids), finely chopped

TO DECORATE
choose from: chocolate coffee
   beans, grated chocolate,
   chocolate curls (see page 274),
   cocoa powder, edible gold
   stars OR confetti

1. Heat the oven to 190°C/375°F/ gas 5. Cut each sheet of foil into a square with 30cm sides, then fold in the edges to make square shallow cases with 28cm sides. Set each case on a baking sheet (if you only have 1 or 2 sheets, you can bake the sponge mixture in batches).

2. To make the sponge mixture, separate the eggs, putting the whites into a large mixing bowl, or a free-standing electric mixer, and the yolks into a large heatproof bowl. Add the salt to the whites and whisk, with a hand-held electric whisk or the whisk attachment of the mixer, until soft peaks* will form. Gradually whisk in the icing sugar, then keep whisking until the meringue will stand in stiff peaks*. Put the bowl on one side for now.

3. Add the caster sugar to the yolks and whisk with a hand-held electric whisk for a few seconds until combined. Set the bowl over a pan of gently simmering water (the base of the bowl shouldn't touch the water) and whisk at full speed until the mixture is very pale and mousse-like, and reaches the ribbon stage*. Lift the bowl off the pan and whisk the mixture until it returns to room temperature.

4. Using a large metal spoon, scoop up a spoonful of the meringue and add it to the yolk mixture, then whisk it in on low speed, to loosen the mixture. Fold* in the rest of the meringue in 4 batches, using the large metal spoon. Sift the flour, ground almonds and cocoa >>>

on to the mixture and carefully but thoroughly fold in. Divide the mixture equally among the 4 cases and spread evenly – it's important to fill the corners and edges evenly so the sponges are all the same thickness.

5. Bake in the heated oven for 9–10 minutes until the sponges feel firm when gently pressed (if you are uncertain, bake for an extra minute as any slight under-baking will make assembly difficult). Slide the sponges, in their cases, off the baking sheets and on to the worktop. Leave until cold.

6. Meanwhile, make the coffee syrup. Put the sugar, water and coffee into a small pan, set over low heat and stir until the sugar has dissolved. Bring to the boil and simmer for 1 minute. Remove from the heat and stir in the liqueur or rum. Set aside.

7. To make the chocolate mousseline, whip the cream until it will stand in floppy peaks. Set aside on the worktop (don't chill it). Melt* the chocolate, then leave to cool. Put the yolks and liqueur or rum into a large heatproof bowl, or a free-standing electric mixer, and whisk until pale and thick. Combine the sugar and water in a medium pan and heat gently, stirring to dissolve the sugar, then bring to the boil and simmer for 1 minute. Remove from the heat. Whisking on full speed, pour the hot sugar

syrup on to the egg mixture in a thin, steady stream – aim for the centre of the bowl, not the edge. Continue to whisk until the mixture is very thick and mousse-like, and reaches the ribbon stage*. Continue whisking until the mousse has cooled to room temperature. Fold in the melted chocolate, followed by the whipped cream. Leave on the worktop while you work on the sponge layers.

8. Invert one sponge on to a board and gently peel off the foil case. Cut the sponge in half to make 2 rectangles, each 14 x 28cm. Lay one of these, crust-side down, on the piece of thin card. Gently reheat the coffee syrup, then lightly brush a very little over the sponge rectangle – if the sponge becomes saturated, it will be difficult to slice neatly. Spread an eighth of the mousseline over the sponge. Set the second sponge rectangle on top – make sure the top is level. Brush with syrup and spread a portion of mousseline over it. Repeat with the rest of the sponges, syrup and mousseline to make a total of 16 layers. Chill for 1 hour to firm.

9. Finally, make the chocolate glaze. Melt the butter in a small pan, then skim off the foam. Carefully pour the clear butter into another small pan, leaving behind the milky residue. Put all but 60g of the chocolate into a heatproof bowl. Reheat the butter until just bubbling, then

pour it on to the chocolate while stirring constantly. Keep stirring until the chocolate is melted and smooth, then stir in the reserved 60g chocolate to make a glossy glaze. Leave to cool for a few minutes until slightly thickened but still easily pourable.

10. Remove the torte from the fridge and set it on a wire rack placed over a baking sheet (to catch the drips). Starting at one short edge, quickly pour the chocolate glaze over the torte to completely cover it. Let the chocolate drip down the sides – they will be trimmed later on. Return the torte to the fridge to chill for at least 1 hour until set and firm.

11. To complete the torte, dip a large, very sharp knife into very hot water and dry it, then use to trim the sides to make a neat rectangle. Transfer the torte to a serving plate and finish with your choice of decorations. Chill for about 2 hours until the glaze is firm before serving. (The torte can be kept in an airtight container in the fridge overnight.) Remove from the fridge about 15 minutes before serving, cut into thin slices with a large knife dipped in hot water and dried.

SABLÉ BRETON
WITH APPLES

Apples make an obvious choice for a Harvest Festival pudding, and this one hails from Brittany, famed for its butter-rich cakes and desserts made with their rather special, local butter. Tart eating apples are quickly fried in butter and arranged in the base of a cake tin, then covered with a buttercup-yellow sponge mixture flavoured with lemon zest. After baking, the whole thing is inverted so that the golden apples are on top. Serve warm with crème fraîche or home-made custard.

1. Heat your oven to 180°C/350°F/gas 4. To make the apple layer, peel, quarter and core the apples. Cut each quarter into 4 slices. Put the apples into a frying pan with the butter and sugar. Add half of the lemon zest (save the rest for the sponge) and the juice. Set the pan over medium-high heat and cook, stirring frequently, for about 5 minutes until the apples are turning golden and all the liquid has evaporated. Tip into the prepared tin and spread evenly without compressing the apples. Leave to cool.

2. Meanwhile, put the eggs and yolks into a mixing bowl, or the bowl of a free-standing electric mixer, and add the reserved lemon zest and the sugar. Whisk with a hand-held electric whisk, or the whisk attachment of the mixer, to the ribbon stage*. Cut the soft butter into small pieces and add to the bowl while whisking at high speed – the mixture will lose volume.

When all the butter has been incorporated, sift the flour and baking powder into the bowl and gently fold* in with a large metal spoon or plastic spatula.

3. Spoon the sponge mixture evenly over the apple layer. Bake in the heated oven for 40–45 minutes until a good golden brown and a skewer inserted into the centre comes out clean, with no damp sponge mixture clinging to it.

4. Remove the tin from the oven and run a round-bladed knife around the inside to loosen the sponge. Hold an upturned serving plate over the top of the tin, then invert the whole thing. Unclip the side of the tin, lift off the metal base and peel off the lining paper. Serve warm with crème fraîche or home-made custard (see Spicy Figgy Pudding, page 209).

Serves 6–8

Kit you'll need: 1 x 20.5cm round springclip tin, greased with butter and base-lined*

FOR THE APPLE LAYER
4 medium/large tart eating apples, such as Braeburn
25g unsalted butter
1 tablespoon caster sugar
finely grated zest
    of 1 medium unwaxed lemon,
    plus 1 tablespoon juice

FOR THE SPONGE
2 medium eggs, plus 2 yolks, at room temperature
150g caster sugar
150g unsalted butter, softened
150g plain flour
1 teaspoon baking powder

PASSIONFRUIT & PINEAPPLE ICE-CREAM ROLL

An impressive dessert for a birthday celebration, made with a decorated lemon sponge and finished with toasted Italian meringue rosettes and chocolate flowers or swirls. This is from the dairy-free ice-cream roll Challenge so coconut milk is used for the custard-based passionfruit ice-cream filling. There is also a fresh pineapple jam to be made, so plenty of work, but worth it!

Serves 6–8

Kit you'll need: a sugar thermometer; an ice-cream maker (optional); a piping bag fitted with a No. 3 fine writing nozzle; a 20 x 30cm swiss roll tin, lined* and lightly brushed with oil; a large piping bag fitted with a large star nozzle; a kitchen blowtorch; a small disposable piping bag

FOR THE ICE CREAM
1 x 400g tin coconut milk (not reduced fat)
6 medium egg yolks, at room temperature
130g clear Acacia honey
55g golden syrup

175ml passionfruit juice (sieved from about 15 passionfruit or ready-squeezed juice), chilled

FOR THE SPONGE DECORATION
1 large egg, at room temperature
30g golden caster sugar
25g plain flour
10g cocoa powder

FOR THE LEMON SPONGE
3 large eggs, at room temperature
100g golden caster sugar
½–1 teaspoon lemon extract, to taste
1–3 drops of yellow food colouring
75g self-raising flour

FOR THE PINEAPPLE JAM
450g ready-prepared chopped fresh pineapple
1 small Bramley apple
265g caster sugar
5 tablespoons lemon juice
3 tablespoons bottled apple pectin

FOR THE ITALIAN MERINGUE
70g egg whites (from 2 large eggs), at room temperature
140g white caster sugar
3 tablespoons water

TO DECORATE
50g dark chocolate (about 70% cocoa solids), broken up
2 passionfruit

1. To make the ice cream, put the coconut milk and egg yolks into a medium pan and stir with a wooden spoon over low heat until the mixture reaches 75°C and has slightly thickened to lightly coat the back of the spoon. Remove from the heat and stir in the honey and golden syrup. When the mixture is smooth, stir in the passionfruit juice. Cool quickly by setting the pan in a sink of icy water. Once the mixture is very cold, transfer it to the ice-cream maker and churn until just frozen. Scoop the ice cream into a plastic container and keep in the freezer until needed. (The ice cream can also be made in a container in the freezer; stir the mixture well every 15 minutes until it is evenly firm.)

2. Heat the oven to 180°C/350°F/ gas 4. Start by making the sponge decoration. Put the egg and sugar into a bowl and whisk with a hand-held electric whisk until the mixture reaches the ribbon stage*. Sift the flour and cocoa powder into the bowl and carefully fold in*. Transfer the mixture to the piping bag fitted with the writing nozzle and pipe a diagonal lattice over the base of the lined swiss roll tin. Put it into the freezer to chill while you make the lemon sponge.

>>>

3. Break the eggs into a mixing bowl, or the bowl of a free-standing electric mixer, add the sugar and whisk to the ribbon stage*. Add lemon extract to taste and the yellow colouring and whisk briefly until evenly combined (without streaks). Sift the flour into the bowl and fold in*. Carefully spoon the mixture into the swiss roll tin, on top of the piped lattice, and spread evenly with a palette knife.

4. Bake in the heated oven for about 13 minutes until the sponge is golden and springy when lightly pressed. Set a sheet of baking paper on top of the sponge and then a chopping board (or wire rack). Holding them together, invert the whole thing. Lift off the tin and carefully peel off the lining paper, then cover the sponge with a second sheet of baking paper. Set a wire rack on top and invert so the sponge is now crust-side up. Leave the sheet of baking paper in place, then quickly roll up the hot sponge, from one short side, around a hollow tube or bottle about 7.5cm in diameter. The lattice pattern will be on the outside. Leave to cool.

5. To make the jam, finely chop the pineapple and put into a large pan. Peel, core and finely chop the apple. Add to the pan with the sugar, lemon juice and pectin. Set over medium/low heat and stir gently until the sugar has completely dissolved, then bring to the boil. Boil, stirring frequently, until the jam reaches

104°C on the sugar thermometer or setting point (see Blackberry and Apple Jam on page 11 for more details). Pour the jam into a heatproof bowl and leave until completely cold and set. The jam will need to be easy to spread (but not a purée) so, if necessary, blitz it briefly in a food processor.

6. To assemble the roll, carefully unroll the sponge and spread it with a thick layer of jam (you won't need all of it). Working quickly, scoop the ice cream out of the container and on to the middle of the sponge to form a neat log 20 x 7.5cm (you may not need all the ice cream), then roll the sponge around the ice cream. Wrap the roll tightly in clingfilm to hold it all together, then place it in the freezer to firm up.

7. In the meantime, make the meringue. Put the egg whites into a large mixing bowl, or the bowl of a free-standing mixer, and whisk just until frothy. Gently heat the sugar with the water in a small pan, stirring until the sugar has dissolved, then bring to the boil. Boil until the syrup reaches 110°C, then start whisking the whites until they will stand in stiff peaks*. As soon as the syrup reaches 118°C, slowly pour it on to the whites while whisking at top speed. Continue whisking until the meringue is stiff and cool.

8. Transfer the meringue to the piping bag fitted with the star nozzle. Unwrap the roll and set it on a freezerproof serving plate.

Quickly pipe the meringue along the top of the roll to make 3 rows of 6 rosettes each. Lightly tinge the peaks brown using the kitchen blowtorch. Return the roll to the freezer.

9. For the piped chocolate decorations, melt* the chocolate in a heatproof bowl set over a pan of steaming hot water, then temper it: slightly increase the heat under the pan so the temperature of the chocolate rises to 45°C – keep stirring so the chocolate heats evenly. Remove the bowl from the pan and set it in a larger bowl of cold water to quickly cool the chocolate. Gently stir until the temperature falls to 27°C. Set the bowl over the pan of hot water again and reheat the chocolate, stirring, until it reaches 29–30°C. Remove the bowl from the pan and cool slightly. Spoon the chocolate into the small disposable piping bag, snip off the tip and pipe small, neat swirls or flowers on to a sheet of silicone paper – you will need 5 perfect decorations but make extra in case of breakages. Leave until set.

10. To serve, peel the chocolate decorations off the paper and gently press into the meringue. Spoon the passionfruit flesh over the roll and serve immediately.

CAPPUCCINO CRÈME BRULÉES

These incredibly rich and creamy coffee-flavoured variations on the classic theme have a more unusual method for creating an extra-crunchy topping. Here the caster sugar is cooked to a caramel and allowed to set, then broken into shards. These are blitzed to a fine sand in a food processer before being sprinkled on to the custards and melted under the grill.

1. Heat the oven to 170°C/325°F/gas 3. Put the egg yolks into a large heatproof bowl, add the sugar and vanilla extract, and mix with a wire whisk until thoroughly combined.

2. Pour both creams into a medium pan and heat until scalding hot. Remove the pan from the heat, add the instant coffee and stir until dissolved. Leave to cool for a couple of minutes, then pour the coffee cream slowly on to the egg yolks, whisking constantly. Strain the custard into a jug, then pour into the buttered ramekins, dividing equally.

3. Set the ramekins in the roasting tin and pour hot water into the tin to come halfway up the side of the ramekins. Bake in the heated oven for 25–30 minutes until the custards are just set. Remove the ramekins from the roasting tin and leave to cool. Once cold, cover the ramekins with clingfilm and chill overnight, or for up to 2 days.

4. To make the caramel topping, put the sugar in a stainless steel pan and add a little water to dampen. Set over medium heat and stir gently until the sugar has completely melted. Turn up the heat to high and cook, without stirring, until the sugar syrup has turned to a pale straw-coloured caramel. Pour the caramel on to the lined baking sheet and leave until cold and hard.

5. Break up the caramel into chunks, then blitz in a food processor to make a fine sandy sugar. Sprinkle the caramel sugar evenly over the chilled custards. Place them side by side on a grill pan or baking sheet.

6. Heat the grill to its highest setting. Slide the pan of ramekins under the grill, as close to the heat as possible, and grill for 4–5 minutes until the sugar has melted and turned to a rich caramel – be careful not to burn the sugar or leave the ramekins under the grill for too long as you risk reheating and overcooking the soft-set custard. Cool briefly until the caramel has set, then serve as soon as possible.

Makes 6

Kit you'll need: **6 x 150ml ramekins, greased with butter; a roasting tin; a baking sheet, lined with baking paper**

4 large egg yolks,
    at room temperature
45g caster sugar
½ teaspoon vanilla extract
300ml single cream
300ml double cream
2½ teaspoons instant
    coffee granules

FOR THE CARAMEL TOPPING
100g caster sugar

INDIVIDUAL CHRISTMAS PUDS

You don't need to circle 'Stir-up Sunday' (the last before Advent) on the calendar for making these little puddings, as they can be left as late as Christmas morning. The children will love helping with the measuring, weighing, zesting and squeezing, and, of course, plenty of stirring! Baked, rather than steamed, the puddings are light, not too sweet or rich, but with bags of flavour. Serve them with fluffy zabaglione or with egg custard or cream.

Makes 6

Kit you'll need: 6 individual pudding basins, about 175ml capacity, greased with butter and the base lined with a disc of baking paper

100g unsalted butter, softened
100g dark brown
    muscovado sugar
finely grated zest and juice
    of 1 medium unwaxed lemon
2 medium eggs,
    at room temperature
1 tablespoon brandy
    OR dark rum
100g self-raising flour
good pinch of salt
¼ teaspoon grated nutmeg
¼ teaspoon ground mixed spice
100g finely grated carrot
    (about 2 medium carrots)
275g luxury dried fruit mix
    OR mixed vine fruit

TO SERVE
Zabaglione (see opposite),
    Custard (see Spicy Figgy
    Pudding, page 209) OR cream

1. Heat the oven to 180°C/350°F/ gas 4. Put the softened butter in a mixing bowl, or a free-standing electric mixer, and beat with a wooden spoon or hand-held electric whisk, or the whisk attachment of the mixer, until creamy and mayonnaise-like. Add the sugar and beat until the mixture is very light and fluffy. Scrape down the side of the bowl, then beat in the lemon zest. Break the eggs into a small bowl, add the brandy or rum and beat with a fork just until combined. Gradually add to the butter mixture, beating well after each addition; add a tablespoon of the weighed flour with the last addition of egg.

2. Sift the rest of the flour, the salt, nutmeg and mixed spice into the bowl and gently fold* in with a large metal spoon or plastic spatula. Add the lemon juice, grated carrot and dried fruit, and carefully mix in until thoroughly combined.

3. Spoon the mixture into the prepared basins, dividing it equally. Tap the basins on the worktop to settle the contents, then arrange them in a roasting tin. Pour enough boiling water into the tin to half fill it. Tightly cover the roasting tin with foil.

4. Transfer to the heated oven and bake for about 1¾ hours until the puddings are starting to shrink away from the side of the basins, and a skewer inserted into the centre comes out clean.

5. Carefully turn out on to a warmed large serving plate, or individual plates, and remove the lining paper discs. Serve the puds piping hot.

Tip

If you want to make the puddings in advance, to serve later the same or the next day, leave to cool in the basins, then cover. To reheat, turn out and microwave using 10-second bursts until piping hot.

ZABAGLIONE

This is a marvellous, and festive, sauce to serve with puddings and beignets as well as with fresh berries and biscotti.

1. Put all the ingredients into a heatproof bowl and set over a pan of barely simmering water (the base of the bowl shouldn't touch the water). Whisk the mixture with a hand-held electric whisk for about 5 minutes until it becomes very pale, thick and mousse-like, and reaches the ribbon stage*.

2. Remove the bowl from the pan and continue whisking the mixture as it cools for 2 minutes. Pour into a warmed serving jug or bowl and serve warm (or within an hour).

Serves 6

4 medium egg yolks,
    at room temperature
4 tablespoons caster sugar
6 tablespoons sweet sherry,
    Champagne OR Marsala
2 tablespoons water

"When the whole family gather at Christmas there might be twenty of us, and the neighbours come in for pudding. So I like to make lots of different ones: some traditional, others classic, but with a twist, and some with different flavours, like ginger and orange.'

FLORA

TIPSY LAIRD'S TRIFLE

Celebrate Burns' Night in true tartan style by making this great trifle with a great name that celebrates Scottish raspberries and Drambuie, the famous liqueur made from whisky, honey and spices. Despite the 'tipsy' description, you only need enough liqueur to moisten and flavour the sponge base – if it's too soggy it won't support the other layers. Old-style almond macaroons add crunch, and, in keeping with tradition, creamy vanilla custard and whipped cream, flavoured with more Drambuie, finish off the whole confection.

Serves 12–16

Kit you'll need: 2 baking sheets, lined with baking paper or silicone sheets; 1 swiss roll tin, 20 x 30cm, greased and base-lined*; a large, deep, straight-sided glass bowl, 20–22cm across

FOR THE MACAROONS
125g ground almonds
175g caster sugar
1 tablespoon cornflour
2 medium egg whites,
   at room temperature
2 drops of almond extract
2 heaped tablespoons
   flaked almonds

FOR THE SPONGE
75g plain flour
pinch of salt
3 medium eggs,
   at room temperature
75g caster sugar
¼ teaspoon vanilla extract

FOR THE CUSTARD
600ml single cream
1 vanilla pod, split open
6 medium egg yolks,
   at room temperature
1 tablespoon cornflour
2 tablespoons caster sugar

TO ASSEMBLE
6 tablespoons good raspberry jam
   OR conserve
6 tablespoons plus 2 teaspoons
   Drambuie, Marsala OR
   sweet sherry
250g fresh or frozen (use straight
   from freezer) raspberries
300ml whipping cream,
   well chilled
1 tablespoon caster sugar

TO DECORATE
25g toasted flaked almonds
50g fresh raspberries OR
   1 tablespoon freeze-dried
   raspberry pieces

1. To make the macaroons, heat the oven to 170°C/325°F/gas 3. Combine the ground almonds, sugar and cornflour in a mixing bowl. Put the egg whites and almond extract into a small bowl and whisk with a fork until frothy, then tip into the almond mixture. Mix with a wooden spoon to make a stiff paste. Spoon the mixture on to the lined baking sheets, using the equivalent of 2 level teaspoons of the mixture for each macaroon and spacing them well apart to allow for expansion – the mixture will settle itself to form discs about 3.5–4cm across. Decorate the macaroons with the flaked almonds. Bake in the heated oven for about 25 minutes until golden and crisp. Leave to cool on the baking sheets. (The macaroons can be stored in an airtight container for up to 4 days.)

2. For the whisked sponge, turn the oven temperature up to 220°C/425°F/gas 7. Sift the flour and salt on to a sheet of baking paper and put to one side. Break the eggs into a mixing bowl, or the bowl of a free-standing electric mixer, and whisk with a hand-held electric whisk, or the whisk attachment of the mixer, for a few seconds until frothy. Add the sugar and vanilla and whisk to the ribbon stage*. Sift half of the flour into the mixture and delicately fold* in with a large metal spoon. Repeat with the rest of the flour, folding until you can no longer see any specks of flour.

>>>

3. Pour the mixture into the prepared tin and spread evenly. Bake in the heated oven for 10–12 minutes until golden brown and springy to the touch. Cover a wire rack with a sheet of baking paper and sprinkle it with caster sugar. Turn out the sponge on to the paper and peel off the lining paper. Leave the sponge to cool. (Once cold, it can be wrapped in clingfilm and kept for up to 2 days.)

4. When you are ready to assemble the trifle, make the custard. Heat the cream with the split vanilla pod until scalding hot, then remove from the heat and leave to infuse for 20 minutes. Lift out the vanilla pod and use the tip of a sharp knife to scrape a few of the vanilla seeds into the cream (wash and dry the pod to use again). Beat the egg yolks with the cornflour and sugar in a heatproof bowl, then stir in the hot cream. When thoroughly combined, return the mixture to the pan and stir over very low heat until thick enough to coat the back of the wooden spoon; don't let the custard boil. Pour into a clean bowl and leave to cool while you assemble the layers.

5. Set the sponge crust-side down on a board and spread the jam over the top. Cut the sponge across into quarters, to make 7.5 × 20cm strips. Sandwich these in pairs, jam sides together, then slice each sandwich across into 8 fingers. Arrange the fingers in a single layer in the bottom of the glass serving bowl so they extend up the sides a little way, making sure there are no gaps. Sprinkle the sponge fingers with the 6 tablespoons Drambuie, Marsala or sherry, then scatter the raspberries on top.

6. Set aside 5 of the best-looking macaroons for the decoration. Crumble 15 macaroons into large chunks and scatter over the raspberries to make a thick, even layer (the left-over macaroons are cook's perks). Pour the cooled custard evenly over the crumbled macaroons, then cover and chill for at least 3 hours, or overnight, until firm and set.

7. Whip the cream with the sugar and remaining 2 teaspoons liqueur until it is floppy and thick enough to spread easily. Spoon on top of the custard and gently spread into swirls. Decorate with the reserved whole macaroons, flaked almonds and raspberries. If not serving immediately, cover the bowl and keep in the fridge for up to 4 hours.

SPICY FIGGY PUDDING

"We all like figgy pudding..." goes the Christmas carol, and everyone will love this old-fashioned baked, rather than steamed, pudding flavoured with dried figs, spices and orange. It harks back to the 16th century when fig trees were common in Britain and such puddings were deservedly popular. The mixture includes breadcrumbs, which lighten the texture. Serve with custard or with zabaglione (see page 205) or warmed golden syrup.

1. Using kitchen scissors or a large knife, cut each fig into about 10 pieces, discarding the stalk. Put into a medium pan with the orange zest. Measure the juice from the orange and make up to 175ml with water, if necessary. Add to the pan with the cinnamon stick. Set over medium heat and bring to the boil. Add the bicarbonate of soda (the mixture will turn foamy) and stir well, then reduce the heat and simmer very gently, stirring frequently, for about 15 minutes until the figs are very soft. Remove from the heat and leave to cool.

2. Heat the oven to 180°C/350°F/ gas 4. Generously grease the mould with butter, then line the base with a small disc of baking paper. Put the 75g softened butter and the sugar into a mixing bowl, or a free-standing electric mixer, and beat well with a wooden spoon or hand-held electric whisk, or the whisk attachment of the mixer, until the mixture is fluffy. Scrape down the side of the bowl. Gradually add the eggs, beating well after each addition. Sift the flour, ginger and mixed spice into the bowl and fold* in with a large metal spoon or plastic spatula.

3. Remove the cinnamon stick from the figs and add the thick sticky mixture to the bowl with the breadcrumbs. Stir in gently until thoroughly combined. Transfer the mixture to the prepared mould. Tap it gently on the worktop to settle the mixture and remove any pockets of air.

4. Place a sheet of buttered foil, butter side up, on the worktop and make a wide pleat (6–7cm) across it (the pudding expands during baking and the pleat will allow the foil to expand too). Cover the mould with the foil, buttered side down, firmly pressing it to the side of the mould. Set the mould in a roasting tin and pour enough hot water into the tin to fill it by three-quarters. Transfer to the >>>

Serves 6–8

Kit you'll need: 1 ovenproof brioche mould OR pudding basin, about 1.5-litre capacity

250g soft-dried figs
finely grated zest and juice
    of 1 large orange
1 cinnamon stick
½ teaspoon bicarbonate of soda
75g unsalted butter, softened,
    plus extra for greasing
150g light brown
    muscovado sugar
2 medium eggs, at room
    temperature, beaten to mix
150g self-raising flour
2 teaspoons ground ginger
½ teaspoon ground mixed spice
50g wholemeal breadcrumbs
caster sugar, for sprinkling

FOR THE CUSTARD
425ml creamy milk,
    such as Jersey or Guernsey
1 vanilla pod, split open
4 medium egg yolks,
    at room temperature
2½ tablespoons caster sugar

heated oven and bake for about 2 hours until a skewer inserted into the centre of the pudding comes out clean.

5. When the pudding is nearly ready, make the custard. Put the milk into a medium pan, preferably non-stick. Scrape in a few seeds from the vanilla pod, then add the pod to the pan too. Bring to the boil, stirring with a wooden spoon. Remove from the heat, cover the pan and leave to infuse for about 20 minutes. Put the egg yolks and sugar into a heatproof bowl set on a damp cloth (to prevent wobbling) and beat thoroughly with a wooden spoon for about a minute until very smooth and much paler.

6. Remove the vanilla pod from the milk, then slowly pour the warm milk on to the yolks in a steady stream while stirring constantly. Tip the mixture back into the pan, set it over medium heat and stir the custard constantly until it thickens enough to coat the back of the spoon – take care not to let the custard get too hot. Pour into a warmed jug. (If not serving immediately, set the jug in a pan or bowl of hot water to keep warm for up to 30 minutes.)

7. Remove the mould from the roasting tin and remove the foil. Run a thin-bladed knife around the inside of the mould to loosen the sponge. Hold an upturned,

warmed serving plate on top of the mould and invert the whole thing. Lift off the mould and peel off the lining paper disc. Sprinkle the pudding with caster sugar and serve hot with the custard.

Tip

Strips of candied orange zest make a lovely decoration. Blanch 8mm-wide strips in boiling water for 2 minutes, then drain and return to the pan. Cover with fresh water and add 1 tablespoon sugar. Bring to the boil, stirring to dissolve the sugar, then simmer for 2 minutes. Drain and dry on kitchen paper.

'I love cinnamon in baking. It feels so warm, wintry and Christmassy. It reminds me of home in Lithuania.'

UGNE

SAVOURY PASTRY & BAKES

From elegant canapés to comforting pies, savoury pastry is the key to baking treats for any celebration. Exquisite bite-sized morsels of flavour, such as Party Palmiers (page 249), Bourekas (page 248), Cheese Beignets (page 220) or prawn-cocktail-filled choux buns (page 219), are perfect party food. Or why not put a new twist on that old favourite, the vol-au-vent? There's an asparagus and Parma ham filling on page 224, but you can be as imaginative as you like. Tamal fills his with coriander chicken, spiked with ginger and chilli, to his mother's recipe.

Elegant Salmon & Asparagus Pies (page 228) or a Smoked Haddock & Baby Leek Tart (page 216) are light and lovely for a smart picnic, but at the other end of the spectrum savoury baking also provides some of the very best warming food. A Cornbread-topped Bonfire Night Chilli (page 237) will keep everyone stoked

up through the fireworks. And nothing beats a robust pie for keeping out the chill. As Marie says, 'a good steak pie made with puff pastry is a celebration meal'. In the game season, you might like to try a Pheasant Pie with a Lemon Suet Crust (page 240).

Dorret knows how lucky she was that from an early age at school she was taught how to make hot-water-crust pastry and raised pies because once you have mastered the art of a raised pie (see page 234 for a masterclass), you can really start to experiment with what you put inside.

'A traditional roast dinner is one of my favourite things to eat, so I decided to put everything into a pie,' Mat says. 'I cooked it all first, then built up layers of stuffing, sausagemeat, turkey, cranberry, chestnut and sprouts. It's a great thing to do for a get-together because you can feed so many people. One good slice can make a meal, and the sprouts and cranberry make it look really colourful.'

It can be fun to put a savoury spin on something traditionally served sweet, for example the Lebanese influence that Stuart brings to his favourite cinnamon swirls, spreading the dough with minced lamb pepped up with mint, cumin, allspice, cardamom and, of course, cinnamon, before rolling it up like a swiss roll, cutting into thick slices and baking.

Although pies are perhaps the most traditional of British dishes, they are incredibly adaptable when it comes to bringing in variations from across the world. 'Some of my mum's side of the family come from southern Spain', Stuart says, 'so I thought I would bring paella-style flavours to a pie, but without the rice: chicken, paprika, chorizo, tomatoes, peppers, all inside shortcrust pastry.'

Smart and sophisticated or satisfyingly substantial, savoury bakes can make the perfect centrepiece for a summer garden party or a cosy winter gathering. As Sandy says: 'When you mention baking for a celebration, people tend to think of cakes and sweet tarts, but for big family get-togethers I like to bake savoury things. I don't think they get nearly enough press.'

SMOKED HADDOCK & BABY LEEK TART

There are many myths about why the leek is a symbol of Wales, the most popular of which is that soldiers wore them in their caps to identify each other in a famous battle against invading Saxons. Even now, it is the tradition amongst soldiers in Welsh regiments to eat a raw leek on St David's Day – though they would most likely prefer to celebrate the occasion with this tremendous combination of tender, sweet young leeks and lightly smoked haddock fillets in a crisp pastry case.

1. To make the pastry, sift the flour and salt into a mixing bowl, add the pieces of butter and toss in the flour so they are lightly coated. Rub* the butter into the flour until the mixture looks like fine crumbs. Break the egg into a small bowl, add 1½ tablespoons icy water and beat with a fork until combined. Add the egg mixture to the rubbed-in mixture and stir in with a round-bladed knife to make a firm dough. If there are dry crumbs or the dough feels hard, work in more water a teaspoon at a time. Shape the dough into a thick disc, wrap in clingfilm and chill for 15 minutes until firm but not hard.

2. You can also make the pastry very quickly in a food processor: put the flour and salt into the bowl and 'pulse' to combine. Add the cold butter and blitz just until the mixture looks like fine crumbs. Slowly pour in the egg mixture through the feed tube while the machine is running. As soon as a ball of dough forms, stop the machine. If it is difficult

to bring the dough together, add more water a teaspoon at a time, pulsing the machine just until a dough forms. Chill for 15 minutes.

3. Roll out the pastry on a lightly floured worktop to a disc about 32cm across and use to line* the flan tin. Leave the excess pastry hanging over the rim of the tin for now. Prick the base well with a fork, then chill for 15–20 minutes. Meanwhile, heat your oven to 190°C/375°F/gas 5.

4. Neaten the rim of the pastry case, trimming off the excess pastry. Line the case with baking paper and fill it with baking beans, then bake blind* in the heated oven for 12–15 minutes until the pastry is set and firm. Remove the paper and beans, then bake for a further 7–10 minutes until the pastry is crisp and golden brown.

5. Set the flan tin on a heatproof surface. Turn the oven down to 150°C/300°F/gas 2 and put the baking sheet in the oven to heat.

>>>

Serve 4–6

Kit you'll need: 1 x 23cm fluted round, deep, loose-based flan tin; a baking sheet

FOR THE PASTRY
175g plain flour
2 good pinches of salt
100g unsalted butter, chilled and diced
1 medium egg
1½–2 tablespoons icy cold water

FOR THE FILLING
150ml milk
150ml double cream
½ teaspoon black peppercorns
small sprig of fresh thyme
425g skinless, undyed smoked haddock fillets
250g baby leeks
½ teaspoon fine sea salt
2 tablespoons rapeseed oil
2 medium eggs
black pepper, to taste

6. While the pastry is chilling and then baking, you can get on with making the filling. Put the milk, cream, peppercorns and thyme sprig into a wide pan – wide enough to lay the fillets in it in a single layer. Arrange the fish in the liquid, skinned side down, taking care they are not overlapping. Set over medium/low heat and slowly bring to the boil. Leave to simmer for 5 minutes, then remove from the heat and leave the fish to finish cooking in the hot liquid and then cooling completely.

7. Trim the ends off the leeks – don't cut off too much of the green tops as they will add plenty of flavour. Thinly slice the leeks on a slight diagonal and put into a colander. Rinse under the cold tap, then sprinkle with the sea salt – this will help the leeks keep their texture. Leave for 5 minutes, then rinse well under the cold tap again and drain thoroughly.

8. Heat the oil in a frying pan over medium/high heat, add the drained leeks and stir-fry for about 5 minutes until softened but not coloured. If necessary, turn up the heat to evaporate any excess liquid. Tip the leeks into a heatproof bowl and leave to cool.

9. When the fish has cooled, lift it out of the liquid with a slotted spoon, draining off as much liquid as possible. Flake the flesh into the bowl containing the leeks, discarding any small bones, and mix together. Strain the cooking liquid into a measuring jug, then measure 250ml (discard the rest). Add the eggs and plenty of pepper and mix well.

10. Spoon the fish and leeks into the pastry case and spread evenly – don't pack firmly as you want the egg mixture to trickle down through the fish and leeks. Set the flan tin on the hot baking sheet and pour the egg mixture into the pastry case. Slide the baking sheet, with the tin on it, back into the heated oven and bake for 30–35 minutes until the filling is lightly coloured and just set (barely a wobble) when you gently jiggle the baking sheet.

11. Remove from the oven and leave to cool for 20–25 minutes before unmoulding. Best eaten the same or the next day, slightly warm or at room temperature. Keep any leftovers, well covered, in the fridge.

PRAWN COCKTAIL PUFFS

Party pieces made with choux pastry are perfect for handing round with drinks. Profiterole-sized savoury choux buns make fun, lidded containers for a classic filling of prawns in marie rose sauce. Both the buns and filling can be made well in advance, then quickly assembled. Another idea for choux canapés follows: incredibly more-ish cheese beignets that are quickly fried, instead of baked, and served hot.

<u>Makes 48</u>

Kit you'll need: a large disposable piping bag; 2 baking sheets, lined with baking paper

FOR THE CHOUX DOUGH
100g plain flour
175ml water
¼ teaspoon fine sea salt
75g unsalted butter, diced

3 medium eggs, at room
  temperature, beaten to mix
beaten egg, to glaze

TO FLAVOUR
2 good pinches of cayenne pepper
2 grinds of black pepper

FOR THE FILLING
400g cooked, peeled prawns
6 tablespoons good mayonnaise

2 tablespoons tomato ketchup
dash of Tabasco sauce
1 teaspoon brandy
small bunch of fresh chives,
  finely snipped
¼–½ fresh, medium-hot
  green chilli, seeded and
  finely chopped
paprika, for dusting

1. Sift the flour on to a sheet of greaseproof paper. Put the water, salt and butter into a medium pan and heat gently until the butter has melted – don't let the water boil yet. Turn up the heat and quickly bring the mixture to the boil, then tip in the flour all in one go. Remove the pan from the heat and beat furiously with a wooden spoon – the mixture will look like a mess at first, but as you beat it will turn into a smooth, heavy dough. Set the pan back on low heat and beat the dough for about 2 minutes to slightly cook it, until it comes away from the side of the pan in a smooth, glossy ball. Tip the dough into a large heatproof mixing bowl, or a free-standing electric mixer, and leave to cool until it is barely warm.

2. Using a hand-held electric whisk, or the mixer whisk attachment, gradually beat in the eggs, beating well after each addition, to make the dough very shiny and paste-like. It should just fall from a spoon when lightly shaken – you may not need the last tablespoon or so of egg as the choux dough needs to remain stiff enough to pipe. (If you have any egg left, save it for glazing, in which case you may not need to use another egg for this.)

3. Flavour the choux dough by beating in the cayenne and black pepper. If you are not going to use the choux immediately, cover the bowl with clingfilm and leave at cool room temperature for up to 4 hours.

4. Heat the oven to 200°C/400°F/gas 6. Spoon the dough into the piping bag, then snip off the tip to make an opening 1.5cm across. Pipe mounds about 3cm in diameter and 2.5cm high on the lined baking sheets, well apart to allow for expansion. Lightly brush with beaten egg, taking care it doesn't drip down and glue the pastry to the paper, which would prevent it from rising properly.

5. Bake in the heated oven for 15 minutes, then reduce the oven temperature to 180°C/350°F/gas 4. Quickly open and close the oven door (this will get rid of the steam), then bake for a further 7 minutes until the choux buns are crisp and golden.

>>>

6 Remove the sheets from the oven. Use a skewer to make a small hole at one side of each choux bun, to let out the steam trapped inside, then return to the oven. Bake for a final 5 minutes until very crisp and firm. Transfer to a wire rack and leave until cold before filling. (The buns can be kept in an airtight container for up to a day – if necessary, crisp up at 180°C/350°F/gas 4 for 5–8 minutes; cool before filling.)

7. To make the filling, drain the prawns well on kitchen paper, blotting moisture from the top too. Combine the mayonnaise, tomato ketchup, Tabasco, brandy and chives in a bowl and mix well. Add chilli to taste. Roughly chop the prawns and add to the sauce. Taste and add more Tabasco or chilli if you like – the mixture shouldn't be bland. If you are not filling the puffs immediately, cover the bowl and keep in the fridge until needed – up to 6 hours.

8. To assemble the puffs, split each choux bun horizontally, then spoon in a little of the filling and replace the lids. Arrange on serving plates, dust lightly with paprika and serve.

Variation

CHEESE BEIGNETS: Make the choux dough as in the Puffs recipe, but instead of cayenne and black pepper, flavour with 75g coarsely grated Gruyère cheese and a dash each of Tabasco and Worcestershire sauces. (If you are not frying the choux immediately, cover the bowl tightly and leave at cool room temperature for up to 4 hours.) Pour enough vegetable oil into a deep-sided medium pan to make a layer about 2.5cm deep and heat to 180°C. Scoop up a rounded teaspoonful of the choux dough and, using another spoon, push it off into the hot oil. Repeat until you have about 5 or 6 beignets in the oil. Fry for 4–5 minutes, turning them frequently, until they are a good golden brown. Lift them out of the oil with a slotted spoon and transfer them to a roasting tin lined with kitchen paper. Keep warm in a moderate oven while you fry the rest of the beignets. Sprinkle with a little flaked sea salt and serve as soon as possible, with Muhammara (see page 113). Makes about 50 beignets

CHEESE & WALNUT BISCOTTI

Savoury biscotti, twice-baked in the same way as the sweet ones, but gently spiced with cayenne pepper, make an excellent base for party canapés and starters. Use them like bruschetta (some topping ideas are below) or serve with salsa and dips such as Muhammara (see page 113). You can adjust the quantity of cayenne to make the biscotti more or less spicy, according to your taste.

Makes about 18

Kit you'll need: 1 baking sheet, lined with baking paper

50g walnut pieces
100g extra mature Cheddar, finely grated
25g Parmesan, freshly grated
about 175g plain flour
½ teaspoon baking powder
¼ teaspoon fine sea salt
⅛ teaspoon cayenne pepper, or to taste
2 medium eggs, beaten to mix

Some topping ideas

HAM AND CHEESE: Spread the biscotti with goat's cheese. Drape a piece of Parma ham over the top and finish with a basil leaf.
PEAR AND BLUE CHEESE: Spread the biscotti with blue cheese – a creamy Gorgonzola dolce works well. Top with thin slices of pear and a walnut half.
TOMATO AND MOZZARELLA: Arrange sliced tomatoes on the biscotti, top with some torn pieces of mozzarella and finish with a drizzle of extra virgin olive oil.

1. Heat the oven to 180°C/350°F/gas 4. Put the walnut pieces in a mixing bowl and gently crush them with the end of a rolling pin or a pestle, just to break them up slightly. Add both cheeses to the bowl, then sift 150g of the flour, the baking powder, salt and cayenne into the bowl. Mix everything together with your hand. Make a well in the centre and add the eggs, then mix with a round-bladed knife to make a slightly soft dough.

2. Sprinkle some of the remaining flour on to the worktop, then turn out the dough and gently knead it for a couple of minutes, working in as much of the remaining flour as needed to make a firm but not dry dough. Flour your hands and shape the dough into a neat brick 22 x 6.5 x 2.5cm.

3. Transfer the dough brick to the lined baking sheet and bake in the heated oven for 25–30 minutes until golden brown. Remove the sheet from the oven (leave the oven on) and set it on a heatproof surface. Leave the dough to cool, on the sheet, for 10 minutes.

4. Using a serrated bread knife, gently cut the brick across, on a slight diagonal, into slices about 1cm thick. Lay the slices flat on the baking sheet and return it to the oven. Bake for 11–12 minutes until starting to colour. Remove the sheet from the oven and, using a palette knife, turn the slices over. Bake for a further 10–11 minutes until the slices are lightly golden and feel firm.

5. Transfer the slices to a wire rack and leave to cool. Store in an airtight container and eat within 5 days.

ASPARAGUS AND PARMA HAM VOL-AU-VENTS

A triumph of the richest puff pastry, vol-au-vents are thought to have been created by the celebrated French chef Marie-Antoine Carême. One elaborate recipe, which included cockscombs, lobster tails and lambs' sweetbreads and brains, was made for a banquet at the Brighton Pavilion hosted by the Prince Regent in 1817. This one is a little more restrained! It makes the most of early summer vegetables dressed with a vibrant pesto and garnished with crisp Parma ham.

Makes 24

Kit you'll need: a 3cm and a 5cm plain round cutter; a large baking sheet, lined with baking paper; a silicone sheet; a disposable piping bag

FOR THE PUFF PASTRY
300g plain flour
½ teaspoon salt
185ml icy cold water
250g unsalted butter, well chilled
1 egg, beaten to mix, for brushing

FOR THE FILLING
60g Parma ham
115g full-fat cream cheese
100g baby asparagus
50g shelled small broad beans
100g shelled fresh young peas
  OR petits pois
50g tiny mangetout, cut in half
1 tablespoon basil oil
sea salt flakes and black pepper,
  to taste
lemon juice, to taste

FOR THE PESTO
50g fresh baby leaf spinach
handful of fresh basil leaves
10g sunflower seeds
10g pine nuts
50g Parmesan, freshly grated
50ml extra virgin olive oil

TO GARNISH
micro herbs (optional)
finely chopped fresh radishes

1. To make the pastry, put the flour and salt into the bowl of a free-standing electric mixer fitted with the paddle attachment. Mix well, then add the cold water and, on low speed, work just until the ingredients come together to make a rough, shaggy dough. If there are dry crumbs add more water a teaspoon at a time. Turn out on to a lightly floured worktop and shape into a rectangle about 1cm thick. Wrap in clingfilm and chill for 15 minutes.

2. Meanwhile, put the butter between 2 sheets of clingfilm and pound with a rolling pin until supple but still very cold. Shape into a square with 12cm sides.

3. Roll out the dough away from you on the lightly floured worktop to a 13 x 25cm rectangle. Set the butter on the dough so it almost covers the bottom half of the rectangle. Fold over the dough to enclose the butter, then press the edges together to seal. Gently roll out the dough away from you to a 15 x 30cm rectangle. Mark the centre of a long side, then fold the bottom edge up to this centre point and fold the top down, so the short sides meet. Now fold the dough over in half to complete your first 'book turn'. Repeat, to give the dough another book-turn, then cover with clingfilm and chill for 20 minutes. Repeat the process 2 more times so the dough has a total of 6 book turns. Wrap and chill for 30 minutes.

4. To shape the vol-au-vents, roll out the chilled pastry to a large rectangle 3.5mm thick. Stamp out 24 discs using the 5cm cutter — you should have slightly over a third of the pastry sheet left. Set the discs slightly apart on >>>

the lined baking sheet. Brush lightly with egg glaze and prick well with a fork. These will be the bases.

5. Now roll the rest of the pastry sheet slightly thinner – to about 2.5mm – and stamp out another 24 discs with the 5cm cutter. Use the 3cm cutter to stamp out the centre of each disc to make a neat ring. Set a pastry ring on top of each base and gently press in place. Lightly brush the tops of the rings with egg glaze – try not to let it trickle down the side as this will prevent the pastry from rising evenly.

6. Stack up all the trimmings and the centre discs cut from the rings (don't knead the pastry together). Re-roll and stamp out 24 more 5cm discs. Cut out the centres as before to make rings and set these on top of the vol-au-vents so each base is topped by 2 rings. Lightly brush the tops with egg glaze, then chill for 20 minutes.

7. Meanwhile, heat the oven to 200°C/400°F/gas 6. Set the silicone sheet over the top of the vol-au-vents (so they rise evenly) and bake in the heated oven for 10 minutes. Remove the silicone sheet and brush the top again

with egg glaze, then bake for a further 13–20 minutes until golden and crisp. Transfer to a wire rack to cool. Leave the oven on.

8. Lay the slices of Parma ham flat on the baking sheet lined with fresh baking paper and bake in the oven for 5 minutes until crisp. Quickly slice into long narrow shards or strips, about 8cm long, if possible – you'll need 24 plus a few extra to allow for breakages. Leave to cool.

9. To make the pesto, put all the ingredients in a food processor and blitz to a smooth paste. Taste and mix in some salt, pepper and lemon juice. Transfer the pesto to a screw-topped jar and keep in the fridge until needed.

10. Beat the cream cheese until smooth and slightly lighter, then season with salt, pepper and lemon juice to taste. Spoon into the piping bag and keep in the fridge until needed.

11. Trim 12 of the asparagus spears so the tips are 5cm long, then cut them in half lengthways. Put into a small pan and pour over boiling water to cover. Bring to the boil and blanch for 2 minutes.

Drain and quickly plunge into a bowl of icy cold water. Leave for a minute, then drain well. Set these tips aside for the garnish.

12. Chop the rest of the asparagus and the leftover stalks into 1cm pieces, then repeat the blanching/cooling/draining process. Set aside. Cook the broad beans, peas and mangetout in the same way – when the beans are cooled, gently slip off their outer grey skins to reveal the vivid green beans. Put all the vegetables into a bowl and gently mix in 2 teaspoons of the pesto and the basil oil. Cover and keep in the fridge until needed.

13. To assemble, gently press down the risen base inside each pastry case. Snip off the tip of the piping bag to make a 5mm opening, then pipe a disc of cream cheese into each pastry case. Spoon about ½ teaspoon of pesto on top. Add enough of the vegetable mixture to fill the case. Pipe a small dot of cream cheese on the top. Garnish with a halved asparagus tip and Parma ham shard. Arrange the vol-au-vents on a serving plate and finish with micro herbs and chopped radishes, then serve immediately. Save any leftover pesto for pasta.

SALMON & ASPARAGUS PIES

Served hot or cool, these pies are a very classy way to celebrate the British asparagus season, which traditionally kicks off on St George's Day on 23ʳᵈ April. They are lovely for a special occasion – maybe a day at the races or a birthday dinner on the patio. The rich, crisp, cream-cheese pastry, encasing the slimmest spears along with flakes of freshly cooked salmon, is easy to make and to shape.

Makes 6

Kit you'll need: I baking sheet; a 13cm plain round cutter (see recipe); a set of 6 individual, oval pie moulds in a tray, each mould greased with butter; a small shaped cutter (optional)

FOR THE PASTRY
300g plain flour
¼ teaspoon fine sea salt
½ teaspoon icing sugar

150g unsalted butter,
    chilled and diced
150g full-fat cream cheese, chilled
I medium egg yolk
grated zest of I medium
    unwaxed lemon, plus about
    I tablespoon juice

FOR THE FILLING
softened butter, for greasing
I x 500g piece salmon fillet
    (preferably from the thick top
    end), pinboned if necessary

24 very fine asparagus spears
    (about 130g)
beaten egg, to glaze

FOR THE HOLLANDAISE
SAUCE (OPTIONAL)
3 medium egg yolks,
    at room temperature
2 tablespoons water
juice of ½ medium lemon,
    or to taste
175g unsalted butter
salt and pepper, to taste

1. To make the pastry, put the flour, salt and icing sugar (this makes the pastry extra crisp) into a food processor and 'pulse' a couple of times to combine. Add the butter and blitz until the mixture looks like fine crumbs. Break up the cream cheese and add to the processor with the egg yolk, half of the lemon zest (save the rest for the filling) and the juice. Blitz just until the mixture comes together to make a firm and slightly waxy dough.

2. Remove the dough from the processor, flatten it to a thick disc and wrap in clingfilm. Chill for at least 45 minutes or up to 3 hours.

3. Meanwhile, make the filling. Heat the oven to 180°C/350°F/ gas 4. Lay a large sheet of foil on the worktop and butter it generously. Set the salmon in the middle of the buttered foil and wrap it up tightly to make a neat, sealed parcel. Set it on the baking sheet and bake in the heated oven for 25 minutes. Remove from the oven and leave the parcel, unopened, until completely cold.

4. Remove the tough ends from the asparagus spears by bending them until they snap. Drop the spears into a wide pan of lightly salted boiling water and boil for I minute. Drain, then quickly plunge the spears into a bowl of icy cold water and leave for 2 minutes. Drain thoroughly and pat dry on kitchen paper. Cut off the tips of the spears in 8cm lengths (save the stalks to flavour the hollandaise sauce, or to use in a salad, risotto or soup).

>>>

5. When the salmon is cold, unwrap the parcel. Tip the juices into a bowl and add the remaining lemon zest. Flake the fish fairly finely into the bowl, discarding the skin and any stray bones. Season the fish lightly with salt and pepper, then mix gently and taste – you may need to add a little more seasoning or even a few drops of lemon juice.

6. Roll out the pastry on a floured worktop to 4mm thickness. Using the 13cm plain round cutter, or a saucer, cut out 6 discs. Gather up the trimmings, re-roll the pastry and stamp out 6 ovals for the lids, using one of the individual pie moulds as a cutter. Save the trimmings for the decoration. Gently lift a pastry disc into each buttered pie mould and press on to the base, then ease the pastry up the sides, pressing out any air pockets and creases with the tips of your fingers. Continue easing the pastry so it extends 4mm above the rim of the mould.

7. Half fill the pastry cases with salmon. Set 4 asparagus tips in each case, arranging the tips head to tail, then cover with the remaining salmon to fill the cases. Finish each case by brushing the pastry rim with beaten egg, then setting a lid on top. Pinch and seal the edges together firmly. Cut a small steam hole in the centre of the lid using the tip of a small sharp knife. Re-roll the pastry trimmings and cut out small shapes such as tiny stars or flowers. Stick these on to the lids with a dab of beaten egg. Chill for 30 minutes.

8. Towards the end of the chilling time, heat the oven to 190°C/375°F/gas 5. Gently brush the tops of the pies with beaten egg, then bake in the heated oven for 30 minutes until a light golden brown. Remove the tray of moulds from the oven and, wearing oven gloves, lift each individual mould out of the tray (hold each end of the mould firmly) and set it on the baking sheet. Let go of the ends so the sides of the mould fall away. Remove them, then brush the top and sides of each pie with beaten egg. Bake for a further 5–7 minutes until a good golden colour all over.

8. While the pies are baking, make the optional hollandaise (if you are intending to serve the pies at room temperature, make the hollandaise later). Put the egg yolks, water and lemon juice into a food processor or blender. Add some salt and pepper and blitz for about 10 seconds until just combined. Melt the butter in a small pan over low heat. Skim off the froth from the surface, then continue to heat the butter until it is very hot but not quite boiling. With the machine running, pour the hot butter into the processor or blender through the feed tube, in a thin, steady stream. Stop the machine as soon as all the butter has been added and the sauce is creamy and thick. Taste and add more salt or pepper (or lemon juice), if needed. If you like, finely chop enough of the saved asparagus stalks to make 3 tablespoons and warm for a few seconds in the microwave, then stir into the sauce. Transfer the hollandaise to a serving bowl and keep warm.

10. Eat the pies hot from the oven, warm or at room temperature, with hollandaise sauce or mayonnaise, new potatoes and salads. The pies can be left to cool, then kept in an airtight container in the fridge overnight; bring back to room temperature before serving.

ROASTED RED ONION TATINS

The famous inverted tart of caramelised apples in puff pastry is attributed to the Tatin sisters who lived in the Loire Valley town of Lamotte-Beuvron in the late 19th century. The same idea also works beautifully with halved red onions, roasted until sticky and tender. The tatins make a great accompaniment to steak or a roast for a special occasion meal.

1. Heat the oven to 200°C/400°F/gas 6. Peel the onions and trim the root and stem ends very slightly so they still hold the onion together at each end. Cut the onions in half across the circumference.

2. Put the butter in a roasting tin just big enough to hold the onion halves in a single layer and set it over medium/low heat. When the butter melts and starts to bubble, sprinkle the sugar over the butter, then set the onions on top, cut-side down. Scatter the thyme leaves over the onions and season with a little salt and pepper. Spoon in the vinegar and stock. Tightly cover the tin with foil, then put it into the heated oven and roast for 20 minutes.

3. Remove the tin from the oven and remove the foil. Baste the onions by spooning the sticky juices over them, then return the tin, uncovered, to the oven. Turn down the temperature to 180°C/350°F/gas 4 and roast

for 10 minutes. Baste the onions again – if the juices are getting very thick and are in danger of burning, add a couple of tablespoons of stock or water to the tin. Check the onions with the tip of a sharp knife – if they are not yet tender, roast for a further 10 minutes and check again.

4. Remove the tin from the oven and leave the onions to cool in the sticky juices until completely cold. At this point the onions can be kept at cool room temperature for up to 4 hours before finishing. When you're ready to bake the tatins, carefully lift the onion halves out of the roasting tin (they'll be very soft and you want them to stay intact) and set them, cut-side down and well apart, on the lined baking sheet.

5. Roll out the pastry on a lightly floured worktop to a 20 × 30cm rectangle. You need to cut out discs that will be big enough to cover the onion halves; if your onions are very large >>>

Makes 6

Kit you'll need: 1 baking sheet, lined with baking paper; a 10cm plain round cutter

3 medium/large red onions
35g unsalted butter
1 tablespoon demerara sugar
small sprig of fresh thyme
1 tablespoon red wine
  or cider vinegar
3 tablespoons vegetable stock
salt and pepper, to taste

TO FINISH
½ quantity Puff Pastry
  (see page 285), well chilled, OR
  375g ready-made all-butter puff
  pastry, thawed if frozen

Tip

All the preparation can be done well ahead so you only have to pop the tatins in the oven about 20 minutes before serving.

you'll need to use a cutter bigger than 10cm, or you could cut around a small dish or saucer. Dip the cutter in flour and stamp out 6 discs. Lay one over the top of each onion dome and gently press and mould it to completely cover the onion. With the rounded end of a palette knife, delicately tuck the edge of the pastry disc under the edge of the onion base. Prick the top of each pastry dome lightly with a fork, then chill for 10–15 minutes.

6. Meanwhile, heat the oven to 220°C/425°F/gas 7. Bake the tatins for about 20 minutes until the pastry is crisp and golden. Carefully turn each tatin over so the sticky cut onion is revealed and serve immediately.

'I always enjoy making pies and tarts and working with pastry. On my travels in Europe I've picked up influences from French, German and Italian baking, and I love Lebanese flavours. I bring ideas home and then put my own spin on them.'

STUART

RAISED GAME PIE

Raised pies have been a favourite of the British table for centuries, at one time majestic, elaborate constructions decorated with pastry columns, crests and coats of arms. This is a slightly more restrained version, but it is still a great-looking centrepiece for an autumnal party. A mixture of venison, rabbit, pheasant, pigeon or wild boar (according to what game you like, and what is available) is encased in crisp and rich, hot-water-crust pastry, which traps all the savoury meat juices without becoming soggy.

Serves 12

Kit you'll need: I large, oval raised/game pie mould OR a 20cm round springclip tin, 7cm deep, greased with lard; a 2.5cm oak leaf cutter OR leaf-shaped cutter; a baking sheet

FOR THE FILLING
700g boneless mixed game meat, diced
200g rindless back bacon, diced
200g minced pork belly (unsmoked)
2 banana shallots, finely chopped
2 garlic cloves, crushed
2 tablespoons Madeira
½ teaspoon ground mace
½ teaspoon ground allspice
2 tablespoons chopped fresh parsley
2 tablespoons chopped fresh thyme
salt and pepper, to taste

FOR THE HOT-WATER-CRUST PASTRY
450g plain flour
100g strong white bread flour
75g chilled unsalted butter, cut into 1cm cubes
200ml water
½ teaspoon salt
100g lard

TO GLAZE
I egg yolk, beaten

1. Start by making the filling so the flavours have time to develop. Put all the ingredients into a large bowl. Add a little salt and pepper, then mix everything together with your hands until thoroughly combined. Take a teaspoon of the mixture, shape it into a small 'burger' and fry it for a minute or so on each side until cooked through, then taste and add more seasoning to the filling mixture, if necessary. Cover and chill while you make the pastry.

2. Heat the oven to 200°C/400°F/ gas 6. Combine both flours and a pinch of salt in a mixing bowl. Add the butter and rub in* lightly using your fingertips. Pour the water into a small pan and add the salt and lard. Heat gently until the lard has melted, then bring to the boil. Pour the hot mixture on to the flour and quickly mix everything together with a wooden spoon to make a dough. As soon as the dough is cool enough to handle, tip it out on to a floured worktop and knead it just until smooth and even.

3. This pastry becomes crumbly as it cools, so you need to work quickly now. Cut off a third of the pastry and wrap it tightly in clingfilm. Roll out the remaining pastry to an oval or disc large enough to line your tin. Carefully lift the pastry into the tin and press it on to the base and side, smoothing out wrinkles. Leave excess pastry hanging over the rim. Check there are no cracks or holes in the pastry case – press the pastry together or patch with small scraps of pastry.

>>>

4. Roll out the remaining pastry to an oval or disc, slightly larger than the top of your tin, to form the lid. Cover with clingfilm and leave on the worktop for now.

5. Spoon the filling into the pastry-lined tin and press it down well, making sure the surface is level. Brush the edge of the pastry case with beaten egg yolk, then lay the pastry lid on top. Press the edges of the case and lid together firmly to seal. Trim off the excess pastry and crimp or flute* the edge neatly. Make a hole in the centre of the lid to allow steam to escape during baking.

6. Gather up the pastry trimmings and roll them out again. Stamp out 20 leaves with the shaped cutter. Attach these to the pastry lid, using a dab of beaten egg yolk as glue. Brush the lid all over with beaten egg yolk to glaze.

7. Set the tin on the baking sheet and bake in the heated oven for 30 minutes. Turn down the oven temperature to 170°C/325°F/gas 3 and bake the pie for a further 1¾ hours until the pastry is a rich golden brown.

8. Leave the pie in its tin until completely cold before unmoulding. Serve at room temperature, on a rimmed plate to catch any juices. Store any leftovers, tightly wrapped, in the fridge.

BONFIRE CHILLI WITH CORNBREAD TOPPING

On Bonfire Night, you need good hot food so a home-made chilli is spot on, here with a tasty, fluffy Texas-style cornbread topping, dropped on top of the bubbling chilli like dumplings, towards the end of its time in the oven. If you want some fire in your cornbread as well, you can use chopped green chilli instead of chives. A bowl of soured cream and a good green salad complete the meal.

Serves 4–6

Kit you'll need: a large flameproof casserole with lid (see recipe)

FOR THE CHILLI
2 tablespoons rapeseed oil
450g lean minced beef
1 large red onion, finely chopped
4 garlic cloves, or to taste, crushed
½–1 teaspoon hot/mild chilli powder, to taste
1 teaspoon ground cumin

1 tablespoon tomato purée
2 x 400g tins chopped tomatoes
3 tablespoons water
2 medium red peppers, cored and cut into 2cm chunks
1 x 400g tin red kidney beans, drained and rinsed
salt and pepper, to taste

FOR THE CORNBREAD TOPPING
140g medium/fine yellow cornmeal OR polenta

125g plain flour
½ teaspoon bicarbonate of soda
1 teaspoon baking powder
¼ teaspoon fine sea salt
small bunch of fresh chives, finely snipped
225ml buttermilk
1 medium egg
1 tablespoon clear honey
50g unsalted butter, melted

TO SERVE
soured cream

1. Heat the oven to 180°C/350°F/gas 4. Heat the oil in the casserole over medium/high heat. (If your casserole isn't flameproof, you can cook the chilli on top of the stove in a large saucepan, then transfer it to a casserole before adding the topping.) Add the beef and fry, stirring constantly, until lightly coloured and broken up. Push the meat to one side and turn down the heat, then add the chopped onion to the other side of the casserole. Cook gently, stirring occasionally, for about 7 minutes until softened but not browned.

Add the garlic, ½ teaspoon chilli powder, the cumin, a good pinch each of salt and pepper and the tomato purée. Stir everything together. Cook for a further 2 minutes, stirring frequently.

2. Add the tomatoes to the casserole. Pour the water into one empty tomato tin and swish it around to clean it out, then tip the water into the second tin, swish it around and pour into the casserole. Stir well and bring the mixture to the boil. Cover with the lid and transfer the casserole

to the oven. Cook for 30 minutes. (If you are simmering the chilli in a covered pan on top of the stove, stir occasionally.)

3. Stir the chilli well, then stir in the red peppers and beans. Cover again and return to the oven to cook for 15 minutes.

4. Remove the chilli from the oven (leave the oven on) and give it a stir. Taste and add more chilli powder, salt and pepper as needed, so it has just the right amount of 'heat' for your family >>>

or guests. If you have made the chilli in a saucepan, transfer it to a casserole. Set aside.

5. To make the topping, combine the cornmeal, flour, bicarbonate of soda, baking powder, salt, chives and 3–4 grinds of pepper in a mixing bowl and make a well in the centre. Measure the buttermilk in a jug and add the egg, honey and melted butter. Mix with a fork, then pour into the well. Stir everything together thoroughly using a wooden spoon – the mixture will be thick and sticky.

6. Drop heaped spoonfuls of the cornbread mixture on top of the chilli to cover the surface. Leave the cornbread mounds looking rough – don't spread them out – so there is a little space between them for the sauce to bubble up. Place in the heated oven and bake for about 30 minutes until the chilli is bubbling and the cornbread topping is set and a nice golden brown. Serve piping hot, with soured cream.

Note

The chilli can be made ahead, then left to cool and kept, tightly covered, in the fridge for up to 3 days. Bring the chilli back to the boil on top of the stove before adding the topping. If the chilli seems dry and lacking in sauce, add a little water to loosen it up. If you have any topping left over, form it into golfball-sized mounds and set, slightly apart, on a baking sheet lined with baking paper. Bake alongside the chilli for 20–25 minutes until golden brown.

LEMON SUET CRUST PHEASANT PIE

Celebrate the relatively short pheasant season (from October to February) with this very light and fresh-tasting combination of pheasant breast chunks and small sausagemeat balls, baked with vegetables and cider under a crisp, quick-to-make, lemony suet crust. It's testimony to the fact that game dishes don't have to be rich and heavy or time-consuming to make.

Serves 4–6

Kit you'll need: 1 pie dish, 1.25–1.5-litre capacity, with a pie raiser OR egg cup

FOR THE FILLING
6 skinless, boneless pheasant breasts (about 500g) OR partridge breast meat
1½ tablespoons plain flour
375g meaty sausages (350g skinned weight)
about 2 tablespoons rapeseed oil

1 medium onion, finely diced
1 medium carrot, peeled and finely diced
1 celery stick, finely diced
leaves picked from a small sprig of fresh thyme
150ml medium dry cider
100ml game, chicken or vegetable stock
salt and pepper, to taste

FOR THE SUET-CRUST PASTRY
200g self-raising flour
50g fresh white breadcrumbs
¼ teaspoon salt
leaves picked from a small sprig of fresh thyme
finely grated zest of 1 medium unwaxed lemon
100g beef or vegetable suet
about 200ml icy cold water, to mix
beaten egg, to glaze

1. Cut each pheasant breast into 8 chunks (if using partridge, cut it into large chunks). Put the flour on a plate or into a plastic bag, add a little salt and pepper and mix well. Add the chunks of pheasant and toss in the seasoned flour to coat. Remove the skin from the sausages. With floured hands, roll the sausagemeat into 18 small balls.

2. Heat the rapeseed oil in a frying pan (preferably non-stick) over medium heat and quickly brown the pheasant, in batches, for about 1 minute on each side until lightly coloured. Remove with a slotted spoon to a clean plate. When all the chunks of pheasant have been browned, add all the sausagemeat balls to the pan (you may need to add a little more oil) and fry until evenly browned. Transfer with the slotted spoon to the plate with the pheasant. Take the pan off the heat.

3. Add the onion, carrot and celery to the fat remaining in the frying pan, then stir in the thyme leaves and set over low heat. Cook gently, stirring frequently, for 5–8 minutes until the vegetables are soft and very lightly coloured (don't let them brown). If there is any seasoned flour left on the plate, add it to the pan and stir well, then pour in the cider. Turn up the heat to medium and bring to the boil, stirring constantly to scrape up all the scraps of meat left on the base of the pan. Add the stock and simmer gently for a couple of minutes. Taste and adjust the seasoning. Remove from the heat and leave the cider mixture to cool (it will be fairly thin) while you make the pastry.

>>>

4. Put the flour, breadcrumbs, suet, salt, thyme leaves and lemon zest in a mixing bowl. Mix well with your hand or a round-bladed knife, then use the knife to stir in enough icy cold water to make a slightly firm, shaggy-looking but elastic dough. Turn out on to a lightly floured worktop and knead for a couple of seconds just to make a smooth ball of dough. Cover with the upturned bowl and leave to rest for 10 minutes.

5. Meanwhile, heat the oven to 180°C/350°F/gas 4 and set the pie raiser (or egg cup) in the centre of the pie dish. Spoon the pheasant and sausagemeat balls into the dish around the pie raiser, then add the cider mixture.

6. Roll out the pastry on the lightly floured worktop to the shape of your pie dish but 3cm larger all around than the dish. Dampen the rim of the dish with water. Cut a strip of pastry about 1.5cm wide from all around the edge of the pastry shape and press it on to the rim of the dish. Brush the strip with water. Wrap the remainder of the pastry shape loosely around the rolling pin and gently unroll over the dish, letting the pie funnel poke through (you may need to make a small slit in the pastry lid for this). Using your thumbs, gently press the edge of the lid firmly to the pastry strip on the rim to seal. Cut off excess pastry with a sharp knife (keep these trimmings).

7 Use the back of a small knife to knock up* the pastry edge, then flute or scallop* it. Brush the pastry lid lightly and evenly with beaten egg, then cut a couple of steam holes using the tip of a sharp knife. If you like, use the trimmings to make cut-out shapes and attach to the top of the pie with a dab of beaten egg.

8 Bake in the heated oven for about 40 minutes until the pastry is crisp and a rich golden brown. Serve hot with steamed green vegetables and creamy mashed celeriac or potatoes.

'For Boxing day, I like to make mini pork pies with pork fillet meat, sage and thyme, packed around a boiled quail's egg, with a jelly made from chicken stock funnelled in after baking.'

PAUL

MATHRI WITH FRESH PEACH & GINGER PICKLE

If you are a fan of tortilla chips with salsa, try these for a change. These spicy, crisp-fried Rajasthani snacks are irresistible eaten warm with a fruity pickle for dipping. The dough, flavoured with peppercorns, cumin seeds and ajwain or carom seeds, is quick to make and the mathri puff up as they fry.

1. Put the butter in a small pan and set over low heat. Once the butter has melted, turn up the heat and bubble the butter for a minute. Remove from the heat and tilt the pan, then carefully skim off and discard all the white foam that's floating on the surface. Slowly pour the clear yellow butter into a heatproof bowl, leaving behind the milky white liquid on the bottom of the pan; discard this. Leave the clear (clarified) butter to cool until needed.

2. Sift the wholemeal flour into a bowl. Discard the pieces of bran left in the sieve, then weigh 110g of the sifted flour and put it in a mixing bowl. Sift the white flour, baking powder and salt into the bowl. Add the cumin and ajwain seeds. Put the peppercorns in a mortar and crack with a pestle (you want large pieces, not ground pepper); add to the bowl. Mix everything together, then make a well in the centre.

3. Pour the clarified butter into the well along with 125ml water. Stir with a round-bladed knife to make a soft but not sticky dough, adding more water as needed. The dough should feel like shortcrust pastry. Turn out on to a lightly floured worktop and roll out 2.5mm thick. Stamp out discs with the floured cutter. Prick them well with a fork.

4. Pour enough oil into a medium saucepan to make a layer about 2.5cm deep. Heat until the oil reaches 160°C. Fry the dough discs, in batches of 3 or 4, for about 1½ minutes on each side until puffed and very lightly coloured – they shouldn't be browned, so adjust the heat as necessary. Use a slotted spoon to remove the mathri from the oil and drain on kitchen paper. Eat the same day, warm or at room temperature, with peach and ginger pickle.

Makes about 24

Kit you'll need: 6.5cm plain round cutter; a deep-frying thermometer

65g unsalted butter
about 125g plain wholemeal flour
110g plain white flour
¼ teaspoon baking powder
3g fine sea salt
½ teaspoon cumin seeds
1 teaspoon (3g) ajwain/carom seeds
½ teaspoon (2g) black peppercorns
125–150ml water, at room temperature
vegetable oil, for frying

TO SERVE
Fresh Peach and Ginger Pickle (see page 246)

FRESH PEACH & GINGER PICKLE

Quick to make and ready to eat the same day, this spicy pickle is delicious with Mathri (see page 244), as well as with poppadoms or cold meats. It is lower in salt than many other pickles.

Makes about 1kg

juice of 1 large lemon
4 large, firm peaches
3g (about ½ teaspoon)
    fine sea salt
3g (about ½ teaspoon)
    brown mustard seeds
3g (about ½ teaspoon)
    cumin seeds
2 good pinches of fennel seeds
1½ tablespoons rapeseed oil
4cm cube fresh root ginger,
    peeled and finely chopped or
    coarsely grated
¼ teaspoon ground turmeric
⅛ teaspoon chilli flakes
200ml cold water
50g demerara sugar

1. Put the lemon juice into a large bowl. Quarter the peaches and remove the stones. Slice each quarter in half, then cut each slice across into 3 chunks. Put these into the lemon juice and toss gently. Sprinkle with the salt and toss again, then leave to macerate until needed.

2. Lightly crack (don't crush) the mustard, cumin and fennel seeds using a pestle and mortar. Heat the oil in a medium pan (large enough to hold all the ingredients) over medium heat and add the cracked seeds. Stir for a couple of seconds until they start to 'pop', then add the ginger (with any juice from chopping/grating) and stir for 20 seconds. Stir in the turmeric and chilli flakes. Pour in the water and bring to the boil, then simmer gently for 10 minutes.

3. Add the peaches with any liquid in the bowl. Bring back to the boil and simmer for a couple of minutes, then stir in the sugar. Boil gently, stirring frequently, for 20–25 minutes until the peaches are very soft and the liquid is thick and sticky. Leave to cool before serving at room temperature. The pickle can be kept, tightly covered, in the fridge for 4 days.

BOUREKAS

Made in various forms from North Africa to the Mediterranean, and from the Middle East to Eastern Europe, bourekas have travelled a long way from their roots in the Ottoman Empire. These crisp, triangular pastries with a cheese and parsley filling make great party fare – try them with the toasted walnut and red pepper dip, Muhammara (see page 113).

Makes 16

Kit you'll need: 2 baking sheets, lined with baking paper

½ quantity Puff Pastry
    (see page 285), well chilled, OR
    375g ready-made all-butter
    puff pastry, thawed if frozen
75g ricotta
75g feta cheese, crumbled
1 tablespoon chopped
    fresh parsley
cayenne pepper, to taste
1 medium egg, beaten to mix
salt and pepper, to taste

TO FINISH
2 teaspoons sesame seeds
2 pinches of nigella seeds

1. Flour your worktop, then roll out the pastry to a square with 40cm sides. Leave to rest for a minute while you make the filling.

2. Put the ricotta, crumbled feta and parsley into bowl and mix well. Season with cayenne, salt and pepper to taste. Add a tablespoon of the beaten egg and mix thoroughly.

3. Lightly brush the pastry square with beaten egg, then, using a ruler and a pizza wheel-cutter or a large floured knife, cut into 16 squares. Spoon a rounded teaspoon of filling on to the centre of each square, then fold the square over in half to make a neat triangle. Press the edges

together firmly to seal. With the back of a small knife, knock up* the edges, then flute* them. It's important to seal the edges well to prevent the filling from leaking out during baking. Arrange the triangles, slightly apart, on the lined baking sheets and chill for 20 minutes.

4. Heat the oven to 200°C/400°F/ gas 6. Lightly brush the triangles with beaten egg. Mix together the sesame and nigella seeds and sprinkle on to the pastries. Bake in the heated oven for 15–18 minutes until crisp and golden. Transfer to a wire rack and leave to cool. Eat warm or at room temperature the same day.

PARTY PALMIERS

Crisp, buttery puff pastry makes lovely canapés for a party, served warm from the oven with drinks. These savoury, heart-shaped palmiers are the elegant cousins of cheese straws and they don't take that much longer to prepare. If you don't want to include prosciutto, just leave it out and increase the quantity of cheese to 90g.

1. Lightly flour your worktop and roll out the pastry to a very thin 50 × 20cm rectangle. If necessary, turn the pastry so it lies horizontally on the worktop (the long sides are top and bottom). Neatly trim the edges with a pizza wheel-cutter or a large, sharp knife.

2. Brush the pastry with beaten egg. Combine the grated cheese and mustard powder, then sprinkle half evenly over the pastry. Cover with the slices of Parma ham, arranging them in a single layer. Scatter the remaining cheese mixture over the top. Gently press the topping on to the pastry with the flat of your hand.

3. Using a ruler, mark the centre point along one long side, then, starting from a short edge, roll up the pastry tightly, like a swiss roll, until it reaches the centre point. Repeat from the other short edge so that the rolls meet in the centre. Carefully brush the edges of the rolls, where they meet, with beaten egg, then press them together.

4. Line one of the baking sheets with clingfilm. Lift the rolled pastry on to the clingfilm and wrap it tightly. Chill, on the baking sheet, for at least 1 hour or up to 2 days.

5. When you're ready to bake, heat the oven to 200°C/400°F/ gas 6. Set the rolled dough on the worktop and unwrap. Line the 2 baking sheets with baking paper. Using a large, sharp knife, cut the rolled dough across into 1cm-thick slices and lay them, slightly apart, on the baking sheets.

6. Bake in the heated oven for 12 minutes. Remove the baking sheets from the oven and carefully flip the palmiers over with a palette knife. Bake for a further 5–7 minutes until golden brown. Transfer to a wire rack and leave to cool. Serve warm or at room temperature the same day.

Makes 20

Kit you'll need: 2 baking sheets

½ quantity Puff Pastry
    (see page 285), well chilled, OR
    375g ready-made all-butter
    puff pastry, thawed if frozen
1 medium egg, beaten to mix
70g Parmesan, freshly grated
2 good pinches
    of mustard powder
90g Parma ham, thinly sliced

SWEET
PASTRY & PATISSERIE

From the crumbly sweet shortcrust encompassing a filling of homely mincemeat, to the rich pâte sucrée base of Florentine Pastries (page 293), or the crisp flakiness of a vol-au-vent holding chocolate and praline, there is nothing like the melt-in-the-mouth sweetness of a delicious pastry to celebrate everything that is seductive about baking.

Many of the pastries in this chapter can be easily made in a food processor, but some need a little investment in time and practice to perfect – though, like Sandy, you might feel the talent for pastry runs in your family. 'Whenever we have a family celebration my mum will bring her famous apple pie,' she says. 'Both my grandmothers made wonderful pastry, and I think my mum, sister and I have inherited "the family fingers" for pastry. The secret is definitely in the cold touch.'

For Sandy, few things beat the 'classic and true' flavours for a tart: lemon (page 266), chocolate (page 276) or fruit (page 254). However, a great pastry base, filled with classic crème pâtissière, invites you to explore a wealth of flavours and toppings. Marie was first drawn to baking by the displays in Parisian pâtisseries of just such stunning tarts, studded with berries, apricots, pears and architectural arrangements of sliced glazed apples. 'I still love to make a classic tart with a spiral of apples, figs or blood oranges,' she says. If you're lucky enough, like Paul, to have fruit growing in your garden, you can ring the changes throughout the seasons with rhubarb, gooseberries, blackcurrants or, in the height of summer, strawberries, 'finished', as he suggests 'with a piping of Chantilly cream'.

The rich, almondy nature of frangipane makes a pastry filling that is easily adaptable to summer or winter toppings. The recipe on page 260 suggests peaches and raspberries, while for Mat, rhubarb 'is right up my street. As someone who generally prefers savoury over sweet, I like the contrasting sharpness.' The Christmas Frangipane Tart (page 289) is redolent with flavours of the festive season: wine mulled with cinnamon, cloves and allspice for poaching pears, set off with a decoration of Christmas trees piped in white icing. You could even create your own special celebration version, as Ian did for 'Super Saturday', the day of six gold medals for Team GB at the London Olympics, by making a frangipane tart and decorating it with a Union Jack design fashioned from red and white currants and blueberries.

All our Bakers also love a spot of chocolate indulgence – 'a chocolate tart always goes down well at the fire station', says Mat, so there are plenty of chocolatey recipes here to satisfy such cravings. And don't forget you can use any egg whites left over from making sweet pastry to whip up some Pistachio Meringue Sea Shells (page 263).

SUMMER BERRY LINZER TORTE

Named after the Austrian town of Linz where it was created, this is a festive latticed confection that is usually filled with raspberry conserve. But when fresh berries are at their peak it seems crazy not to make the most of them. The pastry is so rich it is almost like shortbread, which makes it difficult to line the tin in the normal way, so instead it is pressed on to the base and up the side, and the lattice top is created in layers, rather than woven – an easier but effective alternative.

1. Heat the oven to 180°C/350°F/gas 4. Tip the hazelnuts and almonds into a small baking dish or tin and toast in the heated oven for about 10 minutes until lightly golden. Cool. You can turn off the oven for now.

2. Put the toasted nuts in a food processor with 3 tablespoons of the weighed flour and 'pulse' until fairly coarsely ground. Add the lemon zest, cinnamon and sugar and pulse until finely ground. Scrape down the side of the bowl, then add the rest of the flour and the salt and pulse briefly, just until combined. Add the pieces of butter and blitz until the mixture looks like breadcrumbs. Add the egg and blitz just until the dough comes together in small clumps.

3. Tip half of the dough clumps into the flan tin and set aside. Tip the rest of the dough on to the worktop and knead it briefly until it comes together into a slightly sticky, heavy dough. Shape into a thick disc, wrap in clingfilm and keep in the fridge until needed.

4. Flour your fingers, then press the dough clumps in the flan tin over the base and up the sides to the rim to cover evenly. Chill for 30 minutes until very firm.

5. Towards the end of the chilling time, heat the oven again to 180°C/350°F/gas 4. Line the pastry case with baking paper, fill with baking beans and bake blind* for 11 minutes. Remove the paper and beans and bake for a further 10 minutes until firm and the edge is starting to colour. Leave to cool completely. You can turn off the oven for now.

6. While the pastry case is cooling, make the fruit filling. Put the blueberries, raspberries, lemon zest and juice, and caster sugar into a medium pan and set over medium/low heat. When the juices start to run, stir the fruit gently and turn up the heat so the mixture comes to a fast boil. >>>

Serves 8–10

Kit you'll need: 1 x 23cm fluted round, deep, loose-based flan tin; a baking sheet

FOR THE NUT PASTRY
150g blanched hazelnuts
75g blanched almonds
225g plain flour
finely grated zest
    of 1 medium unwaxed lemon
½ teaspoon ground cinnamon
125g caster sugar
good pinch of salt
160g unsalted butter,
    chilled and diced
1 medium egg, plus 1 yolk,
    beaten together to mix

FOR THE FRUIT FILLING
250g fresh blueberries
250g fresh raspberries
finely grated zest and juice
    of 1 medium unwaxed lemon
75g caster sugar
icing sugar, for dusting

Boil, stirring frequently, for about 7 minutes until the fruit mixture is thick and jammy. Pour into a heatproof bowl and leave to cool, then cover and keep in the fridge until needed.

7. When the pastry case is cold, roll out the thick disc of dough on the well-floured worktop to an 18 × 24cm rectangle. Trim the long edges to neaten them, then cut the rectangle lengthways into 10 strips, each 1.5 × 24cm.

8. Turn the oven on again to 180°C/350°F/gas 4, and put the baking sheet in to heat.

9. Spoon the fruit filling into the pastry case. Now you are going to make a pastry lattice on top. Flour a palette knife and slide it under one pastry strip. Lift it over the filling and lay it vertically down the centre. Press the ends of the strip on to the pastry rim and trim off the excess (keep all the pastry trimmings). Lift a second

strip and lay it parallel to the centre strip about 2cm from the edge. Repeat with a third strip, laying it parallel to the centre strip on the other side of it.

10. Turn the pastry case on the worktop 90 degrees so the strips are now running horizontally in front of you. Repeat the whole process: lay one strip vertically down the centre and place parallel strips on either side.

11. Turn the case 90 degrees again so it is back to its original position. Now place a strip vertically in between the centre strip and second strip you put in place. Lay another strip on the other side of the centre strip, halfway between the centre strip and the third strip you put in place.

12. Finally, turn the pastry case 90 degrees and set the last of the strips in place, each one halfway between the centre strip and the ones on either side.

13. Gather up all the pastry trimmings and roll into a sausage about 1cm thick. Press this around the rim of the pastry case to cover all the ends of the strips – don't worry if there are breaks in the strips or the edging; just push them back together.

14. Set the tin on the heated baking sheet and bake for about 35 minutes until golden brown – check after 25 minutes and rotate the tin if necessary so the torte bakes evenly. Remove from the oven and leave to cool and firm up for 10 minutes before carefully unmoulding. Dust the torte with icing sugar and serve warm or at room temperature. Best eaten the same or the next day.

RICH & TINY ECCLES CAKES

These elegant little cakes are long way from the original version made by James Birch in his shop in Eccles in the 1870s. Dainty enough to serve as petits fours or on a tiered cake stand, they still comprise the traditional spicy filling of fruit and ground almonds encased in flaky pastry and finished with the signature crunchy sugar crust.

Makes about 38

Kit you'll need: **a 6.5cm plain round cutter; 2 baking sheets, lined with baking paper**

FOR THE FLAKY PASTRY
225g plain flour
¼ teaspoon fine salt
175g unsalted butter, chilled
1 teaspoon lemon juice
about 125ml icy cold water

FOR THE FILLING
100g currants
100g raisins
2 tablespoons dark rum
50g unsalted butter, softened
50g light brown muscovado sugar
50g ground almonds
finely grated zest of 1 small
    unwaxed lemon, plus
    1 teaspoon lemon juice
freshly grated nutmeg

TO FINISH
1 medium egg white
caster sugar, for sprinkling

1. Sift the flour and salt into a mixing bowl. Slice off 40g of the weighed butter and cut into small dice, then add to the flour. Rub* the butter into the flour until the mixture looks like fine crumbs. Make a well in the centre. Add the lemon juice to 125ml icy water, then pour into the well and stir together with a round-bladed knife to make a soft but not sticky dough; add more water a teaspoon at a time if necessary. Shape the dough into a thick disc, wrap in clingfilm and chill for 30 minutes.

2. Roll out the dough away from you on a lightly floured worktop to a rectangle about 15 x 45cm. Cut a third of the remaining butter into small flakes and dot them evenly over the top two-thirds of the pastry rectangle. Fold the bottom third of the rectangle up to cover the butter-dotted middle third, then fold down the butter-dotted top third

to make a 3-layer sandwich. Seal the open edges with the side of your hand, then wrap the dough and chill for 20 minutes.

3. Set the chilled piece of dough on the lightly floured worktop so that the folded edges are to the sides. Roll out the dough away from you into a rectangle as before and dot the top two-thirds with half the remaining butter, cut into flakes. Fold up into thirds, wrap and chill as before. Repeat the rolling out and folding a third time, starting with the dough placed so the folded edges are top and bottom, then wrap and chill for 30 minutes (or up to a day) before using.

4. Start the filling while the dough is having its first chilling. Put the currants, raisins and rum in a small bowl and stir well, then cover with clingfilm and leave to soak at room temperature for at least 1½ hours (or up to a day).

5. Combine the soft butter, sugar, ground almonds, lemon zest and juice, and a little nutmeg in another bowl and beat well with a wooden spoon. Add the soaked fruit (with any liquid left in the bowl) and stir in.

6. Roll out the pastry dough on the lightly floured worktop to a square with 39cm sides. Stamp out 36 discs with the cutter. Pile the trimmings on top of each other (don't knead them together), then re-roll and cut out 2 or 3 more discs, if possible. Put a teaspoonful of filling on the centre of each disc. Gather up the pastry edges over the filling and pinch them firmly to seal, then invert the cakes on the worktop so the gathered side is facing down. Very gently roll the rolling pin over the top of each cake so it is slightly flatter and about 5cm across; the fruit should be visible through the pastry. Arrange the cakes, slightly apart, on the lined baking sheets, then chill for 20 minutes.

7. Heat the oven to 220°C/425°F/ gas 7. Beat the egg white with a fork until frothy, then lightly brush over the tops of the cakes. Sprinkle with a little caster sugar. Bake in the heated oven for 10–12 minutes until a good golden brown – check the cakes after 8 minutes and rotate the sheets so that all the cakes bake evenly. Transfer to a wire rack to cool. Store in an airtight container. Best eaten within 2 days.

FRANGIPANE TART

A really good-looking fruit-topped almond tart to make when succulent peaches and berries are in season, or at any time of the year using tinned or frozen fruit.

1. Make the rich sweet shortcrust pastry either by hand or in a food processor. By hand, sift the flour into a bowl, add the diced butter and rub in* until the mixture looks like fine crumbs. Stir in the sugar. Beat the egg with the water until combined, then stir into the crumbs with a round-bladed knife to make a slightly soft but not sticky dough. To use a food processor, put the flour and butter into the bowl and blitz until the mixture looks like fine crumbs. Add the sugar and 'pulse' to combine. Mix the egg with the water and, with the machine running, add through the feed tube. Stop the machine as soon as a ball of dough forms. Wrap the dough and chill for 20 minutes until firm but not hard.

2. Heat the oven to 190°C/375°F/gas 5, and put the baking sheet in to heat up. Roll out the pastry on a lightly floured worktop and use to line the flan tin*. Prick the base of the pastry case well with a fork, then chill for 10 minutes.

3. Line the pastry case with baking paper and fill with baking beans, then set the tin on the heated baking sheet and bake blind* for about 15 minutes until the pastry is set and the edges are lightly coloured. Remove the paper and beans and return the empty pastry case to the oven to bake for a further 10–12 minutes until the base is cooked through (no damp patches) and turning a light golden colour. Set aside to cool (leave the oven on).

4. Now make the almond filling. Put the soft butter and sugar into the food processor (no need to wash the bowl) and blitz until the mixture is creamy and smooth. With the machine running, pour in the eggs through the feed tube. Once combined, stop the machine and scrape down the side of the bowl. Add the ground almonds and almond extract and blitz just until combined. You can also make the filling by hand: cream the butter with the sugar until light and fluffy using a wooden spoon or hand-held electric whisk, then gradually beat in the eggs. Fold* in the almonds and almond extract.

5. Spread a thin layer of raspberry jam over the base of the pastry case. Spoon the almond mixture on top and spread evenly. **>>>**

Serves 8–10

Kit you'll need: 1 baking sheet; a 28cm fluted round, deep, loose-based flan tin

FOR THE PASTRY
225g plain flour
100g unsalted butter, chilled and diced
50g caster sugar
1 medium egg
1 tablespoon icy cold water

FOR THE ALMOND FILLING
175g unsalted butter, softened
175g caster sugar
4 medium eggs, at room temperature, beaten to mix
175g ground almonds
1 teaspoon almond extract
generous ½ jar home-made raspberry jam OR best-quality shop-bought jam

TO DECORATE
3 ripe peaches OR
    1 x 420g tin sliced peaches
200g raspberries
4 tablespoons apricot jam

Bake in the heated oven for 30–40 minutes until the filling is golden and feels springy when gently pressed in the centre. Remove the tart from the oven and leave to cool.

6. Once the tart is cold, start on the decoration. If you are using fresh peaches they need to be peeled. To do this, make a small nick in the skin near the stem end, then lower the peaches into a pan of boiling water and leave for 10 seconds. Drain, then peel off the loosened skins with the help of a small sharp knife. Halve the peaches and remove the stones, then cut into thick slices. If using tinned peaches, drain thoroughly.

7. Arrange the peach slices and raspberries in neat circles on top of the tart. Warm the apricot jam in a small pan over low heat, then press through a fine sieve to remove any lumps of fruit. If necessary, reheat the sieved jam so it is nice and runny, then gently brush it over the fruit to glaze. Leave to set before serving.

PISTACHIO MERINGUE SEA SHELLS

Snowy, sculptured meringues always look special – these, flavoured with chopped pistachios, are shaped, using a couple of spoons, into oval sea shells. Once baked, the flat bases are coated with dark chocolate, and the meringues sandwiched in pairs with whipped cream. They are lovely on their own, but if you want to push the boat out, a hot chocolate sauce or a bowl of fresh berries adds an extra touch of glamour!

1. Heat the oven to 120°C/250°F/gas ½. Put the pistachios into a small pan, add enough water to cover and bring to the boil. Remove from the heat and leave for a minutes, then drain. Tip the nuts on to kitchen paper or a tea towel and gently rub them to remove the papery brown skins. Chop the nuts medium fine.

2. Put the egg whites and cream of tartar into a spotlessly clean mixing bowl, or a free-standing electric mixer. Whisk the whites with a hand-held electric whisk, or the whisk attachment of the mixer, on slow speed until they look foamy. Increase the speed to maximum and whisk until soft peaks* will form. Gradually whisk in the sugar and whisk to make a smooth, glossy meringue that stands in stiff peaks*. Set aside 1 tablespoon of the pistachios, and scatter the rest over the meringue. Gently fold in* with a large metal spoon.

3. Now shape the meringue into neat ovals: using 2 matching spoons with oval bowls – the kind used for eating dessert – scoop up a spoonful of meringue; transfer it to the second spoon, smoothing the sides, then back to the first spoon, again smoothing and shaping the sides to neaten. Gently push the meringue oval off the spoon on to the lined baking sheet. Repeat with the rest of the meringue to make 12 oval shapes.

4. Scatter the reserved pistachios on top of the meringues, then bake them in the heated oven for 2–2½ hours until they are crisp, dry and firm. Cool on the baking sheet for about 15 minutes before transferring them to a wire rack. Leave until completely cold. (If you are not finishing the meringues immediately, you can store them in an airtight container for up to a week.)

>>>

Makes 6 pairs

Kit you'll need: 1 baking sheet, lined with baking paper; a piping bag fitted with a medium star nozzle (optional)

FOR THE MERINGUE
50g pistachios
2 medium egg whites,
    at room temperature
good pinch of cream of tartar
110g caster sugar

TO FINISH
50g dark chocolate (about 70% cocoa solids), broken or chopped up
125ml double cream, well chilled
Hot Chocolate Sauce (see page 264) OR berries, to serve

5. Melt* the chopped chocolate. Leave to cool and thicken for about 5 minutes, then use an offset palette knife to spread the chocolate over the flat base of each meringue in an even coating. Leave to set.

6. Meanwhile, whip the chilled cream until thick and almost at stiff peak stage. Spoon into the piping bag fitted with the star nozzle, if using. Pipe or spread a swirl of cream on the chocolate-coated bases of 6 meringues and sandwich in pairs with the other 6 meringues. Serve immediately (or keep in the fridge for up to an hour) with chocolate sauce or fresh berries.

Hot Chocolate Sauce

Put 100g chopped dark chocolate (about 70% cocoa solids) into a small, heavy-based pan and add 50g diced unsalted butter, 100ml water, single cream or black coffee and 1 tablespoon caster sugar. Warm gently over the lowest possible heat, stirring frequently, until smooth and melted. Taste and add more sugar if necessary. Keep warm until ready to serve.

GLUTEN-FREE FRESH LEMON TART

For a special occasion there is little to beat a lemon tart. The shortbread-like crust for this one is made in a food processor with ground almonds and cornflour instead of flour, and is simply pressed into the tin. The filling is also made in the processor, from whole lemons blitzed with eggs, sugar, cornflour and butter. Those on a gluten-free diet can enjoy the tart along with everyone else.

1. To make the crust, put the ground almonds, cornflour and sugar into a food processor and 'pulse' just to combine. Add the butter and blitz just until the mixture looks like fine crumbs. Tip the crumbs into the buttered tin and press evenly over the base and up the sides (right to the rim) using the back of a spoon – the crust will be about 5mm thick. Chill for 20 minutes.

2. Heat the oven to 180°C/ 350°F/gas 4 and put the baking sheet into the oven to heat up. Bake the crust for 12–16 minutes until a very light gold colour.

3. Meanwhile, make the topping. Set the lemons on a large plate (to catch all the juice) and trim off the ends. Cut each lemon into 8 wedges, removing the pips. Cut each wedge across in half and put into the food processor. Combine the cornflour and caster sugar and add to the processor bowl. Blitz just until the lemon is coarsely chopped. Add the egg and yolk and blitz briefly until combined. With the machine

running, pour in the cooled butter through the feed tube. Stop the machine as soon as all the butter has been added – the mixture won't be smooth but should have a few visible tiny pieces of lemon.

4. Remove the crust from the oven and set it (in its tin) on the heated baking sheet. Turn down the oven temperature to 170°C/325°F/gas 3. Pour the lemon mixture into the hot crust to fill it almost up to the rim. Carefully return to the oven and bake for 30–35 minutes until the lemon filling is just starting to colour and is firm when you gently jiggle the baking sheet.

5. Remove from the oven and leave to cool completely, then cover lightly and chill for at least 3 hours, or overnight. To serve, run a thin, round-bladed knife around the inside of the tin to loosen the crust, then carefully unmould the tart. Dust with icing sugar and serve with whipped cream or ice cream. Store in an airtight container in the fridge. Best eaten within 2 days.

Serves 8–12

Kit you'll need: 1 x 20.5cm round, deep, loose-based sandwich tin, greased with butter; a baking sheet

FOR THE CRUST
200g ground almonds
35g cornflour
50g caster sugar
100g unsalted butter, chilled and diced

FOR THE FILLING
2 medium unwaxed lemons, preferably thin-skinned
15g cornflour
185g caster sugar
1 medium egg, plus 1 yolk, at room temperature
100g unsalted butter, melted and cooled
icing sugar, for dusting

Note

After baking, it is vital that the tart has time to cool and then chill in order to firm up the filling, so be sure to plan ahead.

TOFFEE APPLE TART

A very elegant Bonfire Night sweet, this is made from tart eating apples arranged on a layer of thick toffee sauce in a crisp, sweet pastry case, and topped with a streusel (crumble). During baking the toffee bubbles up to permeate the apple slices and give them that special 'tarte tatin' flavour.

Serves 8

Kit you'll need: 1 x 23cm fluted round, deep, loose-based flan tin; a baking sheet

FOR THE RICH SWEET SHORTCRUST PASTRY
175g plain flour
pinch of salt
20g icing sugar
100g unsalted butter, chilled and diced
1 medium egg yolk
about 1 tablespoon icy cold water

FOR THE TOFFEE SAUCE
100g caster sugar
30g golden syrup
1 teaspoon water
30g unsalted butter, diced
50ml double cream, at room temperature
good pinch of sea salt (fine or flakes)

FOR THE APPLE FILLING
4 large Braeburn or other tart eating apples (about 600g)
¼ teaspoon ground cinnamon

FOR THE STREUSEL TOPPING
150g plain flour
30g caster sugar
30g light brown muscovado sugar
75g unsalted butter, chilled and diced

1. You can make the pastry in a food processor or by hand. For the processor method, put the flour, salt and icing sugar into the bowl and 'pulse' a couple of times, just to combine. Add the pieces of butter and blitz just until the mixture looks like fine crumbs. Add the yolk and cold water and blitz just until the mixture comes together to make a firm dough. If there are dry crumbs and the mixture won't bind together, add more water a teaspoon at a time through the feed tube. To make the pastry by hand, sift the flour, salt and sugar into a mixing bowl. Add the pieces of butter and toss in the flour so they are lightly coated, then rub* into the flour until the mixture looks like fine crumbs. Add the yolk and water and stir in with a round-bladed knife to make a firm dough; if there are dry crumbs, work in more cold water a teaspoon at time. Shape the dough into a thick disc, wrap in clingfilm and chill for 20 minutes.

2. Roll out the pastry dough on a lightly floured worktop to a large disc about 32cm across. Use to line the flan tin*, leaving the excess pastry hanging over the rim for now. Prick the base with a fork, then chill the pastry case for 15 minutes.

3. Meanwhile, make the toffee sauce. Have all the ingredients weighed and ready. Put the sugar, golden syrup and water into a small heavy-based pan and set over very low heat. Cook gently, stirring with a wooden spoon from time to time, until the sugar has completely dissolved – don't let the mixture boil; take the pan on and off the heat if necessary. Now bring the mixture to the boil and leave to bubble gently, without stirring it but carefully swirling it in the pan from time to time, until a rich dark caramel is formed. Remove from the heat, add the butter and stir gently with the wooden spoon (the caramel

will foam up). When the butter has been incorporated, stir in the cream – the mixture will turn a bit lumpy so put it back over low heat and stir until melted and smooth. Pour the toffee sauce into a heatproof bowl, sprinkle the salt on top and leave until cold.

4. Heat your oven to 190°C/375°F/ gas 5. Neaten the edge of the pastry case, trimming off the excess pastry. Line the case with baking paper, fill with baking beans and bake blind* in the heated oven for 12–15 minutes until the pastry is set and firm. Remove the paper and beans, then bake for a further 5 minutes until the pastry is crisp and lightly coloured.

5. While the pastry case is baking, peel and quarter the apples. Cut out the cores, then cut the apples into very thin slices and tip into a bowl. Sprinkle the cinnamon over the apples and toss until evenly coated. Set aside while you make the streusel mixture.

6. Put the flour and both sugars into a mixing bowl and mix together with your hand. Add the pieces of butter and rub in with your fingertips until the mixture looks like fine crumbs (you can also do this in a food processor – 'pulse' the flour with the sugars, then add the pieces of butter and blitz for a few seconds, just until crumbs form).

7. When the pastry case is ready, remove it from the oven and set the tin on a heatproof surface. Reduce the oven temperature to 180°C/350°F/gas 4, and put the baking sheet into the oven to heat up.

8. Spoon the toffee sauce into the pastry case to cover the base evenly – the sauce will have firmed up but it will spread easily thanks to the warm pastry. Arrange the apple slices on top to fill evenly, with no gaps or holes. Scatter the streusel topping over the apples, making sure it is evenly distributed.

9. Set the flan tin on the heated baking sheet and bake the tart for 35–40 minutes until the streusel topping is a nice golden colour and the toffee sauce has started to bubble up. Carefully unmould the tart and leave to cool. Eat warm or at room temperature, the same or the next day, with custard (see Spicy Figgy Pudding, page 209) or cream.

CHOCOLATE PECAN PIE WITH A PECAN CRUST

An extra-special dark chocolate version of the Thanksgiving favourite, this is guaranteed to be the star of the show! The pastry is made with pecans in a food processor, then the shell is baked blind before the chocolate and nut filling is added. This blind baking will keep the pastry crisp for at least 24 hours so that you can give the pie time to deepen in flavour overnight.

Serves 12

Kit you'll need: 1 x 23cm round, loose-based flan tin; a baking sheet

FOR THE PECAN PASTRY
175g plain flour
2 good pinches of salt
50g pecans
2 tablespoons caster sugar
115g unsalted butter, chilled and diced
1 medium egg, beaten to mix

FOR THE FILLING
250g pecan halves
50g unsalted butter, diced
125g dark brown muscovado sugar
150g golden syrup
100g dark chocolate (about 70% cocoa solids), broken up
3 medium eggs, at room temperature, beaten to mix
icing sugar, for dusting

1. Make the pastry in a food processor: put the flour, salt, pecans and sugar into the processor bowl and blitz until the nuts are finely chopped and the mixture looks sandy. Add the pieces of cold butter and blitz again until the mixture looks like fine crumbs. With the machine running, add the beaten egg through the feed tube and blitz just until the mixture comes together to make a ball of slightly soft dough. Remove the ball of dough, flatten it to a thick disc and wrap in clingfilm. Chill for 20 minutes.

2. Roll out the pastry on a lightly floured worktop to a disc about 32cm across and use to line the flan tin*. Chill for 15 minutes. Meanwhile, heat the oven to 190°C/375°F/gas 5.

3. Line the pastry case with baking paper and fill with baking or dried beans, then bake blind* for 15 minutes. Remove the paper and beans and bake for a further 7–10 minutes until the pastry is crisp and a light golden brown.

4. Remove the tin from the oven and set it on a heatproof surface. Turn down the oven to 180°C/350°F/gas 4, and put the baking sheet in to heat up.

5. Tip the pecans into a small baking dish or tin and toast in the oven for 5–7 minutes until they turn a light gold and smell nutty. Remove and cool a bit, then set aside a dozen of the best-looking pecan halves. Roughly chop the remaining pecans.

6. Put the butter, brown sugar, golden syrup and chocolate into a heavy-based pan large enough to hold all the filling ingredients. Set the pan over very low heat and melt gently, stirring frequently. When smooth, remove the pan from the heat and leave the mixture to cool until barely warm. Add the eggs and beat well with a wooden spoon until thoroughly combined. Gently mix in the chopped pecans.

7. Spoon the filling into the pastry case and spread evenly.

Arrange the reserved pecan halves on the surface. Set the tin on the heated baking sheet and bake for about 30 minutes until the filling is slightly puffed and just firm when pressed in the centre – start checking after 25 minutes as you don't want the filling to become too dark (cover with a sheet of greaseproof or baking paper, if necessary) or overcook (it will continue cooking for a few minutes after it comes out of the oven and you want it to have a fudgy rather than set and firm texture).

8. Cool for 10 minutes before carefully unmoulding, then leave to firm up for at least 30 minutes before lightly dusting with icing sugar and slicing. Serve slightly warm or at room temperature, with whipped cream or vanilla ice cream. The rich flavours of the chocolate and nuts deepen if the pie is kept, tightly covered, in a cool spot (not the fridge) for a day or so before serving.

'There is always room for a sense of adventure and for experimentation, but also there are some classics like pecan pie, chocolate tart and lemon tart whose flavours are just so right, they can't be bettered.'

SANDY

PRALINE & CHOCOLATE VOL-AU-VENTS

Literally 'flying with the wind', vol-au-vents are intended to be the lightest, wispiest of pastry mouthfuls, so this is a recipe to show off your pastry skills. The little cases are filled with dark ganache, hazelnut praline 'butter' and crème légère, the lightest of all crème pâtissières, to create layers of flavour. Beautifully presented, with curls of dark chocolate and flowers, these would make a sensational tiered display.

Makes 24

Kit you'll need: a 3cm and a 5cm plain round cutter; a baking sheet, lined with baking paper; a silicone sheet; 2 disposable piping bags

FOR THE PUFF PASTRY
300g plain flour
½ teaspoon salt
185ml icy cold water
250g unsalted butter
1½ tablespoons cocoa powder

FOR THE PRALINE BUTTER
70g blanched hazelnuts
70g caster sugar
2 teaspoons water

FOR THE GANACHE
60g dark chocolate (50–60% cocoa solids), finely chopped
2 teaspoons espresso
60ml double cream (not extra-thick or 'spoonable')

FOR THE CRÈME LÉGÈRE
100ml full-fat milk
1 large egg yolk, at room temperature
1 tablespoon cornflour
20g caster sugar
10g unsalted butter, at room temperature
¼ teaspoon vanilla bean paste
75ml double cream (not extra thick or 'spoonable'), well chilled

TO FINISH
50g chopped toasted hazelnuts
50g dark chocolate (about 70% cocoa solids)
24 small purple pansies (optional)

1. Make the puff pastry as for the Asparagus and Parma Ham Vol-au-vents (see page 225), with one difference: after rolling out the pastry for the second 'book fold', sift the cocoa over the rectangle before folding. Shape the vol-au-vent cases exactly as given on pages 225–6, then bake at 200°C/400°F/gas 6 in the same way. Leave to cool while you make the fillings. Reduce the oven temperature to 180°C/350°F/gas 4.

2. To make the praline butter, put the hazelnuts in a small baking dish or tin and toast in the oven for 5–7 minutes until just starting to colour. Leave to cool. Line the baking sheet with clean baking paper or the silicone sheet. Put the sugar and water in a small pan, set over low heat and stir gently until the sugar has completely dissolved. Turn up the heat and boil, without stirring, until the syrup turns to a light caramel.

3. Add the hazelnuts and stir gently with a metal spoon, then cook for a few seconds longer until you have a rich caramel. Pour on to the lined baking sheet and leave to cool. Once completely cold and set, break into chunks, then put into a food processor and 'pulse' long enough to make a smooth, creamy 'butter'. Transfer to a bowl, cover and set aside until needed.

>>>

4. For the ganache, put the chopped chocolate and coffee into a heatproof bowl. Heat the cream until it just comes to the boil, then pour it over the chocolate. Leave to melt for a couple of minutes before stirring gently until smooth. Allow to cool and thicken up slightly, then transfer to a piping bag.

5. Press down the risen base in each pastry case, to make room for the filling. Snip off the tip of the piping bag to make a 5mm opening, then pipe a spiral of ganache into each pastry case. Leave to set at room temperature.

6. Meanwhile, make crème légère. Heat the milk in a small pan until almost boiling; remove from the heat. Beat the egg yolk with the cornflour and sugar in a heatproof bowl until smooth and light, then stir in the hot milk. When thoroughly combined, pour the mixture back into the pan and stir over medium/low heat until it boils and thickens. Remove from the heat and stir in the butter and vanilla. Transfer to a clean, heatproof bowl and press a piece

of clingfilm on the surface to prevent a skin from forming, then leave to cool. Chill for 30 minutes.

7. Whip the cream until it will stand in soft peaks*. Stir the chilled crème until it is very smooth, then fold it into the whipped cream. Transfer to the other piping bag and keep in the fridge if not using immediately.

8. To assemble the vol-au-vents, spoon a little praline butter on top of the set ganache in each pastry case. Snip off the end of the piping bag to make a 5mm opening and pipe a little crème légère on the praline butter. Sprinkle with a few chopped hazelnuts, then cover with a little more piped crème légère. Decorate one half of each filled vol-au-vent with a sprinkling of chopped hazelnuts.

9. Make shavings from the dark chocolate (see right) and use to decorate the top of the vol-au-vents. Arrange the pastries on a serving plate and decorate with some purple pansies, if you like. Serve immediately.

Chocolate curls & shavings

Gently melt* 50g dark chocolate (about 70% cocoa solids), then pour it on to a clean marble slab or worktop. Working quickly, before the chocolate sets, use a palette knife to spread the chocolate thinly. Keep working the chocolate with the knife, spreading it back and forth, until you have a rough rectangle about 20 x 30cm and 2–3mm thick. As soon as the chocolate becomes matt and dull, rather than shiny, and starts to set, stop working it. Hold a large, sharp knife (pointing away from you), with the blade at an angle of about 45 degrees, on one side of the chocolate slab and scrape off a very thin sheet, which will curl as you go. For large curls, scrape from one side of the chocolate slab to the other. Take shorter shavings too. Use a palette knife, rather than your fingers, to gently lift the curls or shavings into place.

CHOCOLATE & CARAMEL CUSTARD TART

Custard tart meets millionaire's shortbread (a big favourite amongst the Bakers) in this elegant twist on a classic recipe. The crisp pastry case, reminiscent of shortbread, is filled with a rich, creamy, caramel custard and finished with a thick layer of dark chocolate shavings. Don't waste the left-over egg whites – keep them for meringues (see page 263). If you can't use them straight away they freeze well.

Serves 8–10

Kit you'll need: 1 x 23cm fluted round, deep, loose-based flan tin; a baking sheet

FOR THE SWEET SHORTCRUST PASTRY
175g plain flour
pinch of salt
1 tablespoon caster sugar
100g unsalted butter,
   chilled and diced
about 2 tablespoons
   icy cold water
1 medium egg white, for brushing

FOR THE FILLING
125g caster sugar,
   plus 1 tablespoon
125ml water
90g unsalted butter,
   at room temperature, diced
500ml double cream,
   at room temperature
7 medium egg yolks,
   at room temperature
pinch of fine sea salt

TO FINISH
50g dark chocolate (about 70% cocoa solids), chopped

1. You can make the pastry in a food processor or by hand. For the processor method, put the flour, salt and sugar into the bowl and 'pulse' a couple of times to combine. Add the pieces of butter and blitz until the mixture looks like fine crumbs. Add the cold water and blitz just until the mixture comes together to make a firm dough – if there are dry crumbs and the mixture won't bind together, add more water a teaspoon at a time through the feed tube.

2. To make the pastry by hand, sift the flour, salt and sugar into a mixing bowl. Add the pieces of butter and toss in the flour to lightly coat, then rub* the butter into the flour until the mixture looks like fine crumbs. Add the water and stir into the crumbs with a round-bladed knife to make a firm dough; if there are any dry crumbs work in more cold water a teaspoon at time.

3. Shape the dough into a thick disc, wrap it in clingfilm and chill for 20 minutes.

4. Roll out the pastry dough on a lightly floured worktop to a large disc about 32cm across and use to line the flan tin*. Leave the excess pastry hanging over the rim for now. Prick the base with a fork and chill the pastry case for 15 minutes.

5. Heat the oven to 190°C/375°F/gas 5. Neaten the edge of the pastry case, trimming off the excess pastry. Line the case with greaseproof paper, fill with baking beans and bake blind* in the heated oven for 12–15 minutes until the pastry is set and firm. Remove the paper and beans, then bake the empty case for a further 5–7 minutes until the pastry is crisp and lightly coloured.

6. Transfer the tin to a heatproof surface and quickly brush the inside of the hot pastry case with a thin layer of beaten egg white. This will help to seal the pastry and keep it crisp. Reduce the oven temperature to 170°C/325°F/gas 3, and put the baking sheet into the oven to heat up.

>>>

7. Start making the filling while the pastry case is chilling (end of step 4). Put the 125g sugar and the water in a medium pan, set over low heat and stir occasionally to help dissolve the sugar – do not allow the syrup to boil before all the sugar has dissolved. Once the syrup is clear, bring it to the boil and let it boil rapidly until it has turned a rich chestnut brown. Remove from the heat and stir in the pieces of butter, followed by the cream – the mixture will turn lumpy, so return the pan to medium/low heat and stir until melted and smooth. Leave to cool until lukewarm.

8. Put the yolks in a heatproof bowl with the remaining tablespoon of sugar and beat well with a wooden spoon for about 1 minute until very light and smooth. Stir in the lukewarm caramel cream and the salt, then transfer the caramel custard to a large jug.

9. Set the flan tin on the heated baking sheet and place this on the oven shelf. Carefully pour the custard into the pastry case, then gently slide the shelf in and close the oven door. Bake the tart for 25–30 minutes until the custard is just set when you jiggle the baking sheet. Remove from the oven and set the tin on a wire rack. Leave the tart until completely cold.

10. Meanwhile, make chocolate shavings to decorate the tart (see page 274).

11. Carefully unmould the tart and set it on a serving plate. Transfer the chocolate shavings to the top of the tart using a palette knife rather than your fingers. Serve at room temperature, the same or the next day – keep in an airtight container in the fridge but remove 30 minutes before serving.

SWEET LITTLE BEIGNETS

During the Jewish festival of light, Chanukah, a candle is lit at dusk on each of the eight days. On the first night it is traditional to eat food cooked in oil (and open a small gift). Often this will be latkes (potato pancakes), but doughnuts like these beignets are very popular. They are delicious on their own or with a chocolate sauce, zabaglione or maple syrup.

1. Put the sultanas and sherry into a small bowl and mix well, then cover with clingfilm and leave to macerate for at least I hour, or up to 6 hours if possible.

2. When you are ready to make the choux pastry, sift the flour on to a sheet of greaseproof paper. Put the water, milk, butter, sugar and salt into a medium pan and heat gently until the butter has melted – don't let the water boil yet. Turn up the heat and quickly bring the mixture to the boil, then tip in all the flour in one go. Remove the pan from the heat and beat furiously with a wooden spoon – the mixture will look like a mess at first, but as you beat it will turn into a smooth, heavy dough. Set the pan back on low heat and beat the dough for about 2 minutes to slightly cook it, until it comes away from the side of the pan in a smooth, glossy ball. Tip the dough into a large heatproof mixing bowl and leave to cool until barely warm.

3. Using a hand-held electric whisk, gradually add the eggs to the dough, beating well after each addition. After the last portion of egg has been incorporated, beat the mixture on high speed for a minute to make a smooth, shiny paste. Mix in the sultanas and any sherry left in the bowl – the choux dough will be slightly softer than that used for baked choux pastries such as éclairs. At this point the dough can be covered and kept at room temperature for up to 3 hours.

4. Heat 3cm of oil in a deep medium pan to 175°C (you can also use a deep-fat fryer, if you have one). Scoop up a tablespoon of the choux dough (a measuring spoon or a soup spoon) and use a second spoon to gently push the dough off the spoon and into the hot oil. Add 4 more beignets to the pan (don't overcrowd it) and fry for about 5 minutes until a fairly dark golden brown all over (just as with baked choux buns, the shell should be crisp and the dough thoroughly cooked to leave a hollow centre cavity). Carefully remove the beignets with a slotted spoon and drain on kitchen paper.

5. Transfer to a warm serving dish, sprinkle with caster sugar and eat warm with zabaglione, chocolate sauce or maple syrup.

Makes 15; serves 4–6

Kit you'll need: **deep-frying thermometer**

30g sultanas
I tablespoon sweet sherry
vegetable oil, for deep-frying
caster sugar, for sprinkling

FOR THE CHOUX PASTRY
75g plain flour
100ml water
2 tablespoons milk
20g unsalted butter, diced
2 teaspoons caster sugar
¼ teaspoon fine sea salt
2 medium eggs, at room
    temperature, beaten to mix

TO SERVE
Zabaglione (see page 205),
    Hot Chocolate Sauce
    (page 264) OR maple syrup

RUGELACH

Made from a rich, sweet-cheese dough, these crescent-shaped pastries are traditionally baked to celebrate Chanukah. This version is filled with a sweet, spicy, nutty mixture, making them rather like rich cookies. Other recipes use apricot jam and raisins, which makes them very sticky indeed. These are perfect with a cup of coffee.

Makes 24

Kit you'll need: **2 baking sheets, lined with baking paper**

FOR THE SWEET CHEESE PASTRY
275g plain flour
1 tablespoon caster sugar
good pinch of fine sea salt
150g unsalted butter, chilled and diced
150g full-fat cream cheese
1 medium egg yolk
½ teaspoon vanilla extract

FOR THE FILLING
150g walnut pieces
1½ teaspoons ground cinnamon
150g caster sugar

1. Heat the oven to 180°C/350°F/gas 4. Make the pastry in a food processor: put the flour, sugar and salt into the bowl and 'pulse' a few times to combine. Add the butter and blitz until the mixture looks like fine crumbs. Break up the cream cheese and add to the bowl with the egg yolk and vanilla extract. Blitz just until the mixture comes together to make a heavy, firm dough. Remove the dough from the processor bowl, divide it into 3 equal portions and wrap them in clingfilm. Chill for an hour.

2. Meanwhile, prepare the filling. Tip the walnuts into a small baking dish or tin and toast in the heated oven for 5–7 minutes until a very light golden colour. You can turn off the oven for now. Leave the walnuts until cold, then put into the (clean) processor bowl with the cinnamon and sugar, and 'pulse' until the nuts are fairly finely chopped. Set aside.

3. When you are ready to shape the rugelach, unwrap one portion of pastry dough. Divide the nut mixture into 6 equal portions and, instead of using flour, sprinkle a portion of the nut mixture on

the worktop. Roll out the dough, on the nut mixture, to a disc 26cm across. Using a pizza wheel-cutter, or a large, sharp knife, cut the disc into 8 triangular wedges (like a cake). Sprinkle another portion of nut mixture on top of the dough and gently press it on to the surface with your hand.

4. Gently lift out one of the triangles and roll it up, starting from the short side and tucking the pointed end underneath when you reach it, then gently curve into a crescent shape and set it on a lined baking sheet. Repeat with the other 7 triangles. Cover lightly and chill while you roll out and shape the remaining 2 portions of dough. When all have been shaped, chill for 30 minutes.

5. Heat the oven to 180°C/350°F/gas 4. Uncover the baking sheets and bake the pastries for about 20 minutes until the tips are just turning a light golden colour – it's important not to overcook the rugelach and let them get brown or they will be hard and dry. Transfer to a wire rack to cool. Store in an airtight container. Best eaten within 3 days.

GALETTE DES ROIS (TWELFTH NIGHT CAKE)

From medieval times in France, this 'kings' cake' was made to celebrate the Epiphany on 6th January, the last day of the Christmas festivities. The tradition is to bury a dried bean inside; whoever finds it is crowned Lord (or Lady) of Misrule, and can choose the entertainment until midnight. The 'cake' is actually made from puff pastry and filled with a rich combination of crème pâtissière and almond-rum cream.

1. Lightly flour your worktop and roll out half the pastry to a disc about 25cm in diameter and the thickness of a pound coin. Cut out a neat disc about 24cm across – use a pan lid, cake tin or plate as a guide. Lay the pastry disc on the lined baking sheet and cover with a sheet of clingfilm. Lightly dust the clingfilm with flour.

2. Roll out the remaining dough in the same way and cut out a second disc of the same size. Set this on top of the floured clingfilm, then cover the whole lot with clingfilm. Put into the fridge to chill while you make the filling.

3. For the crème pâtissière, which will need time to firm up in the fridge, heat the milk in a medium pan until bubbles start to form around the edge. Remove from the heat. Put the egg yolks, sugar and cornflour in a heatproof bowl set on a damp cloth on the worktop (the cloth will prevent the bowl from wobbling). Whisk together with a wire whisk for a couple of minutes until very

smooth, then whisk in the hot milk. Tip the mixture back into the pan and whisk constantly over medium heat until the mixture boils and thickens – take care it doesn't catch on the bottom of the pan. Remove from the heat and whisk in the butter. Transfer the crème to a clean heatproof bowl and press a piece of clingfilm or dampened baking paper on the surface to prevent a skin from forming. Cool, then cover the top of the bowl with clingfilm and chill for at least 1 hour.

4. Meanwhile, make the almond-rum mixture. Beat the soft butter with a wooden spoon or hand-held electric whisk until creamy, then beat in the sugar. Continue beating until light and fluffy. Gradually beat in the egg a tablespoon at a time. When the mixture is very light in colour and texture, gently stir in the ground almonds, flour, almond extract and rum followed by the cold crème pâtissière. Cover the bowl and chill for 15–20 minutes.

>>>

Serves 8–10

Kit you'll need: 1 baking sheet, lined with baking paper; a ceramic or dried bean; a gold paper or card crown

1 quantity Puff Pastry (see page 285), well chilled, OR
   750g ready-made all-butter puff pastry, thawed if frozen
beaten egg, to glaze

FOR THE CRÈME PÂTISSIÈRE
150ml creamy milk
2 medium egg yolks,
   at room temperature
30g caster sugar
10g cornflour
15g unsalted butter, softened

FOR THE ALMOND-RUM CREAM
75g unsalted butter, softened
75g caster sugar
1 medium egg, at room
   temperature, beaten to mix
100g ground almonds
10g plain flour
¼ teaspoon almond extract
1½ tablespoons dark rum

5. When ready to assemble, uncover the pastry and lift off the top disc and clingfilm. Spoon the filling on to the pastry disc on the lined baking sheet, mounding it slightly in the middle and leaving a 2cm border of pastry all around the edge. Push the bean into the filling – not too close to the centre, to avoid confusion when cutting into slices.

6. Brush the pastry border with beaten egg, then lift the second pastry disc over the filling and lay it centrally on top. Gently smooth the pastry lid down to push out any air bubbles before pressing the pastry edges together firmly to seal. Knock up* the edge, then scallop* it. Brush the pastry lid very lightly with beaten egg to glaze and chill for 20 minutes.

7. Meanwhile, heat the oven to 220°C/425°F/gas 7. Brush the pastry lid a second time with beaten egg, then very lightly score a diamond pattern with the tip of a sharp knife, without cutting through the pastry. Make a couple of small steam holes in the centre of the lid. Bake in the heated oven for 15 minutes, then reduce the temperature to 180°C/350°F/gas 4 and bake for a further 25 minutes until the pastry is a good golden brown and crisp (for best results, check after 15 minutes and, if necessary, rotate the sheet so the pastry bakes evenly).

8. Leave to cool slightly, then serve warm with the paper crown on top (ready for the Lord or Lady of Misrule to wear). If making in advance, gently reheat in a 170°C/325°F/gas 3 oven before serving. Remember to tell your guests to look out for the inedible bean.

PUFF PASTRY

This is the lightest, richest and flakiest of all pastries – and the trickiest. What makes it so delicious is its butteriness. Save all the trimmings: just stack them up, then re-roll; don't knead them together.

1. Put the flour and salt into a food processor and 'pulse' to combine. Cut 50g of the butter into small pieces and add to the bowl, then blitz until the mixture looks like fine crumbs. Mix the lemon juice with the water. With the machine running, add through the feed tube to make a ball of slightly moist dough. You can also make it by hand: rub* the butter into the flour, then stir in the liquid with a round-bladed knife. Turn out on to a lightly floured worktop and score a deep cross in the top of the dough ball. Wrap and chill for 15 minutes.

2. Meanwhile, sprinkle a little flour on the remaining piece of butter, then set it between sheets of clingfilm. Pound it with a rolling pin until half its original thickness. Remove the film and fold the butter in two, then re-cover and pound again. Keep doing this until the butter is pliable but still cold. Beat it into a 13cm square.

3. Put the ball of dough on the floured worktop. Roll out the dough 'flaps' from the scored cross in 4 directions – the dough should end up looking like a cross with a thick rough square in the centre. Dust the butter lightly with flour, then place on top of the central square. Fold the flaps of dough over the butter to enclose it and gently press the seams with the rolling pin to seal.

4. Turn the dough upside down, brush off excess flour and lightly press with the rolling pin to flatten – don't squeeze the butter out. Gently roll out the dough away from you to a rectangle about 54 x 18cm. Fold it in thirds – fold up the bottom third to cover the centre third, then fold down the top third to cover the other layers and make a neat square. Lightly press the open edges with the rolling pin to seal. This is your first 'turn'. Brush off excess flour.

5. Lift up the dough and give it a quarter turn anti-clockwise so the folded edges are now to the sides. Roll out the dough to a rectangle and fold it in 3 again, just as before. Wrap and chill for 15 minutes.

6. Give the dough 2 more turns, alternating the position of the folded edges each time, then wrap and chill as before. Make a final 2 turns, to make a total of 6, and chill well before using.

Makes about 750g

300g plain flour
3g fine salt
300g unsalted butter, cold but not rock-hard
1 teaspoon lemon juice
about 140ml icy cold water

Note

After the fourth turn, the dough can be kept in the fridge for 4 days, or frozen. Before using, thaw if frozen, then give the dough another 2 turns to make a total of 6.

HOME-MADE MINCEMEAT PIE

Mince pies are one of the great treats of Christmas, but for a change, why not bake a big pie for Boxing Day and serve it with leftover brandy butter, or cream? It's well worth making your own mincemeat for the pie, as it will taste wonderfully fresh and fruity, quite unlike anything you can buy. This easy version has no suet and combines apples, fresh citrus juice and zest, glacé ginger and ginger wine with the sweet dried fruit. The shortcrust pastry is easily made in a food processor with ground almonds and icing sugar to give a rich flavour and a light, crisp texture, which contrasts beautifully with the moist fruity-spicy filling.

Serves 8–10

Kit you'll need: 1 large, round pie plate or dish, about 20cm across the base, 25cm across the top and 5cm deep; small shaped cutters (optional); a baking sheet

FOR THE MINCEMEAT FILLING
300g mixed dried vine fruit (raisins, sultanas, currants)
75g chopped glacé ginger
125g dark brown muscovado sugar
finely grated zest and juice of 1 medium unwaxed lemon
finely grated zest and juice of 1 small orange
½ teaspoon ground mixed spice
1 cinnamon stick
250ml ginger wine
2 medium/large Bramley apples (about 550g)
70g unsalted butter

FOR THE ALMOND SHORTCRUST PASTRY
350g plain flour
¼ teaspoon salt
85g ground almonds
100g icing sugar
250g unsalted butter, chilled and diced
1 medium egg, beaten to mix

1. To make the mincemeat, put the dried vine fruit, glacé ginger, sugar, lemon and orange zest and juice, mixed spice, cinnamon stick and ginger wine into a large saucepan. Peel, quarter and core the apples, then cut each quarter into 6 chunks. Add to the pan with the butter. Set over medium heat and bring to the boil, stirring frequently. Adjust the heat so the mixture boils gently and cook, stirring frequently, until the apples are tender and the liquid is thick and sticky – you want the mixture to be jammy, so don't let it become dry or stiff. Transfer to a heatproof bowl and cool, then cover and leave at room temperature overnight. (The mincemeat can be kept in a covered container in the fridge for up to 5 days.)

2. To make the almond pastry, put the flour, salt, ground almonds and sugar into a food processor. 'Pulse' several times to combine, then add the diced butter and blitz until the mixture looks like fine crumbs. Add the egg and blitz briefly until the mixture comes together to make a ball of soft but not sticky dough. Remove the dough from the bowl, weigh it and cut off 300g. Shape this into a thick disc and wrap in clingfilm. Shape and wrap the rest of the dough, then chill both portions for 15–20 minutes until firm but not hard. (You can keep the dough overnight in the fridge, but remove it about 15 minutes before using.)

3. Roll out the larger portion of dough fairly thinly to a disc about 32cm across and use to line >>>

the pie plate*. Leave the excess pastry hanging over the rim for now. Roll out the second, smaller piece of dough to a disc about 26cm across for the lid and set it aside.

4. Stir the mincemeat filling and remove the cinnamon stick, then spoon into the pastry case and spread evenly. Brush the rim of the pastry case with cold water. Roll the pastry lid around the rolling pin and lift it on to the pie to cover. Press the pastry edges together to seal firmly. Trim off the excess pastry with a sharp knife, then flute* the edge. Make a steam hole in the centre of

the lid. If you like, gather up the pastry trimmings, re-roll and cut out stars or tiny Christmas trees with shaped cutters; attach these to the top of the pie with dabs of water. Chill for 20 minutes.

5. Heat the oven to 180°C/ 350°F/gas 4, and put the baking sheet in to heat up.

6. Set the pie plate on the heated baking sheet in the oven and bake for 30–35 minutes until the pastry is golden – rotate the pie after 20 minutes and then check it frequently to be sure the pastry lid doesn't get too brown before the base is fully cooked;

if necessary, cover the top lightly with baking paper, or, if the edge is browning before the centre of the lid, wrap a long strip of foil around the edge.

7. Leave the pie to cool until just warm before carefully unmoulding it and setting it on a serving plate. Serve warm or at room temperature, the same or the next day (keep in an airtight tin in a cool spot – not the fridge).

'For Christmas I make wide, flat, individual mince pies, more like French tarts than the traditional dumpy English pie. I add cranberries to the mincemeat, and orange zest to the pastry, then insert a star-shaped piece of brandy and orange zest butter into the pastry top.'

IAN

CHRISTMAS FRANGIPANE TART

This festive tart uses ingredients that really say Christmas: sweet pears poached in mulled red wine; rich almond frangipane; and a generous scattering of flaked almonds with an apricot glaze. The tart is decorated with white icing piped in the shape of delicate Christmas trees in between each crimson-coloured pear.

Serves 8

Kit you'll need: 1 x 25cm fluted round, deep, loose-based flan tin; a large disposable piping bag (optional); a baking sheet; a small disposable piping bag

FOR THE POACHED PEARS
400ml red wine (preferably
   Cabernet Sauvignon)
1 cinnamon stick
6 whole cloves
4 whole allspice berries
freshly grated nutmeg, to taste
1 orange, peeled and halved
100g caster sugar
4 large Bosc or Conference pears,
   just ripe (pick even-sized fruit)

FOR THE SWEET PASTRY
250g plain flour
50g caster sugar
125g unsalted butter,
   chilled and diced
1 large egg yolk
about 3 tablespoons
   icy cold water

FOR THE FRANGIPANE
150g salted butter, softened
150g caster sugar
3 large eggs, at room temperature
½ teaspoon almond extract
150g ground almonds

TO ASSEMBLE
2 tablespoons ground almonds
40g flaked almonds

FOR THE FRESH
APRICOT GLAZE
170g fresh ripe apricots (3–4)
1 tablespoon orange juice
30g caster sugar
small pinch of sea salt flakes

FOR THE ICING
75g icing sugar
about 1 tablespoon lemon juice

1. Start by poaching the pears. Pour the wine into a pan large enough to hold the halved pears in a single layer. Add all the spices, the orange halves and sugar and stir over low heat until the sugar has dissolved. Peel and halve the pears, then scoop out the cores with a teaspoon. Add to the pan, cut side uppermost, and bring the wine to the boil. Lower the heat so the wine just simmers, then cover the pan and poach gently for 20–30 minutes until the pears are just tender when prodded with a cocktail stick.

2. Remove the pears from the wine with a slotted spoon and carefully drain on a wire rack, then transfer to a plate lined with kitchen paper and leave until cool. The wine can be re-used to poach more fruit or for drinking.

3. To make the pastry, put the flour and sugar into a food processor and 'pulse' just to combine. Add the butter and blitz until the mixture looks like fine crumbs. Add the egg yolk and 3 tablespoons cold water and blitz until the mixture comes together to form a ball of soft but not sticky dough. If there are dry crumbs and the dough won't come together, add more water a teaspoon >>>

at a time. Remove the dough from the bowl, shape it into a thick disc, wrap in clingfilm and chill for about 15 minutes until firm but not hard.

4. Roll out the pastry on a lightly floured worktop and use to line the flan tin*. Prick the base well, then chill for 15 minutes.

5. Meanwhile, heat the oven to 190°C/375°F/gas 5, and make the frangipane filling. Put the soft butter and sugar into a mixing bowl and beat with a wooden spoon or a hand-held electric whisk until light and creamy. Break the eggs into a small bowl, add the almond extract and beat with a fork until combined. Gradually add to the butter mixture, beating well after each addition. Fold in* the ground almonds. If you want to pipe the filling, transfer to the large piping bag. Set aside on the worktop until needed.

6. Line the pastry case with baking paper, fill with baking beans and bake blind* for 10 minutes until the pastry is set and firm. Carefully remove the paper and beans and bake the empty case for a further 7–8 minutes until it looks dry and is just starting to colour. Remove from the oven and set aside to cool for 15–20 minutes. Leave the oven on, and put the baking sheet in to heat up.

7. To assemble the tart, sprinkle the ground almonds over the base of the cooled tart case. If piping the frangipane, snip off the tip of the bag to make an opening

about 1.5cm across, then pipe the frangipane into the pastry case in a spiral. Alternatively, spread out the frangipane in the case in an even layer.

8. Using a sharp knife, make 6 cuts across the rounded top of each pear half, cutting about halfway through. With a spatula or off-set palette knife, carefully set 6 of the pear halves on top of the frangipane in a neat star pattern. Cut a circular slice, about 4cm across, from another pear and set in the centre of the tart (you won't need the last pear half). Scatter the flaked almonds between the pears.

9. Set the tart tin on the heated baking sheet and bake in the heated oven for 35–40 minutes until the frangipane is golden brown and just firm when gently pressed towards the centre.

10. While the tart is baking, make the apricot glaze. Quarter the apricots and remove the stones, then put the fruit into a medium pan with the orange juice, sugar and salt. Heat gently, stirring, until the sugar has dissolved. Bring to the boil, then simmer, stirring frequently, for 5–10 minutes to make a thick, coarse purée. Push through a sieve into a small pan. Set aside until the tart has finished baking.

11. Transfer the tart, in the tin, to a wire rack. Gently reheat the glaze, then brush it all over the top of the tart. Leave to cool and firm up before unmoulding.

12. To finish, sift the icing sugar into a bowl and stir in enough lemon juice to make a smooth, runny icing. Spoon into the small disposable piping bag, snip off the tip and pipe Christmas tree decorations in between the pears. Transfer the tart to a serving plate and eat at room temperature.

Note

When fresh apricots are not available, use 100g ready-made apricot glaze or glaze made from 115g apricot jam, warmed until melted and sieved.

FLORENTINE PASTRIES

Traditional Florentine biscuits, combining sticky nuts and candied fruits, are lacily thin and fragile. In this more substantial version, the mixture is held together on a crisp, rich pâte sucrée base – made in the classic way, straight on the worktop, not in a bowl, using egg yolks rather than water to bind. Once baked and cooled, the rectangular slab of pastry, fruit and nuts is inverted and the pastry is anointed with a thick layer of bitter chocolate before cutting into squares.

1. To make the pâte sucrée, sift the flour and salt on to the worktop and make a large well in the centre. Place the butter between 2 sheets of clingfilm and pound with a rolling pin until very supple but still cold. Unwrap the butter and cut it into small pieces, then put it into the well with the egg yolks, sugar and vanilla extract. Gather the fingertips of one of your hands together to form a beak shape and use to mash together the ingredients in the well. When they are thoroughly combined, gradually work in the flour with your fingers, using a plastic dough scraper (or metal spatula) to help you draw the flour in. When the mixture looks like coarse crumbs, gather the whole lot together to make a ball of dough.

2. Lightly dust the worktop with flour, then work the dough gently (pâtissiers call this 'fraiser'): press down on the side of the dough furthest from you with the heel of one hand and push it away from you, then gather up the dough into a ball once more (use the scraper) and repeat. Continue working the dough like this for a couple of minutes – no more – until the dough is silky-smooth and very pliable, so pliable it can be pulled off the worktop in one piece. Form the dough into a thick disc, wrap in clingfilm and chill for 15 minutes.

3. Roll out the pastry dough on the lightly floured worktop to a 20 × 30cm rectangle. Dust the rolling pin with flour, then gently roll the pastry around the pin and lift it into the prepared swiss roll tin. Press it evenly over the base, making sure the corners are filled and there are no gaps between the pastry and the sides of the tin. Prick the pastry base all over with a fork, then cover the tin lightly with clingfilm and chill for 15 minutes.

4. Heat the oven to 180°C/350°F/gas 4. Uncover the pastry and bake for about 15 minutes until lightly golden and firm. Remove the tin from the oven and set it on a heatproof surface. Reduce the oven temperature to 170°C/325°F/gas 3.

>>>

Cuts into 24 squares

Kit you'll need: 1 swiss roll tin, 20 × 30cm, greased with butter and base-lined*

FOR THE PÂTE SUCRÉE
200g plain flour
¼ teaspoon fine sea salt
100g unsalted butter, chilled
4 medium egg yolks
100g caster sugar
½ teaspoon vanilla extract

FOR THE TOPPING
90g unsalted butter
50g caster sugar
50g clear honey
175g flaked almonds
50g pistachios, halved
15g chopped candied peel, chopped finer
45g glacé cherries, quartered
3 tablespoons single or whipping cream

TO FINISH
150g dark chocolate (about 70% cocoa solids), broken up

5. To make the topping, put the butter, sugar and honey into a large frying pan (preferably non-stick) and heat gently until smoothly melted. Add the almonds, pistachios, peel and cherries and cook over medium/low heat, stirring constantly, for 2–3 minutes until the mixture is a pale straw colour. Stir in the cream and cook for a few more seconds until bubbling, then pour over the pastry base and spread out into an even layer.

6. Bake in the heated oven for about 15 minutes until the topping is a rich golden brown – check after 10 minutes and rotate the tin so the mixture bakes evenly. Transfer the tin to a wire rack. Carefully run a round-bladed knife around the inside of the tin to loosen the sticky mixture, then leave until completely cold.

7. When you're ready to finish the pastries, carefully invert the tin on to a large sheet of baking paper laid on the worktop or a chopping board, then lift off the tin; the underside of the pastry base will now be on top. Put the chocolate into a heatproof bowl and melt* gently. Pour the melted chocolate on to the pastry and spread it out evenly in a thick layer using an offset or regular palette knife. Allow to firm up for a few seconds, then use a fork or a plastic pastry comb to mark waves through the chocolate.

Leave on the worktop for about 10 minutes until the chocolate is no longer glossy-looking but is matt, set and firm.

8. Turn the Florentine pastry nut-side up on the chopping board. Trim off the edges with a very sharp knife to neaten them, then cut into squares. Press any nuts that fall off back in place. Store in an airtight container at cool room temperature. Best eaten within 4 days.

CONVERSION TABLES

Weight

METRIC	IMPERIAL
25g	1oz
50g	2oz
75g	2½oz
85g	3oz
100g	4oz
125g	4½oz
140g	5oz
175g	6oz
200g	7oz
225g	8oz
250g	9oz
280g	10oz
300g	11oz
350g	12oz
375g	13oz
400g	14oz
425g	15oz
450g	1lb
500g	1lb 2oz
550g	1lb 4oz
600g	1lb 5oz
650g	1lb 7oz
700g	1lb 9oz
750g	1lb 10oz
800g	1lb 12oz
850g	1lb 14oz
900g	2lb
950g	2lb 2oz
1kg	2lb 4oz

Linear

METRIC	IMPERIAL
2.5cm	1in
3cm	1¼in
4cm	1½in
5cm	2in
5.5cm	2¼in
6cm	2½in
7cm	2¾in
7.5cm	3in
8cm	3¼in
9cm	3½in
9.5cm	3¾in
10cm	4in
11cm	4¼in
12cm	4½in
13cm	5in
14cm	5½in
15cm	6in
16cm	6½in
17cm	6½in
18cm	7in
19cm	7½in
20cm	8in
22cm	8½in
23cm	9in
24cm	9½in
25cm	10in

Volume

METRIC	IMPERIAL
30ml	1fl oz
50ml	2fl oz
75ml	3fl oz
125ml	4fl oz
150ml	¼ pint
175ml	6fl oz
200ml	7fl oz
225ml	8fl oz
300ml	½ pint
350ml	12fl oz
400ml	14fl oz
450ml	¾ pint
500ml	18fl oz
600ml	1 pint
725ml	1¼ pints
1 litre	1¾ pints

Spoon Measures

METRIC	IMPERIAL
5ml	1 teaspoon
10ml	2 teaspoons
15ml	1 tablespoon
30ml	2 tablespoons
45ml	3 tablespoons
60ml	4 tablespoons
75ml	5 tablespoons

INDEX

ACKNOWLEDGEMENTS

Hodder & Stoughton and Love Productions would like to thank the following people for their contribution to this book:

Linda Collister, Sheila Keating, Norma MacMillan, Alice Laurent, Rita Platts, Emma Marsden, Louie Waller, Nicky Ross, Sarah Hammond, Alasdair Oliver, Kate Brunt, Claudette Morris, Joanna Seaton, Damian Horner, Auriol Bishop, Jonathon Scrafton, Jake Senior, Jane Treasure, Sharon Powers.

Thank you to Mary Berry and Paul Hollywood for contributing their recipes and also to the amateur Bakers: Alvin, Dorret, Flora, Ian, Mat, Marie, Nadiya, Paul, Sandy, Stuart, Tamal, Ugne.

– DON'T JUST BAKE. BAKE IT BETTER. –

Go from first-time baker to star baker with the *Great British Bake Off: Bake It Better* series, the 'go to' cookery books which give you all the recipes and baking know-how you need in one easy-to-navigate series.

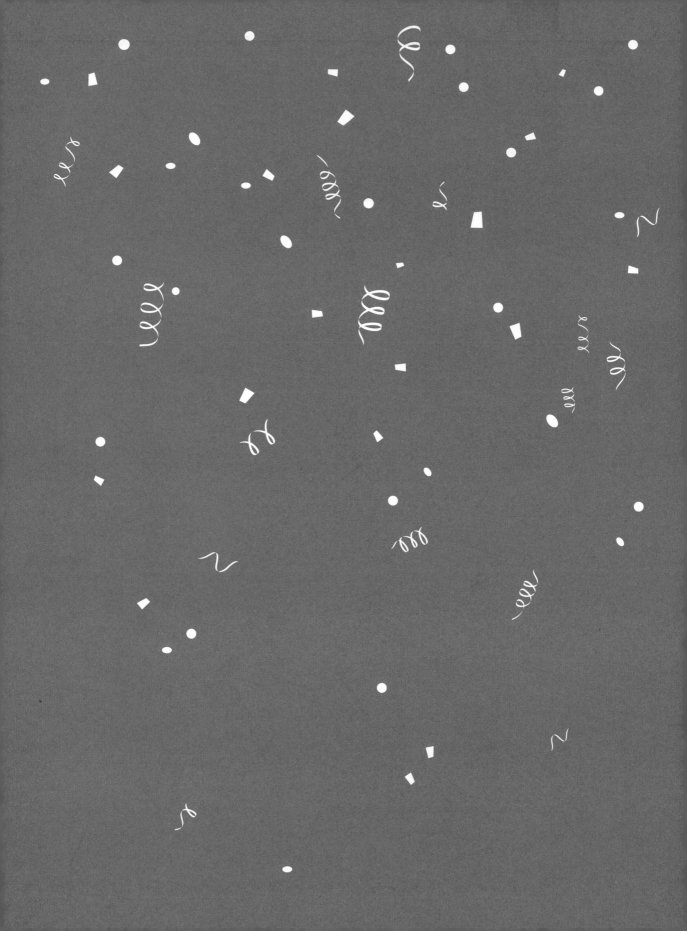